THE GREAT AMERICAN WEST

A PICTORIAL HISTORY FROM CORONADO TO THE LAST FRONTIER

Books by James D. Horan

THE GREAT AMERICAN WEST

JAMES D. HORAN

REVISED AND EXPANDED EDITION
WITH A PORTFOLIO OF PAINTINGS BY
CHARLES SCHREYVOGEL

CROWN PUBLISHERS, INC. NEW YORK

For the Jingle Bob riders:
Pat, Brian Boru, Gary, Jimmy, Arlene, Donna,
and Little Pat, along with the littlest outlaws,
Christopher, Brian, Jeffrey, and Stephanie.
And Gertrude, beloved boss wrangler

Printed in the United States of America

Published simultaneously in Canada by
General Publishing Company Limited

Library of Congress Cataloging in Publication Data

Horan, James David, 1914–
  The great American West.

  Bibliography: p.
  Includes index.
  1. The West—History. 2. Frontier and pioneer life
—The West. I. Title.
F591.H74 1978 978 78–17424
ISBN 0–517–53491–6

Contents

Illustrations

The many hundreds of black-and-white illustrations are integrated with the text and therefore are not listed here.

Color Plates

The Great American West Revisited

IT is almost twenty years since the first edition of this book was published. It has been reprinted many times but finally I decided to revise the book and include a great deal of new material.

When I first began seeking out rare books, prints, maps, diaries, newspapers, and especially photographs on the American West shortly after the end of World War II, there were still glass plates and prints available. Backtracking over my old trails, I soon discovered that few remain; I can only marvel at the prime discoveries I made years ago, which are in this book.

One was the collection of glass plates taken by General John T. Pitman, head of the army's ordnance in the Dakota Territory, who photographed everything in the West. In this book, published for the first time, is a sampling from his four hundred glass plates.

There are also other finds: a collection of superb photographs taken by Theodore Roosevelt of a small band of outlaws he and a posse had captured. Roosevelt, "all mouth and teeth," as one Dakota doctor recalled, had gathered his posse and trailed the band after they raided his Elk Horn ranch. The future president of the United States brought his camera along, photographed his posse and his prisoners, then had someone take him guarding them. Each mounted print is carefully captioned in his own hand.

Finally you will see the biggest gem of all my Western strikes: the original photographs taken by Timothy O'Sullivan on the King Expedition, the first geological survey to enter the West after the Civil War. Even twenty-five years ago photographs of the King Expedition were difficult to find. Today they are exceedingly rare, usually found only in libraries, historical societies, or private collections.

O'Sullivan, Mathew B. Brady's greatest protégé, established his reputation as a photographic genius at Gettysburg and on other Civil War battlefields. The large mounted photographs in this book compose a stunning pictorial history of an unspoiled American West that knew only the tread of a moccasin. One dramatic series contains the first mine photographs taken in Virginia City. An apoplectic foreman later told O'Sullivan that the magnesium he ignited as a primitive flashgun could not only have blown him and the miners to bits if it had ignited the deadly tunnel gases but could also have de-stroyed the world's most valuable silver mine.

Certainly the outstanding addition in this revised edition is the collection of Charles Schreyvogel's thrilling paintings of the Indian Wars. For years I had researched Schreyvogel's life, curiously finding that much of the material was to be found not in the deep West but only a short distance from my home in New Jersey. I discovered Schreyvogel had done most of his major works on the roof of his narrow row house in Hoboken, using a local athlete as his Indian model. Since my biography on Schreyvogel was published years ago—now out of print—many of the paintings have been sold, disappeared, or vanished into private collections. The portfolio of his works gathered for this book may be the last time they will appear as a complete collection.

Also in this new edition are photographs I consider to be the most extraordinary in the history of Western outlawry. They show Billy the Kid, as Henry McCarty, growing up in the mining camp of Silver City, New Mexico Territory, in the early 1870s; his mother, Catherine, who kept a boardinghouse on Silver City's Main Street; street scenes as Billy knew them, and the interior of Morrill's Opera House where Billy as a schoolboy loved to sing and dance in amateur theatricals. It is difficult to visualize the handsome boy in the photograph as America's immortal legend of the Wild West. Permission to use this collection, published in a book for the first time, was given by Robert N. Mullin, a noted expert on the life and times of Billy the Kid who found the photographs many years ago. Mr. Mullin also located and interviewed Chauncey Truesdell, Billy the Kid's classmate in Silver City, and with the assistance of his daughter, Mrs. Frances Daseler, discovered the marriage certificate of Billy's mother, Catherine McCarty, and his stepfather, William Antrim.

I have included in Billy's story the little known but very romantic and authenticated tale of Frank Warner Angel, the Jersey City lawyer who was sent by President Rutherford Hayes to explosive Lincoln County, New Mexico, scene of the bloodiest of frontier wars, to uncover a ring of corrupt government officials. Among the first to give Angel an eyewitness affidavit to the murder of John Tunstall was Billy the Kid, who had adopted the cultured English rancher as a father image. It doesn't require too much imagination to picture the city lawyer dressed in a broadcloth suit, shirt and tie, sitting across from the slender boy in cowpuncher's garb who even then was becoming a frontier legend. What an incongruous pair they made!

I have been asked countless times who I consider the most dangerous man in the Wild West; my candidate has always been Harvey Logan, Montana's Kid Curry. I have researched his life since the 1940s, interviewed men who knew him, and trailed him and his brothers through frontier newspapers, court records, and government documents. Only recently I was given information about his family background that shows that he had links to a vice-president of the United States! The life and times of Kid Curry easily became a highlight of this revised edition.

Since *The Great American West* was first published, Butch Cassidy has been resurrected in articles, newspaper series, and has become the subject of at least one book. There are two theories: he returned to the bosom of his family driving a 1925 Ford; the other insists he was William Phillips, a Seattle businessman. I believe the one-word comment made by Percy Seibert, the American engineer and official of the Concordia Tin Mines in Bolivia where Cassidy and the Sundance Kid worked for many years, when he was asked what he thought about the stories of Cassidy's return: "Rubbish," he snapped. A chapter in this book describing how a Wyoming historian has shattered the growing myth that Cassidy could have been Phillips underscores Mr. Seibert's comment.

As an epilogue the reader will find a shocking present-day racket linked to the Wild West, which in comparison makes Jesse James and his bravos, the Daltons, and the riders of the Wild Bunch to have been unimaginative pikers.

I feel saddened revisiting this list of the friends and strangers who helped me years ago and finding that too many have passed on. I hope this book will be a memorial to their love and interest in the Great American West.

Mrs. Virginia Gilmore, assistant librarian, Montana Historical Society; A. W. Lund, assistant church historian, The Church of Jesus Christ of Latter-Day Saints; M. T. Jensen, vice-president, Aermotor Company, Chicago, Ill.; Carroll D. Hall, monument supervisor, Sutter's Fort, Sacramento, Calif.; Frank H. Roberts, Jr., director, Bureau of American Ethnology, Washington, D.C.; Clarkson A. Collins III, librarian, Rhode Island Historical Society; Mrs. Sadie Schmidt, reference librarian, and Eleanor B. Sloan, historical secretary, Arizona Pioneers' Historical Society; Cheryle Hughes, assistant, Iconographic Collections, State Historical Society of Wisconsin; Virginia Daiker, Alice Parker, and the staff of the Department of Prints and Photographs, Library of Congress; Marjorie M. Pyle, cataloger, Hispanic Society of America; W. G. Burder, director of public relations, Union Pacific Railroad; Mrs. Drucilla Denny, secretary, and Dr. David Gebhard, director, Roswell Museum and Art Center, Roswell, N.M.; Robert Zimmerman, administrative assistant, New Mexico State Tourist Bureau, Santa Fe, N.M.; Josephine Cobb, formerly of the Still Pictures Branch, National Archives; David R. Watkins, chief research librarian, Yale University Library; Archibald Hanna, Coe Collection, Yale University; Harry Brown, public relations department, United States Steel Corporation; Mrs. Margaret Fuller, librarian, American Iron and Steel Institute; Stewart H. Holbrook, Joseph J. Fucelli; Virginia Walton, librarian, Montana Historical Society; Mrs. Paul M. Rhymer, curator of prints, Chicago Historical Society; the late R. G. Vail, director, New-York Historical Society; Sarah Guitar, reference librarian, Missouri State Historical Society; Leo A. McCoy, Red Bluff, Calif.; Don Baxter, managing editor, *Westward;* George D. Wolfe, Knoxville, Tenn.; Preston McMann; the late Mari Sandoz; Clifton Waller Barrett; H. J. Swinney, director, Idaho Historical Society; George Oslin, Western Union; Mrs. C. E. Cook, curator of the museum, Oklahoma Historical Society; Kenneth W. Duckett, librarian, and Thomas Vaughan, curator, Oregon Historical Society; Eugene D. Becker, curator of pictures, Minnesota Historical Society; D. W. Thompson, secretary, Hamilton Library and Historical Association of Cumberland County, Pa.; Mrs. Alys Freeze, head, Western History Department, Denver Public Library; Mrs. Katherine Schmeltekopf, library assistant, Barker Texas History Center, University of Texas; Robert W. Hill, keeper of manuscripts, and Paul Rugen, his assistant, Manuscript Room, New York Public Library; David S. Fotte, assistant director, Springfield Museum of Fine Arts, Springfield, Mass.; Pat McDonough; Mrs. Margaret Shepherd, curator of photographs, Utah Historical Society; Beaumont Newhall, director, George Eastman House, Rochester, N.Y.; Paul Vanderbilt, Wisconsin State Historical Society; Francis W. Cunningham, curator, Oneida Historical Society; Roscoe P. Conkling, Inglewood, Calif.; Wesley R. Hurt, director of the museum, G. Johnson, Ruth Bergmann, librarian, State University of South Dakota, Vermillion, S.D.; Nick Eggenhofer; Helen and Donald R. Foyer of Alexandria, Va.; Glen Dawson, Los Angeles; Peter Decker; Cedric L. Robinson; J. E. Reynolds; Mrs. Clark Kellett, Brown County, Minn.; Dr. A. Carlson, former curator of prints, New-York Historical Society; Florence and Maureen who watched the hearth; the late Sylvester Vigilante; the late Montagu Hankin; the late Melvin J. Nichols of Summit, N.J.; the late Vincent Mercaldo; the late J. Leonard Jennewein, Mitchell, S.D., and his friends in the North Dakota and South Dakota historical societies who gave so much of their time to help establish dates and identify individuals and places shown in the Pitman plates; Helen Staeuble for her editorial skill and devotion to this book, Judy Weismiller for her careful corraling of our pictures, and the late C. Leo Henrichs, one of New Jersey's finest photographers, who spent so many hours carefully developing prints from the fragile Pitman glass plates.

There is ancient authority that the last shall be first. What man can write a book without the assistance, seen and unseen, of his wife? I least of all. Thus to Gertrude, the biggest thanks of all.

The Notch
Spring 1978

The First White Men in the West

THE area of the West, as the term will be used in this book, is all of that vast land bounded on the north by the Canadian border, on the south by the Mexican border, on the west by the Pacific Ocean, and on the east by the western edge of the Mississippi River Valley, including also western Wisconsin, as well as Minnesota, Iowa, Missouri, Arkansas, and western Louisiana.

The first white men to set foot in this land were the Spanish. The overture to their entrance took place in March, 1536, when a man almost naked, with a thick beard and tangled hair, stumbled toward a party of soldiers on the plain some 80 miles north of Culiacan, Mexico. He was accompanied by eleven Indians and a Negro. Tears rolling down his cheeks, he told them they were the first white men he had seen in eight years. He gave his name as Alvar Nuñez Cabeza de Vaca, and he called the Negro with him Estevanico, better known to history as Estevan, or "an Arab Negro from Azamor." Two other Spaniards, he told the soldiers, Alonzo del Castillo Maldonado and Andres Dorantes, were a day's journey in the rear, with a number of Indians who had followed them from the north. When the soldiers had recovered from their surprise, they brought the ragged man back to Diego de Alcaraz, commander of an outpost, who sent out a party to bring the other Spaniards back.

According to his own account, translated into English in 1905 by Fanny Bandelier, de Vaca told his story—and told it well—in Mexico City. Never before in this city of nobles and adventurers had such a tale been heard. He and his companions had been in the expedition of Panfilo de Narvaez, which eight years before had set sail to conquer Florida for His Catholic Majesty. After landing on the Florida coast they moved inland. They hacked and pushed their way through the tangled jungle, fought off Indians, and finally, on the verge of starvation, killed their horses for food.

After fantastic adventures they made their way to the west coast of Florida. There the ingenious blacksmith of

The title page and an extract from de Casteñada's account of Coronado's expedition.

the expedition made a forge and horsehide bellows, then hammered their swords into saws and nails for the purpose of building several small boats. These indomitable men made several boat frames, covered them with horsehide, fashioned ropes from manes and tails, and set sail.

A storm and heavy seas defeated them. Some of the boats capsized and their occupants drowned, others were blown out to sea, never to be seen again. Only de Vaca and a small number survived. Somehow in the wild gale they were blown up on the shore of what is now Galveston, Texas. Friendly Indians found them and helped them. When they recovered their strength they made their way westward, moving from tribe to tribe. De Vaca became a medicine man and, as he recalled in his memoirs, the tribes accepted him "without asking to see my diploma."

It was appropriate that de Vaca's strange tale should be told in the square of Mexico City. It was only eight years since Hernando Cortez had entered the ancient Aztec city to begin the conquest of Mexico. In the crowd listening to de Vaca were men who had marched with Cortez; there were also many nobles and knights who had sailed for New Spain, eager for adventure, conquest and gold. But after Mexico it seemed that there were no new worlds to conquer. . . .

Now de Vaca was telling them not only about shining Cities of Gold, but of the "copper hawk's-bell, thick and large, figured with face" which an Indian had given him, along with a tale of how it had come from the earth. Other Indians, de Vaca told the crowd, had informed him that in the place from which it came were many plates of the same metal.

Actually, there was little fact to the whole tale; the only real evidence was the bell. But the imagination of the people was unleashed. The towns that the Indians had described to de Vaca were now lined with gold; silversmith shops and the doors of houses were inlaid with turquoise. Precious gems and gold were commonplace. The strange copper bell figured with a face now had a name—the Gilded Man.

At last de Vaca was summoned by Don Antonio de Mendoza himself. Undoubtedly the Viceroy was now convinced that perhaps there might be another Peru or Mexico with new lands to conquer, new riches for His Catholic Majesty, the Emperor Charles V. And, more importantly, now that Spain had made herself the champion of Rome, more souls to bring to Holy Mother Church.

Mendoza, however, was cautious; he decided that first he would send his own men north to see what there was to this story. In the meanwhile he dispatched de Vaca to Spain to regale the king with his wondrous tales.

There was a delay of a few years, but finally, in 1539, Friar Marcos de Niza of the Franciscan order, who had gained experience in the jungles of conquered Peru, was selected to go north. With the Negro Estevan and some other native Indians he set out to find what everyone was calling the Seven Cities of Gold. But Estevan, the former slave, was beginning to believe his own lies and impor-

Friar Marcos de Niza.

tance. He wore gaudy robes to which were sewed many tiny bells so that he walked across the wild land to a strange symphony of tinkling bells and the rattling of the red-painted "magic gourd" which he carried.

Women and his unbearable arrogance led to his murder by the Zuñis. Friar Marcos, however, pushed on and finally reached Cibola, which he saw only from a distance. He returned to Mexico City repeating the tales of the Indians—that Cibola was larger than Mexico City and "has some large houses ten stories high . . . they say that the portals and fronts of the chief houses are of turquoise. . . ."

The restless nobles and adventurers unconsciously polished the friar's story, which actually was only gossip he had heard.

King Charles was besieged by petitions from nobles, among them Hernando Cortez, to lead an expedition to conquer the golden cities. But the king decided that Mendoza should select the leader, and thus the Viceroy summoned his close friend, Francisco Vasquez de Coronado, a thirty-year-old Salamanca aristocrat who had come to the New World with Mendoza to seek his fortune only a year before the ragged de Vaca had walked into the plaza of New Mexico. He was a dashing, handsome man, liked by both men and women.

Now there was a kind of madness in the land. Men of every station in life, from nobleman to tutor, begged to be allowed to join Coronado. Nobles sold their land and belongings and rode to New Galicia, the desert province where Coronado was stationed. Large sums were collected and sent to New Galicia. Galleons from Madrid delivered artillery from the royal armory—although later the bronze cannons would fail to penetrate a mud wall—as well as food, pack horses, the best of soldiers. Nothing was too good for the mightiest expedition Spain was to launch in the New World.

But it was the horses, some sent by Mendoza himself from his best stock farms, that were most important, not only to the success of this expedition, but to the history of the American West. In fact they would produce a revolution among the American aborigines comparable only to the introduction of the gasoline engine to the civilized world.

The Spanish horses that Coronado used were tough and durable. They were horses of the Moors, of the desert, animals that could live on grass and forage and not entirely on grain. The Spanish mustang, the Indian pony, would someday be the cow horse of the cattle kingdom.

With their mail and mounted on horses, the Spaniards were invincible. They were mobile against a race that was on foot. They could now move across a land at will, with its occupants barely able to impede their advance.

When the horses, the arms and provisions had been gathered, Mendoza announced that in addition to the overland march he intended to dispatch three ships under Hernando de Alarcon with the army's extra baggage and supplies. The *San Pedro, Santa Catarina* and *Santa Gabriel* were to move up along the coastline with orders to contact Coronado whenever possible.

In February, 1540, Coronado announced that the expedition was ready to start.

As Pedro de Castañeda, a chronicler of the expedition, described the scene, Coronado was resplendent in armor and plumed helmet. Some of his troops were dressed in buckskin or nondescript dress of the period. In addition to the professional *conquistadores* there were some 800 Mexican helpers, grooms, sheep-herders, Negro servants. There were also three women, all wives of members of the party. Mother Church was represented by four friars, led by Friar Marcos, who had been elevated to the post of Father Provincial for his report on Cibola.

The army moved out on a March morning, and from de Castañeda's manuscript—he was a superb reporter—one can see the bright sunshine glinting on the huge two-handed swords and cannons, the colorful banners flapping in the morning breeze, the clouds of dust rising from under the hoofs of the horses. That morning there were brave speeches, gay music and high hopes as the first army of white men moved into the great vastness of the American West.

What Coronado Found

Coronado's expedition lasted about two years; he returned to Mexico in midsummer, 1542. He, or elements

Coronado. No contemporary portrait of Coronado is known to exist, but the upper picture, from the permanent collection of the Roswell Museum and Art Center (Roswell, New Mexico) appears to have some documentary support.

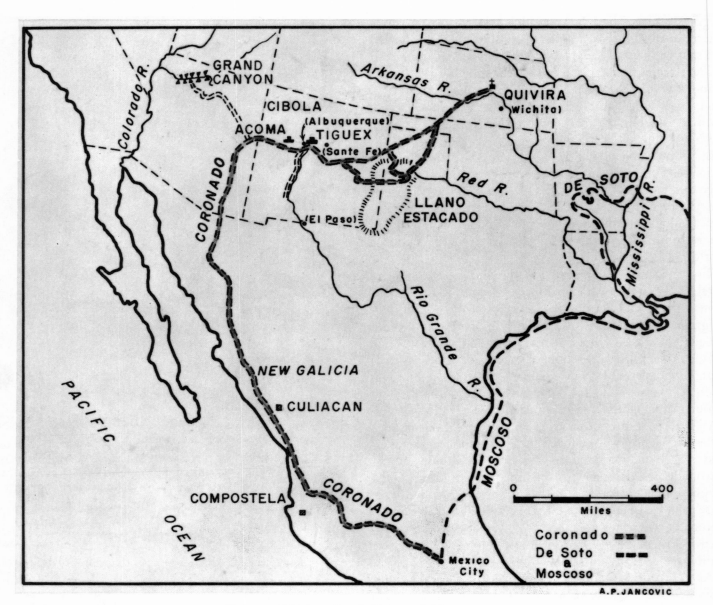

Routes of Coronado, de Soto and Moscoso.

of his expedition, traversed Lower California, Arizona, New Mexico, Texas, Oklahoma, and probably southern Kansas. They camped and explored along the Rio Grande, Colorado and Canadian Rivers (and others), crossed the Yuma Desert and the Painted Desert, "discovered" the Grand Canyon and the Rock of Acoma and wintered in the Rio Grande Valley near what is now Albuquerque. In the second year they reached as far northeast as the fabled site of Quivira (generally believed to be near Wichita, Kansas). What Coronado and his men found in all this territory and did not find determined the future history of the West, and of the world.

They did not find gold or other treasure. They found Indians—Zuñis, Hopis, Apaches and others living in pueblo settlements—who were friendly at first but then went on the warpath when the Spaniards plundered their towns and massacred the inhabitants. Word of the brutal massacre at Tiguex on the Rio Grande, where the army wintered, spread among the tribes.

South of Cibola, the Zuñis, who had never seen white men or heard sounds of guns or had seen horses, attacked the army, touching off the first large-scale engagements between red men and white men. The veteran fighters sent the Indians flying back to the walls of Cibola. Coronado then sent one of his captains to the pueblo with an interpreter to ask peace, but he was greeted by a flight of arrows.

The commander gave the order for attack. Crying "Santiago," the traditional Spanish war cry, the army stormed the pueblo, with Coronado in his glittering armor and plumed helmet leading the attack.

Showers of boulders thundered down from the walls. Arrows hissed through the narrow streets, which echoed with the roar of the big muzzle-loaders. Coronado himself was badly hurt by a boulder and removed from the battle. His enraged troops, even though weakened by the long march and attendant hardships, brought the battle to the enemy until the Zuñis fled.

Cibola

The following description is an example of the thoroughness of Pedro de Casta-ñeda's report of the expedition:

The seven Cities are seven little villages, all within a radius of four leagues (15 to 20 miles). . . . The largest is called Mazaque. . . . The largest may have 200 houses, and two others about 200, and the others somewhere between 30 and 60. . . . There might be in all 500 hearths. . . . Hawikuh has 200 houses all surrounded by a wall. . . . The walls are of stone and mud. . . . The houses, as a rule, are three and four stories high, but at Mazaque there are houses four and seven stories high. . . .

The natives here are very intelligent. . . . They cover the privy and immodest parts of their bodies with cloths resembling table napkins, with fringes and a tassel at each corner, tying them around the hips. . . . They wear cloaks made with feathers and rabbit hair, and cotton blankets. . . . They wear shoes of deerskin. . . . The women wear blankets wrapped tightly around their bodies and fastened or tied over the left shoulder, drawing the right arm over them; they also wear well-fashioned cloaks of dressed skins. . . . They gather their hair over their ears in two wheels that look like coif puffs. . . . An Indian woman will carry a jar of water up a ladder without touching it with her hands.

These Indians cultivate maize, which does not grow tall, but each stalk bears three and four large and heavy ears with 800 grains each. . . . They have very good salt in crystals. . . . They make the best tortillas that I have ever seen anywhere. . . . There are in this province large numbers of bears, mountain lions, wildcats, porcupines, deer, wild goats and otters. . . . They have no knowledge of fish. . . . There are very fine turquoises although not in the quantity claimed. . . . The natives gather and store pine nuts for the year. . . . A man has only one wife. . . .

There are *estufas (kivas)* in the pueblos, in which they gather to take counsel. . . . They have no rulers, but are governed by the counsel of their oldest men. . . . They have their priests, whom they call papas. These priests mount the high terrace of the pueblo in the morning as the sun rises, and from there, like public criers, preach to the people, who all listen in silence, seated along the corridors. The priests tell the people how they should live. I believe that they give them some commandments to observe, because there is no drunkenness among them, nor do they eat human flesh, or steal. . . . They hold their rituals and sacrifices before some idols. . . . What they worship most is water. . . . They make the cross as a sign of peace.

The copper-skinned Indians Cortez brought back from the New World to the Spanish court excited lively interest, for they were exotic beings "from a land two thousand miles away, where gold is found in the water." A German artist and silversmith, Christoph Weiditz, made watercolors of them about 1529 and commented on their colorful regalia. It was believed that these savages wore precious stones in their faces and breasts.

The shaggy-coated buffalo of the American plains appeared in Gomara's *Historia de las Indias Saragossa*, c. 1554. When Cortez's forces reached Montezuma's capital they reported having seen "a rare Mexican bull, with crooked shoulders, a hump on its back like a camel and with hair like a lion." Both Cabeza de Vaca and Coronado saw the "crooked-back oxen" on its native range.

Although these photographs were taken by Tim O'Sullivan in the course of Wheeler's geographical surveys (1871-73), they might have been recorded, had cameras been available to Coronado's men, as early as 1540. Coronado and his men saw and described such sights as the Zuñi and Hopi Pueblos, Acoma, the "Sky City," herds of buffalo, great canyons and rivers, including the Grand Canyon and the Colorado River.

Explorers Column, Canyon de Chelly, Arizona.

Grotto Spring, Grand Canyon of the Colorado River.

Zuñi Indian girl, with water olla.

A Zuñi war chief.

When Coronado found Cibola to be far from the fabled golden city he sent Friar Marcos back in disgrace but kept on, always hopeful that the next tale would be true, the next pueblo would offer the golden temples and doorways studded with precious gems.

But they found only heat, dust, endless distances, high, keening winds and numbing cold. The land was forbidding—either desert-dry or rocky and wild, unfit for cultivation.

The remnants of the expedition—about one-third of the force that had started out with such high hopes in 1540—returned to Mexico in 1542.

Coronado's troubles were many in the years to come. He was removed from office and brought to Mexico City to face charges of the misconduct of the expedition. But he was found to have fulfilled his duties faithfully and was exonerated in full.

The trial did not end the accusations. His enemies continued to denounce him and blame him for what they called a dismal failure. Few would realize in their own lifetime that Coronado had discovered far greater things than gold-sheathed walls or doors studded with turquoise. . . .

He had discovered a new and mighty land in which he had left a heritage of hatred—and several mustangs.

De Soto and the Mississippi

Spain's other elaborate expedition to explore the interior of North America was that of Hernando de Soto's, who, like Coronado, failed to find golden cities but did discover the mightiest river in America.

The report of the expedition made by an anonymous Portuguese of Elvas fails to cite dates. Ranjel, De Soto's secretary, kept a day-by-day journal, but unfortunately his diary breaks off before the death of De Soto, leaving no account of the westward march when the command was under Moscoso. Like Coronado's, De Soto's expedition was disappointing to the royal court because he failed to find treasure.

De Soto's expedition was the last of the full-scale attempts by the Spanish to move into the West. Santa Fe was occupied by 1599, but between that place and St. Augustine, Florida, there was a great sag where Spain had failed to move northward.

Spanish Colonization

While Spain hesitated, the great revolution of the plains was beginning. It was some time in the seventeenth century or possibly earlier that somewhere on the western plains an Indian buck carefully approached one of the lost horses of the Spaniards, put out a trembling hand to touch the velvet coat. When he found it was not a courier of the strange white man's gods he threw a leg over and mounted the steed. One can only guess at the wild triumph which filled the heart of this copper-skinned man as he found himself soaring across the sea of grass.

After that initial adventure he and his tribe must have figured out the technique of riding. Once they learned to stay on, they discovered the horse could not only be used for fast travel but also for hunting. Now he could race along the flanks of the thundering herds of buffalo, now he could lean over and drive home his lance, again and again, leaving the shaggy beasts behind for the women to skin and carve.

Now also he was a fearsome man of war. He could strike a blow and vanish speedily. He could move whole

Indian pueblo of Zuñi, New Mexico. View from the interior.

A Zuñi woman with her hair over her ears in two wheels, as described by de Casteñada. *Photo by C. C. Pierce.*

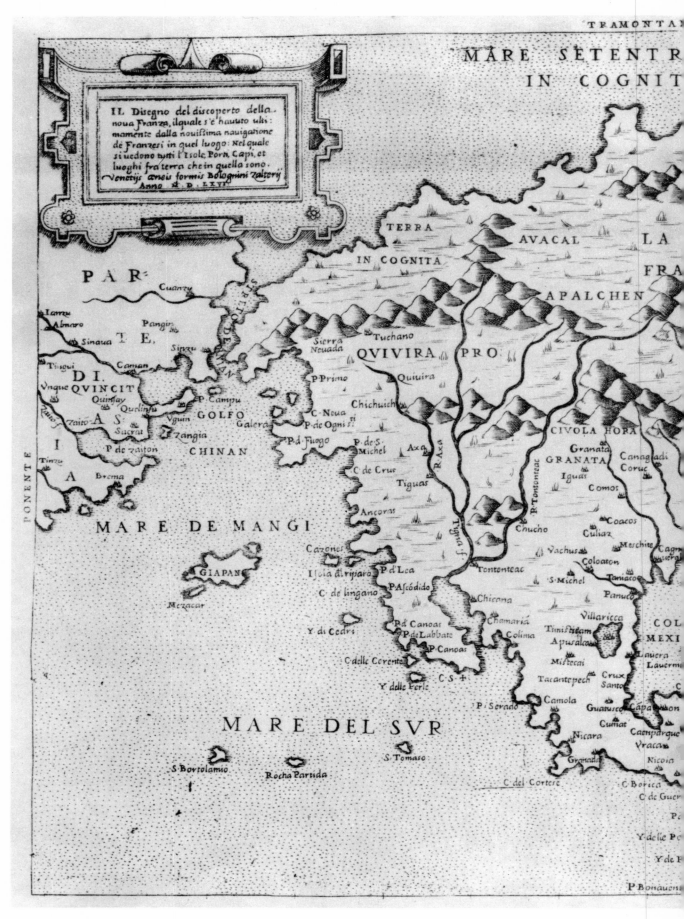

Map of North America made in Bologna, Italy, dated 1566.

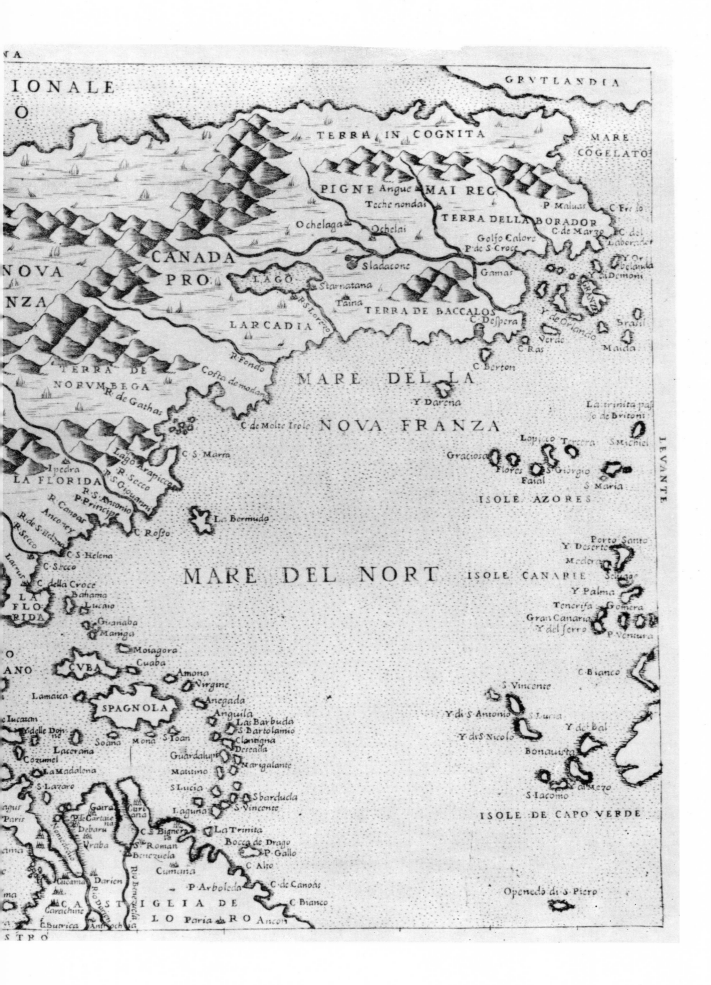

GRVTLANDIA

IONALE

TERRA IN COGNITA

MARE
COGELATO

PIGNE Angue MAI REG
Teche nondai
P. Maluas C. Fredo
TERRA DELLA BORADOR
Ochelaga Ochelai
Golfo Calore C. de Marzo FC. del
P. de S. Croce Laborador

CANADA
PRO.
LAGO
NOVA
Starnatana
FRANZA Slasacone
Taina
R. S. Lorenzo
Gamar
Y. Or
belanda
Y. de Demoni

TERRA DE BACCALOS
Y. de Orlando
C. Despera
Verde
Brasil
LARCADIA
C. Ras
Maida
R. Fondo
C. Berton
TERRA DE
MARE DELLA
Costa de madan
NORVMBEGA
La trinita paſ
R. de Gathas
Y. Darena
ſo de Britoni
NOVA FRANZA
C. de Molte Isole
Lopizo Tercera S. Michiel
C. S. Marta
Gracioso

Lago Arapico
Ipedra R. S. Giouanni
R. Secco
Flores S. Giorgio
Faial S. Maria
LA FLORIDA R. S. Antonio
P. Principe
ISOLE AZORES
R. Canoa
Antonvey
R. de S. Helena
La Bermuda
R. Secco
C. Rosso

Porto Santo
C. S. Helena
Y. Deserte
Madera
C. S. Secco
MARE DEL NORT ISOLE CANARIE Selzar
C. della Croce
LA
FLO
RIDA
Bahama
Lucaio
Y. Palma
Tenerifa Gomera
Gran Canaria
Y. del Serro P. Ventura
Guanaba
Maniga

Moiagora
C. Bianco
CVBA Cuaba
ANO Amona
Virgine
S. Vincente
Lamaica
Anegada
SPAGNOLA Anguila
Y. di S. Antonio S. Luia
Lucaten Lai Barbuda
Y. del Sal
delle Don S. Bartolamio
Y. di S. Nicolo
Soana Mona S. Toan Clanigna
Lacerona Deseada
Bonauista
Cozumel Guardalupi Marigalante
LaMadalena Matino
S. Lazaro S. Lucia
S. Iacomo a. Mezo
Gaira Curi S. barducla
Paris P. de Cartage na ana S. Vincente ISOLE DE CAPO VERDE
Debaru C. S. Bignera La Trinita
S. Roman Vraba Boca de Drago
Benezuela P. Gallo
Cumana C. Alto
Cicama Darien P. Arboleda C. de Canoas
CA Caracchine Rio Benezuela C. Bianco Openedo di S. Pietro
Butrica Antiochia S T I G L I A DE
STRO LO Paria RO Ancon

towns in one-fifth the time he had been accustomed to. Before, as the Spaniards had noted with amazement, the travois, the Indian vehicle, had been attached to the dog; now it could be attached to the horse and piled high with skins, poles, utensils and weapons.

By the beginning of the eighteenth century, when Spain started to establish missions from California to Florida, the Indians on horseback were a strong foe. If it hadn't been for the friendly Pimas it is doubtful if any of the early settlements would have survived.

In 1757 the red men demonstrated how effective they were as a mounted foe. A large band of Comanches, now the undisputed cavalrymen of the plains, swept in to massacre all but four persons in the mission of the San Saba River near the present town of Menard, Texas.

The aroused Spaniards were determined to avenge the martyred San Saba dead. An army of 600 or more Spaniards, Mexicans and a large band of Apaches raided a Comanche village on the Red River near Ringgold. But the villagers had been warned of the approach of the Spanish expedition and were waiting. In the ensuing battle the Comanches, equipped by the French, defeated the Spaniards and sent them fleeing back to San Antonio.

More than a decade later Charles III of Spain had a more serious problem to consider than the defeat of a frontier expedition. The Spanish court was now shaken by the far-off rumbling of the cannons of General Wolfe, who had smashed the French army under Montcalm on the Plains of Abraham. The significance of that defeat was quite obvious to the royal statesmen in the quiet of the Escorial, where King Charles was deciding the future policies of Spain in the New World.

When news of the battle reached him Charles was rightly disturbed. A look at the map of New Spain could easily show him how the situation was altering: Spain's colony of New Spain—Mexico—now had on its borders the aggressive English colonists. Not even the close family ties of the kings of France and Spain had been able to stop the English. Even when her armies were not on the march her daring seamen like Drake were striking the Pacific coast.

Spain's weakest points were in the northern borders of New Spain. Here the line consisted only of a rag-tag line of missions, ranches and presidios, which extended from the French border of Louisiana across Texas and as far north as Pimeria Alta, the southern part of Arizona. The northwest province of Sonora, the outpost of Spanish colonization, was constantly under attack from the fierce Apaches, while lower California was under the firm rule of the Jesuits, who had virtually carved out of the wilderness a series of missions.

The English colonists were not the only threat to the empire; there were the Russians gradually edging down the Pacific Coast from Siberia. In 1723 Vitus Bering sailed into the strait that bears his name, opening the way for his countrymen, who began moving down the coast in their feverish search for the skin of the sea-otter.

Father Junipero Serra.

All explorations of the California frontier in the seventeenth century had been done by missionaries, usually Jesuits, working from their base in Mexico. After the English victory in Canada, Spain decided to abolish the Jesuits from Alta California and replace them with an order easier to govern.

In their place were substituted the Franciscans as the colonizers of Alta California. The supervision of the missionary efforts was given to Father Junipero Serra, who already had a reputation not only as a learned man but as a missionary and explorer.

Serra, born on the Island of Mallorca in 1713, abandoned a life that had offered scholastic and religious honor and chose to go to the frontiers of New Spain. In February, 1768, Serra and 16 brother Franciscans boarded the packet boat *Concepcion*, which had brought back the Jesuit missionaries, and set sail for Alta California. On Easter Sunday he took up his duties as father-president of the missions in lower California.

In the years Serra was in California, he extended the missions north to the bay of San Francisco. In time they became known as "Serra beads." The missions established by Serra and his successors extended in a ragged line from San Diego y Alcala to San Francisco del Solano de Sonoma in the north, a distance of more than 600 miles. All but three were founded prior to 1800. They were spaced a day's journey apart and were connected by a trail called El Camino Real—the King's Highway.

The missions contained a unique collection of artisans, farmers, priests and educators. They occupied millions of acres of the richest pastureland in the West, on which were raised thousands of head of cattle, horses and livestock. Confined within the mission walls were bakers, cooks, shoemakers, soap-makers, musicians, carpenters, tile-makers, plasterers, shepherds, cart-makers, weavers, vine-yardists, hunters, blacksmiths, silversmiths, tallow-ren-derers and of course, the *vaqueros*—cowboys whose dress would become an integral part of the costume of the cow-punchers of the plains.

All of the missions were built by native labor. The massive walls were usually at least four feet thick and composed of sun-dried clay bricks (adobe). Across the tops of the walls were laid hand-hewn timbers which were fastened with rawhide. On these was placed a layer of reeds, then the traditional red tile. Mission life was active, with the first monk up at five and the chapel filled soon after with kneeling Indians. The sun was peering over the hills when they trooped into the fields, the vineyards, the mill, the shop, while the shepherds and their dogs moved out with their flocks to the grassy slopes.

Father Serra, the missions' founder, was a tireless, devoted humble man who was adored by the Indians, the soldiers, and his religious colleagues alike. At his death his faithful friend and brother priest, Fray Palou, wrote the simple words in the burial register of Carmel Mission —words which can still be read today—"On the twenty-ninth of August, 1784, in this Church of San Carlos, in the sanctuary before the altar of Our Lady of Dolores, the office of the dead having been recited, and a Requiem Mass having been sung, I gave ecclesiastical burial to the

San Diego del Alcala Mission (1769), the first of Father Serra's missions, as it appeared in the 1890's.

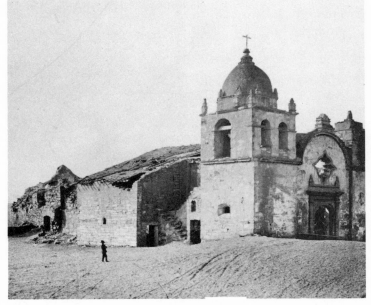

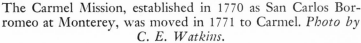

The Carmel Mission, established in 1770 as San Carlos Borromeo at Monterey, was moved in 1771 to Carmel. *Photo by C. E. Watkins.*

San Juan Capistrano Mission before the earthquake of 1812.

San Gabriel Mission.

[19]

Buffalo cow and calf.

Antelope.

Prairie dogs.

Deer, buck and doe.

Jackrabbit.

Elk.

Black bear.

Coyote.

Wildcat.

Rattlesnake.

Mountain lion.

Sage hen.

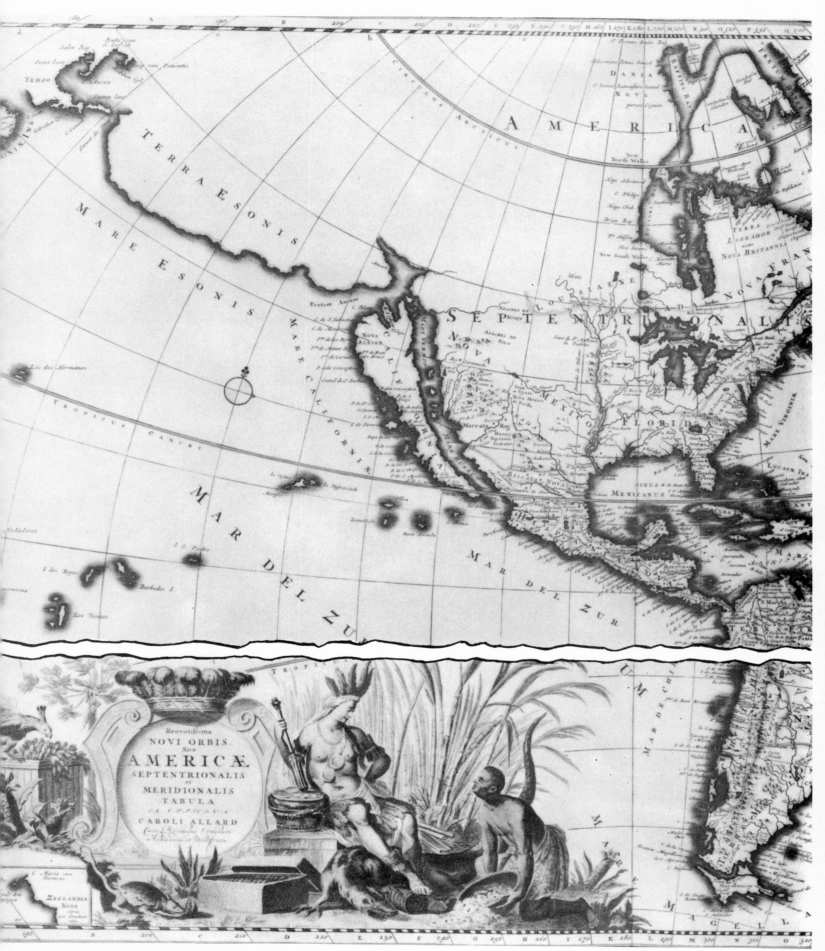

Part of a map of North America, made in Amsterdam, Holland, about 1700. Even
as late as this, California was believed to be an island.

body of Father Lecturer, Fray Junipero Serra, President and Founder of the Missions." Palou's further service to his beloved friend was to write a biography of Serra, one of the most valuable source-books of early western history including descriptions of the Indian tribes and the wild life of the area.

Besides the ecclesiastical reorganization, additional steps were taken to insure the safety of Spain's American frontier. In 1766 the Marqués de Rubí was appointed to make a tour for the purpose of a possible military and administrative reorganization. His party journeyed from Louisiana to California and made a report on conditions, with recommendations for a radical change in policy. The king accepted Rubí's proposal and in 1772 issued a royal order for the establishment of 15 presidios in southern Texas to ensure a firm frontier, leaving everything to the north "to nature and the Indians," as Rubí had put it.

The presidios were to stretch from Bahia del Espiritu Santo to the Gulf of California. Santa Fe and San Antonio, far to the north of the line, would remain as outposts. The royal order also included some of Rubí's recommendations for solution of the Indian problem. They were simple: wipe out the Apaches, who were making trouble with the Comanches. Thus with the Apaches out of the way, the Comanches would calm down and let the settlements alone.

It took the Spaniards five years to try to carry out the king's proposal to wipe out the Apaches. In 1777 El Caballero de Croix arrived in Chihuahua and immediately set the wheels in motion for a mighty Indian campaign. In the end, it was decided to join forces with the Comanches.

The plan called for three large forces to converge on the Apaches from three different directions and force them into an ambush on the Rio Grande. There the Apaches were to be exterminated to the man or else forced into reservations. De Croix proposed that after the Indians were wiped out the Spanish frontier could be advanced further northward and made into a line of demarcation: all those above it were to be considered enemies, all those below it friends, of New Spain.

But the grand plan which certainly would have changed the history of the West was never carried out. Spain suddenly found herself embroiled in European affairs and had no time to think about savages on an endless frontier.

But the Franciscans were still arriving to make Father Serra's dream come true. The last of "Father Serra's beads," San Francisco Solano de Sonoma, was established in 1823. The later missions, many of which can be seen today, were much more successful and effective than the earlier ones and exerted a notable influence on American life not only in California but throughout the Southwest.

In 1821 Mexico rebelled against Spain, won its independence and took over sovereignty of Spanish North America. In 1832 the Mexican government seized church property, and the missions were virtually abandoned (until years later when the property was returned and in some degree restored). By 1848, Mexico itself had lost all its sovereignty over the southwest part of what is now the United States, and the active, direct influence of the Spanish and the Mexicans on American life ceased. What remained was the Spanish heritage.

What did the Spanish leave for the Anglo-Americans who were coming from the East? As we have seen, they implanted a hatred for white men in the hearts of red men. They had also given the Plains Indians horses. To their credit they had cemented an unbreakable friendship with many Indian tribes, especially in California. They introduced longhorn cattle, a colorful fibre in the tapestry of western history; they introduced into the American West the cultivation of orange and lemon trees, as well as orchards and vineyards all of which had a strong effect on the economy and the life of the West. They left behind another kind of seed and fruit—Spanish culture, which is still visible in language, dress and tradition.

The Presidio of San Francisco, 1822.

[23]

Pioneers from the East

IT was after the American Revolution that the colonists on the Atlantic Seaboard looked to the West. Within a few years after Yorktown they began their trek, headed for a new and different world. For generations they had glimpsed this unploughed sea of grass through the leaves and boughs of their eastern forests with mingled fears and dreams. Now they were ready to mold the dream to reality.

But the West and its great future were nothing new to the planners of our infant republic. Even during the Revolution, George Washington had his mind on the West. In 1779, although his Continentals and the Redcoats were deadlocked on the Hudson, he was engaged in a vast strategy that would affect the history of the American West.

By this time Washington was sure that the end of the war was in sight. He saw that when the terms of settlement were drawn, if the young nation got nothing but a strip of land along the East Coast there would be no room for expansion westward. A study of Washington's papers of this period shows that he was carrying on a heavy correspondence with rangers, scouts, travelers, trappers, soldiers and missionaries seeking information about trails, routes, waterways, traders' posts, settlements and the temper of the western tribes. While George Rogers Clark's rifles were storming Vincennes, secret American agents were moving among the western tribes trying to persuade the great Sioux Chief Wabasha to remain neutral, despite the offers made by British agents from Detroit.

Before Yorktown, General Schuyler in his Albany mansion was already moving a pointer across a map of the western frontier and telling his officers that America's destiny lay westward.

After the Revolution many of the men who had fought from Valley Forge to Yorktown moved west to claim their bounty lands. Many Americans, independently of their infant government, rode westward across the Mississippi to seek adventure, to trade with the Indians, to trap and bring back furs, to survey the land. But there were also many organized expeditions and explorations, arranged and financed by companies of merchants as well as by the government.

Captain Gray and the Columbia River

One of the first of these was the expedition of the Boston Marine Association. Its ship, the *Columbia*, with

Captain Robert Gray.

Captain Robert Gray in command, set sail in 1790 for the Pacific Northwest. After making several attempts to penetrate the breakers of the body of water known as Deception Bay, in the spring of 1792 Captain Gray finally succeeded, naming the river he discovered the Columbia in honor of the ship. This discovery gave the United States clear claim to the Oregon country—Oregon, Washington and Idaho—which Great Britain recognized in the Oregon Treaty of 1846. And the reports of the discovery and the nature of the land in the Columbia valley did much to stimulate interest in and emigration to Oregon.

Lewis and Clark

It was Thomas Jefferson who conceived, sponsored and organized the Lewis and Clark expedition, authorized by Congress in 1803. He knew it was important for the young nation to make a survey of the unexplored western lands. Jefferson's secretary, Meriwether Lewis, was in charge, William Clark was selected as associate commander.

The year 1803 is probably best known to most Americans for the Louisiana Purchase, and this great event had a curious impact on the Lewis and Clark expedition. It was the popular opinion that the purpose of the expedition was to map out the new territory, rather than to survey the West to the Pacific. As a result of the Purchase, national interest was stimulated in the expedition and all news of it was eagerly awaited, repeated and discussed

Meriwether Lewis.   William Clark.   Zebulon Pike in the uniform of an officer
                                                                        of the War of 1812.

throughout the country. This accounts, in part, for the great fame of the Lewis and Clark expedition, which was and is probably greater than it deserves, for it did not really accomplish the satisfactory survey which was its purpose. In comparison to the records kept by chroniclers of Coronado's expedition, the journals and reports kept by its members are vague and lack scientific detail.

The expedition assembled near St. Louis and on May 14, 1804, started up the Missouri River. When it neared the Columbia River it made portages over the intervening land, went down the Columbia to the Pacific and was back in St. Louis on September 23, 1806. Their return sparked nation-wide excitement and spurred the organization of many emigrant parties to the West. In this clarion "call to the West" lies its real significance.

The Louisiana Purchase and the Influence of the French on the West

The Louisiana Purchase from France for about $15,000,-000 in 1803 more than doubled the size of the United States. Included in this vast territory west of the Mississippi was the land incorporating the states of Arkansas, Missouri, Iowa, most of Minnesota, North Dakota, South Dakota, Nebraska, most of Kansas, Oklahoma, parts of Montana, Wyoming and Colorado and almost all of Louisiana, including New Orleans.

France had owned this territory until 1762, when she ceded it to Spain. Then, in 1800, Spain ceded it back again to the French. In 1803 Napoleon, needing the money, sold it to the United States. The importance of the addition of this great area to the territory of the United States cannot be overestimated. The fur trade out of St. Louis accounted for the few white settlements at the time.

The French influence on the American West was rather negligible. Apart from the area near New Orleans, where the French culture put down enduring roots, there is little in the rest of the Louisiana Territory to show the French had ever been there, except for place names, of which there are many.

The Zebulon M. Pike Expedition

While the Lewis and Clark expedition was moving across the West, Zebulon M. Pike set out from St. Louis on a July day in 1806. He had 23 white men and 51 Indians and a plan to cross the plains to the Rocky Mountains. He went up the Arkansas River to its source, then moved southward to the Rio Grande country, where he was captured and brought before the governor of (Spanish) New Mexico at Santa Fe. Eventually he was taken across Texas and brought to the Louisiana border. Pike left behind careful journals of his expedition, especially of Texas and the plains country.

Summit of Pike's Peak. *Photo by W. H. Jackson.*

To the Senate & House of Representatives of the United States

In pursuance of a measure proposed to Congress by a message of Jan. 18. 1803. and sanctioned by their appropriation for carrying it into execution, Capt Meriwether Lewis of the 1^t regiment of in-

copies of his map of the river, from it's mouth to the Hot-springs, make part of the present communications. the ex--amination of the Red river itself. is but now commencing.

Th: Jefferson

Feb. 19. 1806.

Portion of Jefferson's letter to Congress, February 19, 1806, reporting on the Lewis and Clark expedition.

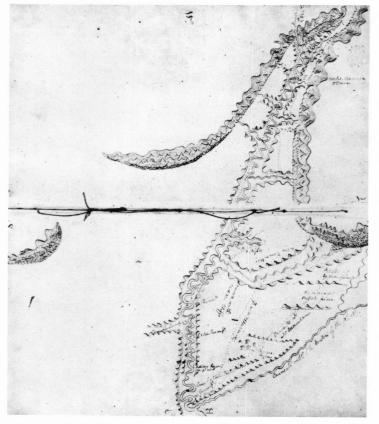

A map of the Pike's Peak region, 1806, from Pike's journal.

The Yellowstone or Stephen H. Long Expedition

In 1819 the United States launched one of its most important western explorations. Not only soldiers and adventurers but also men of science accompanied Major Stephen A. Long's small army, which was ordered to seek sites for posts which would offset the British strength which had been spreading and growing in the north. The party spent the winter of 1819-20 at Engineer Cantonment, near Council Bluffs. Congress changed its plans and, following its instructions, in the spring the party went up the River Platte, sighted the Rocky Mountains and encamped at what is now Denver. At the Arkansas River the party split; one division came down the Arkansas; the other, under Long, set out for the Red River, but by mistake struck the Canadian. The reports of Long's expedition by Edwin James, a physician, which were full of botanical, geological and other scientific data, proved to have great value and importance.

Trappers, Fur Traders, Mountain Men

Besides these three major expeditions there were a number of other explorations during this period and shortly after it. More important perhaps were the commercial activities of trading and fur companies, which helped to blaze trails and prepare the way for emigrants. Outstanding among these were the companies founded by John Jacob Astor, Manuel Lisa and General William H. Ashley.

In 1811 Astor established an important post on the Columbia River and later set up outposts on the Willamette, Spokane and Kanogan Rivers in the Northwest.

In 1870 Manuel Lisa, the St. Louis fur trader, led an expedition up the Missouri and Yellowstone to establish a trading post at the mouth of the Little Bighorn. He set up many trading posts and settlements, made friends of the Indians, loaned them traps, taught them much more about agriculture and medicine and helped them in many other ways.

In the War of 1812 Lisa defeated the attempts of the British to unite the Sioux. More than a year before the war he had warned General Clark that secret agents of the British were attempting to bribe the Sioux to take up arms against the Americans. Had they done so it would have been impossible to estimate the damage done to the posts on the Missouri.

When the war was over the chagrined British agents discovered that more than 40 chiefs whom they had counted as supporters "had intelligence from Lisa" and

Manuel Lisa.

"Jim Bridger Crossing a River." *Sketch by Alfred Jacob Miller.*

Antoine Clement, mountain man, scout and hunter.

Bill Burrows, a Rocky Mountain trapper.

were preparing a campaign of several thousand warriors against the tribes of the Upper Missouri. Only then was is learned that Lisa had quietly sent his own agents among the tribes during the war, inciting them to make war against one another and thus "keeping them too busy with their own affairs to permit them to interfere with the war between England and the United States."

General Ashley and the men he led on his fur-trading ventures in the 1820's were notable for the trails they blazed in the northern Rocky Mountain country. Among Ashley's "mountain men" were a number who became famous and established their places in Western history as scouts, fur-traders, keelboatmen, Indian fighters—Jedediah Smith, the five Sublette brothers, Jim Bridger, Mike Fink, Robert Campbell, Jim Beckwourth and others.

Smith and Bill Sublette "discovered" the South Pass across the Rocky Mountains. At least they were the first to report about this passage, which became a crucial factor in the Oregon Trail migration in the years to come. They also found and gave full details about the Cimarron cut-off and other shortcuts on the way west.

Not only did these mountain men provide much valuable information about the previously unknown mountain country but also they cleared and eased the way—by marking trails, establishing landmarks and posts—for the great wagon-trains of emigrants, a number of which they guided.

Britain's Hudson's Bay Company was quite active in the Northwest country at the time and made many trespasses into the United States' Oregon territory. The mountain men helped to defend the territory against the British company. (Their resistance was an important factor in the celebrated "54-40 or fight" controversy with the British, which was resolved by the Oregon Treaty in 1846, which defined the Oregon border at 49° North Latitude.)

Forts and Cavalry Posts

As the trappers and traders moved into the West they established at strategic points supply and trading posts, fortified against attacks by Indians. The Army also set up military posts as the need for them became apparent (Fort Leavenworth was established in 1827), but there was not much of an organized program of frontier defense until 1845, when Congress voted to establish a series of military posts along the trail to Oregon, and to organize a regiment of expert "Mounted Riflemen" to garrison the forts.

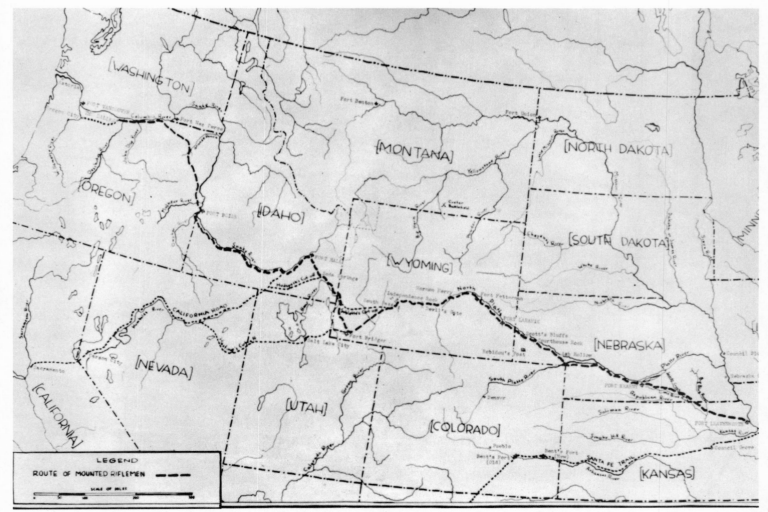

The route of the Mounted Riflemen, May-October, 1849.

Fort Leavenworth, 1849.

The Mexican War broke out before the regiment of mounted riflemen could start on their western orders. But in 1849, after distinguished service at Cerro Gordo, Chapultepec and elsewhere in Mexico, they started on their route from Council Bluffs along the Oregon Trail to Oregon City. The posts they established became the nucleus of the War Department's network of forts and garrisons to protect and police the western lands, all exclusively under federal jurisdiction until the establishment of state governments. The "cavalry" had taken its stand.

The explorations and ventures of the traders and trappers and many others like them were opening up the West. Though Lewis and Clark chose to travel on the rivers, later expeditions and venturers into the West found it better and easier to travel overland. By about 1840 there were two fairly well established Trails across the West—the Santa Fe Trail and the Oregon Trail.

Fort Laramie, 1849.

Landing at Weston, May, 1849.

Fort Hall, 1849.

Texas: Province, Republic, State

Stephen Austin.

Sam Houston. *Photo by Mathew Brady.*

IT was in 1821 that Stephen F. Austin led a group of Americans into the Mexican province of Texas and founded a colony along the Brazos and Colorado Rivers. It was highly successful; word of it spread to the East, and the colony of Americans flourished and expanded.

Austin was astute in his dealings with the Indians, but the colony was not without trouble with some of the tribes, especially when it spread beyond the original borders. In 1826 Austin called a conference at which it was arranged to have 20 to 30 mounted guards constantly ranging the borders of the colony. These rangers were the forerunners of the famed Texas Rangers.

The Texan colonists had trouble not only with the Indians but also with the Mexican government, and this eventually, in 1835, erupted into revolution. Sam Houston was made commander-in-chief of the Texas army and the bitter struggle with the Mexicans, led by Santa Anna, began. The climax of the war was the famous battle of the Alamo, which lasted from February 23 to March 6, 1836.

One hundred and eighty Texans, commanded by Colonel W. B. Travis and including Davy Crockett, James Bowie and other well-known heroes were surrounded by a Mexican army of 1,600 and besieged in a fort that was formerly a mission known as the Alamo. The Texans fought until the last defender was killed. Their heroic

fight and the rallying cry "Remember the Alamo" inspired the Texans and undoubtedly was a factor in speeding victory for the revolutionists. In the battle of San Jacinto months later Sam Houston defeated Santa Anna, independence was won and the Lone Star Republic of Texas was established with Sam Houston as its president.

During the Revolution the Texas Rangers had been given official status as a law-enforcement agency. The new Republic was not recognized by Mexico, and besides the chaos of the war there was constant harassment by both the Mexicans and Indians. In time the Rangers became a guardian force of the young nation.

By 1840 the Rangers had become a permanent fixture on the frontier, with headquarters at San Antonio under Colonel John Coffee Hays. Their weapons were those of the frontier: cap-and-ball rifle, which took a minute to load—a minute which could be fatal—the horse pistol, single-action revolver or the smaller derringer. The hard-riding Texans were desperate for a better weapon when Sam Colt appeared on the scene. The former sailor whittled a model of the famous six-shooter when he was serving aboard a clipper enroute to Calcutta from Boston. He took out his first patent in 1836, the year Texas established its independence.

In 1838 Colt began manufacturing revolvers in Paterson, New Jersey. He could not get the U. S. Army or

Commandancy of Bejar ⎱ 1836,
Feby 23d 3 o'clock P.M. ⎰
To Andrew Ponton judge &
to the Citizens of Gonzales —
The enemy in large force
is in sight — We want men & pro
visions — Send them to us — We
have 150 men & are determined
to defend the Alamo to the last —
Give us assistance —
W.B. Travis
Lt. Col. Comdt

P.S. Send an express to San
Felipe with this news — night
& day —
Travis

The last message of Colonel Travis, "We have 100 men and are determined to defend the Alamo to the last. Give us assistance—"

Colonel Jack Hays.

From a daguerreotype of Captain Samuel H. Walker.

Unofficial.
Dear Sir.
I am induced to believe
from all the facts communicated to us
that the Alamo, has fallen, and all our
Men are murdered! We must not depend
upon Forts; the woods, and Cavins suit
us best.
12 th Mar 1836
Your friend
Sam Houston

Sam Houston's famous letter of March, 1836.

DAILY BULLETIN---EXTRA.

GAZETTE OFFICE, JANUARY 18, 1842.

FROM SANTA FE.

Capture of the Texian Expedition confirmed—Indignity to the American Consul, and the Resident Americans in Santa Fé!!!

Under the above caption we find in the Missouri Republican of the 24th, three letters, received from Independence the evening previous, announcing painful intelligence from Santa Fé, and confirming the news of the capture of the Texian Expedition. The recital of the treatment shown the American citizens (the Republican thinks) will rouse the blood of every one, and calls for revenge. "The treatment of our Consul, Senor Alvarez, and the destruction of the property of

Howland, with two more, was sent in advance as spies, to ascertain the disposition of the Mexicans towards them.

Not understanding the nature of their embassy sufficiently, and from their contradictory statements concerning the place from whence they hailed, they were stripped and ordered not to leave the bounds. In the meantime they made their escape—but after travelling five days and only progressing fifty miles, they were taken by some shepherds, brought in and shot. Seven more from the company were again sent in---among them was Kendall, the editor of the Picayune, a son of Leslie _____ and a Mr. Lewis—they had in

A newspaper report of the Santa Fe massacre.

28th Congress. Second Session. Begun and held at the city of Washington, in the District of Columbia, on Monday the second day of December, eighteen hundred and forty-four.

Joint Resolution for annexing Texas to the United States.

Resolved by the Senate and House of Representatives of the United States of Amer-

that the sum of one hundred thousand dollars be, and the same is hereby, appropriated to defray the expenses of missions and negotiations, to agree upon the terms of said admission and cession, either by treaty to be submitted to the Senate, or by articles to be submitted to the two Houses of Congress, as the President may direct.

J W Jones Speaker of the House of Representatives.

Willie P. Mangum President, pro tempore, of the Senate.

Approv'd March 1. 1845

John Tyler

Resolution of Congress for the annexation of Texas.

[32]

Navy to buy his revolvers; but orders began to come in from Texas and the six-shooter got to be known as the "Texas." In the forties Ranger captain Sam H. Walker came to New York to buy revolvers and met the inventor.

Walker made several suggestions and a new and improved weapon, which Colt called the "Walker Pistol," was made. This new six-shooter made its great reputation in the battle of Pedernales, in which Colonel Hays and 14 rangers were engaged by 70 Comanches. Before the battle ended, 30 redskins were killed. It was a major victory, and the success was clearly due to the newly designed six-shooter that a mounted man could use easily. It gave the Ranger, or any mounted man who had it, the edge to outfight and outgun the Indians. It helped to establish the Colt as a major weapon, a firearm of crucial importance in the history of the West for the next 50 years. But national and world fame did not come until war with Mexico broke out and the Rangers offered their services to General Zachary Taylor. Under pressure from the Rangers, Taylor ordered a thousand Colts at a price of $28,000.

Every soldier in the war marveled at the Rangers' finely balanced six-shooter. With widespread recognition and enthusiasm for his revolver, Colt soon became a millionaire. Now no one went west without a Colt on his hip.

The Mexican War

The United States' war with Mexico started in 1846, primarily because the Republic of Texas, which in 1836 asked to be admitted to the Union, was finally annexed as the twenty-eighth state, in December, 1845. Mexico still regarded Texas as Mexican territory. There were other frictions and pressures in addition to claims of aggression by Mexico, which could not be resolved by negotiation. The was began in May, 1846. In rather rapid succession, Santa Fe was captured; California came under U. S. control and Santa Anna and his army were defeated, but not at all routed, at Buena Vista (February, 1847). In March, 1847, Winfield Scott, with Navy help, took Vera Cruz. The war virtually ended when Mexico City was occupied September 14, 1847.

The peace treaty was ratified in March, 1848. Mexico ceded about half its territory—its provinces of New Mexico and California—out of which also parts of the states of Nevada, Utah, Colorado and Wyoming were carved. The Texas-Mexico border was fixed at the Rio Grande.

A portion of northwestern Texas was ceded to the United States for $10,000,000, by the Compromise Act of 1850. This land eventually became part of the States of New Mexico, Colorado, Wyoming, Kansas and Oklahoma.

In 1853, through the Gadsden Purchase, the United States acquired from Mexico another 45,000 square miles —for the most part south of the Gila River—now the tip of southwest New Mexico and the southern extreme of Arizona. This fixed the southwest boundary of the United States as it is today.

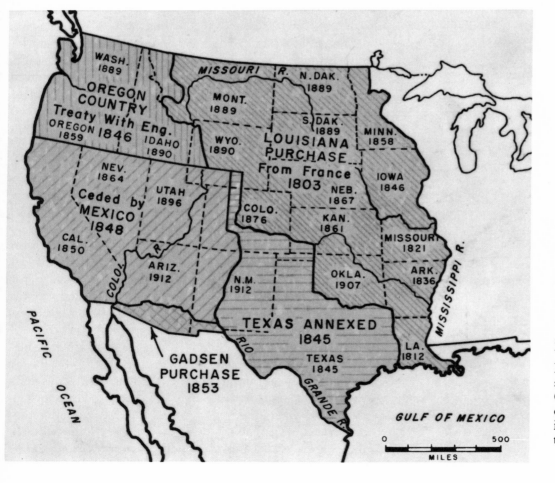

The acquisition and annexation of the western territory, with dates of admission of the states. Though the United States' claim to the Oregon territory dated back to 1792, the British disputed it and the area was under joint jurisdiction from 1816 to 1846. Wisconsin and eastern Minnesota were part of the Northwest Territory organized in 1787. British claims to the area were abandoned in 1814 (Treaty of Ghent). The area shown as part of the 1845 Texas annexation that is not now Texas was ceded to the United States for $10,000,000 by the Compromise of 1850.

Trails West

IN 1834 Congress passed the Indian Intercourse Act designed to resolve relations with the tribes. Among other things, this act provided that an area be set aside for the resettlement in the West of eastern and southern Indians including the Five Civilized Tribes—Cherokees, Creeks, Seminoles, Choctaws and Chickasaws. The territory set aside was part of what is now northeast Oklahoma, and it came to be known as Indian Territory. The program of forcible removal of the Indians actually started following the War of 1812, when some property of the Creek nation was confiscated because some of their

John Ross, the Scots-Indian chief of the Cherokees.

warriors had followed their great chief Tecumseh to the side of the British. This war loot was sold to white settlers four decades later for $11,250,000. In 1817 a delegation of Cherokee chiefs journeyed to Washington. They left with their X's drying on the parchment, suffering monstrous hangovers and with most of their land gone. The liquor bill for getting the chiefs so drunk they didn't know what they were signing was $1,298.50.

The shattering blow fell after Andrew Jackson became President. With the discovery of gold in northern Georgia, whites began to encroach on the treaty lands of the Cherokee—with the connivance of the backwoods President, no friend of the Indians. The tribes struck back with the white man's weapon: an appeal to the courts. They, finally, under the leadership of John Ross, the Scots-Indian chief of the Cherokees, fought the case up to the Supreme Court, where Chief Justice John Marshall said they were right but the court couldn't help them. Under relentless pressure, the Indians were forced off their ancestral lands.

At last the Five Civilized Tribes were rooted up and transferred to lands in the present state of Oklahoma. For many of the refugees, the trip which the red men knew as the "Trail of Tears" was a death march. Many of the old, the infirm, the sick and the children died on the way. Of 1,000 Choctaw emigrants, Captain Jacob Brown wrote in 1830, "only 88 survived."

For some 40 years they would live in relative peace until once again the white man could covet the lands of the Five Civilized Tribes, dreaming of his plow biting deep into the sweet green grass that bent under the prairie wind.

The Oregon Trail

The mass emigration from the East to the Promised Land of Oregon's beautiful Willamette Valley has no precedent in American history, perhaps none in the world. The Promise started with Captain Gray and his reports on the discovery of the Columbia River. It was renewed by Lewis and Clark and reinforced by the accounts of such fur traders and trading companies as John Jacob Astor, the Northwest Company, the Hudson's Bay Company, Frémont and others.

In the 1830's, when some of the older employees of the Hudson's Bay Company, especially the French trappers and bateauxmen, began to talk of retirement, the company urged them to settle in the Willamette Valley.

A tall, young minister, Reverend Jason Lee, who had established a small mission in this valley, helped touch off the great emigration. In an attempt to raise funds for the mission, he had embarked on a lecture tour in the East. Lee's magnetic descriptions of the valley excited audiences wherever he went. It seemed all America was repeating the stories told by the Reverend.

There were many others, like the pioneer Jesse Applegate, who helped to spur on the great emigration. At first, small groups started out, but the real movement came with the development of the "emigrant train," a large, organized self-sufficient party of many families, perhaps hundreds, each skilled at a trade or profession. Almost all went by wagon, oxen-drawn, starting from Missouri. The jumping-off places were chiefly Independence and Kansas

City (then Westport Landing), and sometimes Omaha.

As many noted in their diaries and memoirs, Independence teemed with life. On the dusty streets the emigrants stared at the swarthy-faced Spanish traders with large black hats, or the mountain men, whose fringed buckskin jackets rustled softly as they walked toe in. There were also impeccably dressed gamblers, drunken bucks and snarling Indian dogs. One thing they all recalled: above the noise of the creaking wagons, the whooping and shouting and the cracking of the whips was the steady, constant clanging of hammers on anvils from the numerous blacksmith shops where the wagons were being readied or repaired.

When the trappers or the company men brought in word that the plains were again green, the wagon-master, always a man of much experience with the tribes and the trails, gathered his captains and gave the word to pull out. The next day at sun-up the wagon-master would stand in his stirrups, wave his hat and point west. The long line of canvas-covered prairie-schooners would begin covering the first 50 miles to the Platte, then along that boiling river to the North Platte and the Sweetwater, across the Rocky Mountains at South Pass to the Bear and Snake, then through the Blue Mountains to the Columbia and down that river to the valley and the Pacific.

At the Raft River some trains headed south on the California trail, but most kept on the Snake to the Oregon border 300 miles away. In this journey that spanned half a continent the average wagon traveled two miles an hour, 12 miles a day.

When they reached the Platte the emigrants were in buffalo and hostile Indian country. There they found also that firewood was buffalo dung—"buffalo chips" or "prairie coal." One woman proudly noted in her journal that her son could fill a basket in one minute. Once on the Great Plains the pioneers saw herds of buffalo and were

Wagon trains at Independence Rock. The Sweetwater River is seen at the left.
From a painting by W. H. Jackson.

awed. Armies of the big shaggy-haired beasts seemed to come out of the ground, making the earth tremble as they moved across the land, the pall of dust rising to the empty sky. One man who had waited for hours for a herd to pass wrote in wonderment: "They are still here."

Oxen were chosen by the first pioneers for three reasons: they were more durable; they could be used for plowing in Oregon, and they tasted better than horseflesh. A team usually cost fifty dollars. An average wagonload consisted of 150 pounds of flour, 15 of coffee, 25 of sugar and baking soda. Matches were kept in a corked bottle. Then there were pots, pans and the inevitable gutta-percha bucket for water. Percha was a paintlike waterproofing substance. The head of the house also carefully selected spare wagon parts, along with a Colt, rifle and ammunition.

It was in 1842 that the first emigrant train (led by Elijah White) reached Oregon, but in 1841 an earlier train did reach California. Thereafter, for many years the "trains" rolled in constantly.

The many journals, diaries and letters left by these "men of destiny" paint a vivid picture of the almost unbelievable human tenacity, ingenuity and raw courage that enabled the thousands of men, women and children to cross 2,000 miles of an alien, hostile land. They stopped only for birth and death. They battled sandstorms, snow, sleet, freezing cold and boiling heat; cholera left a trail of graves from Missouri to Oregon. So did the arrows of the Sioux. But the emigrants did not turn back. They were pointed West and nothing could turn their heads.

The Santa Fe Trail

There was another old route west, starting from Missouri at Independence or Westport Landing. That was the Santa Fe trail, used since the 1820's, but almost exclusively by traders. It ended, more or less, at Santa Fe.

In addition to the overland routes there was a waterway which the more wealthy used. Clipper ships sailed from New York around South America to Hawaii, then to

Francis Parkman. *Photo by Benjamin Kimball.*

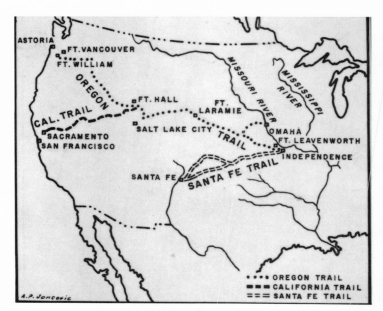

The trails west.

Crossing the Platte.

San Francisco and on to Fort Vancouver. Fare: $500. During the gold strike of '49 miners sailed from New York to the Isthmus of Panama, crossed the mountains with a pack horse or mules and sailed on up the Pacific Coast to San Francisco. The time of the grueling trip was about six weeks.

The Pathfinder—John Charles Frémont

In the 1840's the foremost individual stimulator of "Oregon fever" was the popular idol John Charles Frémont, who came to be known as "The Pathfinder." In 1842 he explored the Trail as far as South Pass, Wyoming. He also ascended the summit of the second peak of the Wind River Mountains, today known as Frémont's Peak. In 1843 he was sent to complete the survey of the trail to the mouth of the Columbia River. His guide on this trip

General John C. Frémont. *Photo by Mathew Brady.*

was Kit Carson, one of the West's greatest scouts. They traveled south and east by way of Klamath Lake to Northwestern Nevada, continuing to the Truckee and Carson Rivers. The reports Frémont sent back captured the imagination of the country and stirred the wanderlust to fever pitch. Emigration boomed.

In the spring of 1845 Frémont led his third expedition to the Great Basin and Pacific Coast. But this time he carried secret orders. He and a party of 62 men traversed the Great Basin down to the valley of the Humboldt. In January, 1846, he reached California.

When news of the outbreak of the Mexican War reached California, Frémont carried out his secret orders and all of the northern region of California fell into American hands. In January, 1847, Frémont and Commodore Stockton had completed the conquest of California, but the young Pathfinder found himself between two opposing army factions and resigned after a bitter court-martial.

Following his resignation, Frémont set out on a fourth expedition to find passes for the Pacific Railroad. This time, instead of the reliable Carson, he had the erratic Bill Williams as a guide. The party was caught in a blizzard and 11 men died. Frémont's party finally wound up in California, to be greeted by the news of the great gold strike at Sutter's Mill.

On to Zion

In between the first great emigration to Oregon and the mad rush to the gold fields of California there was another notable movement of Americans across the wilderness of the West. This time it wasn't the yellow metal or the yearning for new lands that lured them on. It was the more important desire for religious freedom.

The men, women and children who would take part in the march to a new Zion were Mormons, members of Joseph Smith's Church of Jesus Christ of Latter Day Saints. The movement west actually grew out of the fron-

This photograph of an Indian village may possibly be one taken by S. N. Carvalho. The plate which was found in the Mathew Brady daguerreotype collection, Library of Congress, may have been copied by wet-plate by Brady.

October 5. Hot Springs. The morning was calm and clear and at sunrise the thermometer was at 32. The road to day was occasionally extremely rocky with hard volcanic fragments, and our travelling very slow. In about nine miles the road brought us to a group of smoking hot springs with a temperature of 164. There were a few helianthi in bloom with some other low plants and the place was green round about, the ground warm and the air pleasant with a summer atmosphere that was very grateful in a day of high and cold searching wind. The rocks were covered with a white and red incrustation, and the water has on the tongue the same unpleasant effect as that of the Basin spring on Bear river. They form several branches and bubble up with force enough to raise the small pebbles several inches.

Fremont's Report

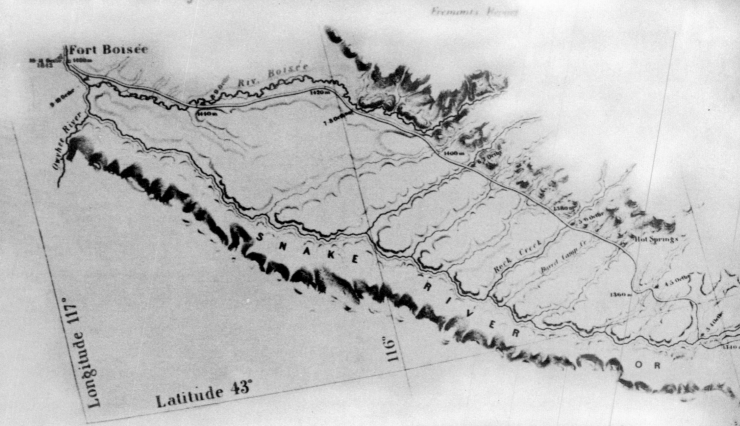

October 1. Fishing Falls. Our encampment was about one mile below the Fishing Falls, a series of cataracts with very inclined planes, which are probably so named because they form a barrier to the ascent of the salmon; and the great fisheries from which the inhabitants of this barren region almost entirely derive a subsistence commence at this place. These appeared to be unusually gay savages ... and merry character struck me as being entirely different from the Indians we had been accustomed to see. From several who visited our camp in the evening we purchased in exchange for goods dried salmon. At this season they are not very fat, but we were easily pleased. The Indians made us comprehend that when the salmon came up the river in the spring they are so abundant that they merely throw in their spears at random, certain of transfixing a fish.

Fremont's Report

1. The figures on the road indicate the distance in miles from Westport Landing.
2. This is the most trying section for the traveller on the whole route. Water, though good and plenty, is difficult to reach, as the river is hemmed in by high and vertical rocks and many of the by streams are without water in the dry season. Grass is only to be found at the marked camping places, and barely sufficient to keep strong animals from starvation. Game there is none. The road is very rough by volcanic rocks, detrimental to wagons and carts. In sage bushes consists the only fuel. Lucky that by all these hardships the traveller is not harassed by the Indians, who are peaceable & harmless.
3. West of the Fishing Falls salmon, fresh and dried, can be obtained from the Indians.

Section six of a seven-section topographical map based on the field notes and journal kept by Frémont, compiled by Charles Preuss, 1846. The notes for October 1—Fishing Falls—and for October 5—Hot Springs—have been enlarged.

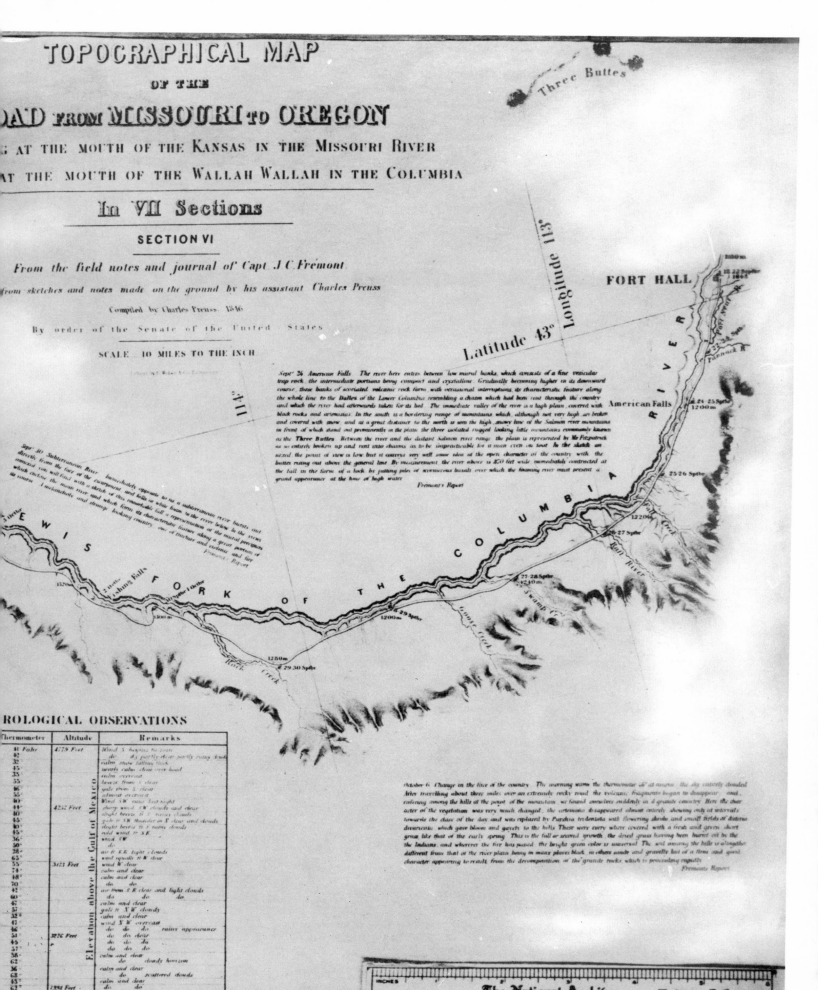

TOPOGRAPHICAL MAP
OF THE
OAD FROM MISSOURI TO OREGON

AT THE MOUTH OF THE KANSAS IN THE MISSOURI RIVER
AT THE MOUTH OF THE WALLAH WALLAH IN THE COLUMBIA

In VII Sections

SECTION VI

From the field notes and journal of Capt. J. C. Fremont

from sketches and notes made on the ground by his assistant Charles Preuss

Compiled by Charles Preuss 1846

By order of the Senate of the United States

SCALE 10 MILES TO THE INCH

Three Buttes

Latitude 43°

Longitude 113°

FORT HALL

American Falls

LEWIS FORK OF THE COLUMBIA

ROLOGICAL OBSERVATIONS

Joseph Smith.

Brigham Young.

tier's antagonism toward the Mormons, which finally exploded when a mob of 200 men with blackened faces stormed the jailhouse at Carthage, Illinois, to murder Smith and his brother. Brigham Young, who inherited the Prophet's mantle, decided that he and his people must find a new Zion.

In March, 1846, Brigham Young and a band of Mormons, after spending a terrifying winter at Nauvoo, Illinois, began moving toward they "knew not what." Food was scarce and the roads were almost impassable. Despite great hardships, the Mormons displayed a powerful sense of organization. Teams were formed to build and repair wagons, and to make chairs, stools, beds, tubs and barrels for sale on the road. Others split logs, and still others roamed the countryside to "invite" rich Gentiles to contribute to the needs of the Saints. Because of the wet weather which delayed them for weeks a main camp was set up in a day at a point called Mount Pisgah. When the weather broke, the train set out with the Saints "coming in all directions from hills and dales and groves and prairies with their wagons, flocks and herds by the thousands. It looked like the movement of a nation."

When they reached the banks of the Missouri, near the present city of Council Bluffs, they erected a ferry and began moving their people across. So great was the number that the task was not completed until late fall, when a winter camp was established across the river.

In the meantime other groups were preparing a more sturdy winter camp about six miles north of Omaha, Nebraska. Called "Winter Quarters," it spread across some 800 acres. Within a short time there were 558 log cabins and 83 sod buildings.

A Mormon emigrant train.

In addition to the homes and workshops, a grist mill and a large tabernacle were erected. Not only men but women worked from dawn to dusk. However, the regular diet of salt pork, corn bread and no vegetables brought on scurvy and finally death. By mid-year one in ten was seriously ill. But death, suffering and hardship were no strangers to the Mormons and could not break their spirit.

Finally spring came and Young and a select corps of men moved out to explore the land for their new Zion. This body, known officially as the Pioneers, gathered on the Elkhorn River and left on April 14, 1847. An advance group went ahead to scout out the land. Every ten miles guideboards were erected. Sometimes messages were put inside or on a buffalo skull, stuck in a split board or a buckskin pouch.

The train was again delayed when mountain fever laid low most of the Pioneers. Brigham Young ordered those who were still physically able to move on while he remained with the sick. The advance scouts found the valley now known as Salt Lake City Valley and on July 24, Brigham Young arrived. After silently gazing over the valley, he said, "This is the place." A week later houses were springing up and 50 acres were under the plow.

In August word was sent back to Winter Quarters, or "Misery Bottom," as the veterans called it, and a second party, 1,500 Saints in 560 wagons, left the following June.

For the next 20 years emigrants left from some point or other on the Mississippi or Missouri to cross the plains to Salt Lake City Valley.

In the year 1849 a plan was put into effect which brought many Mormons to America and across the plains to Salt Lake. The tide of emigration was so strong that Young introduced hand carts, the strangest method of transportation in the history of the West.

The carts were two-wheeled vehicles about the width of a wagon with a four-foot-long box balanced on the axle with a handle and long cross-bar to pull and balance the cart. The carts could hold a load of 500 pounds, although the only iron part was the wheel rim. During four

Main Street, Salt Lake City, probably in the 1850's.

years more than 3,000 Saints pulled these carts across the 1,031-mile journey.

In 1856 the largest hand-cart expedition, known as the Hand Cart Brigade, started out. Unfortunately, the lack of vehicles had delayed the departure until late in the season.

For many, the trip was a grim one. One man recalled how his infant sister died and a tiny grave was dug. Services were quickly over and the weary, heartsick mother stepped back into her position at the cross-bar. In South Pass more than 15 Saints died. In another company starvation and the bitter cold claimed one-sixth of its numbers.

Yet, on the whole not all the hand-cart expeditions were disasters. Those that started in a sensible time of the year walked and dragged their carts the 1,400 miles from Iowa City in nine weeks and had fewer deaths than the wagon trains. Some days they made as much as 30 miles, twice the mileage of the oxen teams.

Mormon hand-cart train.

Gold Strike

ON the morning of January 24, 1848, as James W. Marshall set to work to widen the mill race of the mill he and John Sutter had built on the south fork of the American River in California, he saw a glittering stone in the water, reached down and picked it out. For more than ten years he had heard the Mexicans talk of finding gold in the waterways.

Now as he examined the stone he felt mounting excitement. He hurried back to the camp and put the nugget into boiling lye. Late that afternoon when he retrieved it, the dull gold look had not been tarnished. Almost surely his stone was a nugget of gold.

That night he brought the nugget to Sutter and they made further tests. It was undeniably gold.

Before they parted both men had agreed to keep the news secret. Sutter had good reason; he knew what would happen to the pleasant frontier barony he had established on a 43,000-acre land grant from Mexico's Governor Alvarado. He had built a mill, factory, blacksmith shop and even a distillery. He had Hawaiians and Indians tilling the fertile soil; he even had schooners moving up and down the Sacramento River. There were few trappers or travelers who didn't know of New Helvetia, as he called his empire. Lately Americans from the States had leased some of his land. It was not only profitable but homey. But if word of the gold strike got out, Sutter knew, a human avalanche would pour into his peaceful domain.

The news did leak out. In June, 1848, it was being discussed freely in New York and in Honolulu. One of the biggest gold rushes of world history was on.

Down in drowsy Monterey, the capital, Walter Colton, the *alcade*, or town magistrate, wrote in wonderment: "The blacksmith dropped his hammer, the carpenter his plane, the mason his trowel, the baker his loaf . . . some came on crutches . . . one man was carried in a litter . . . !"

The editor of the New York *Herald* remarked, "Even the bachelors are departing their comforts . . ."

Commodore Jones, commanding the U. S. Naval Squadron in Monterey harbor, reported that shiploads of men had deserted for the gold fields, "even men who are owed nine months' pay."

In the year 1852 the fields actually produced $200,000,-

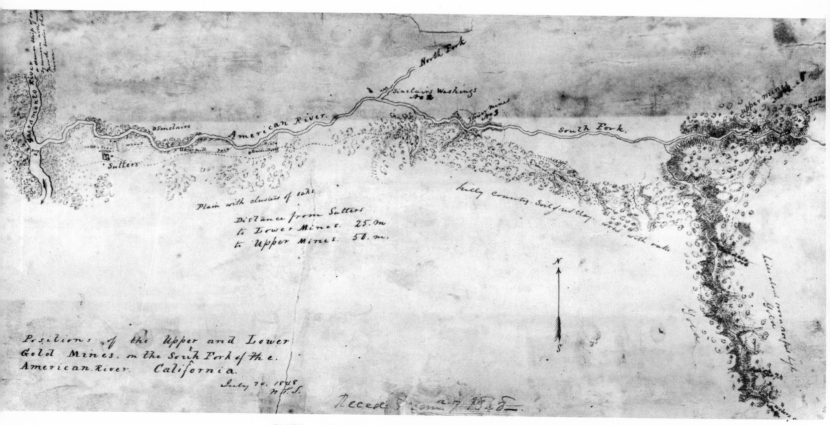

William T. Sherman's map of the gold regions, 1848.

000 in gold. That same month John Sutter was writing this sad entry in his diary: "Hosts are arriving by water and land for the mountains." These same "hosts" would swarm over his peaceful land like a horde of locusts, finally driving him into bankruptcy.

How many people were lured to the fields is anybody's estimate. But the census figures show that in 1848, prior to the strike, there were 20,000 residents in California. By 1852 this had grown to 225,000. However, the population was so transient it is almost impossible to arrive at an exact figure.

The miners traveled the same trail—up to a point—that the settlers took to the Oregon Trail. They also could use the water route to San Francisco or the overland trail or Sante Fe Trail via the Isthmus of Darien (Panama) which could be crossed in six weeks by mule train.

Countless thousands died on the way; almost as many graves marked the southern arm of the Oregon Trail as marked the one which led to the Willamette Valley. At sea many clippers sank off the Horn. The terrible jungle heat of Darien also claimed many lives.

And when the gold-seeker did reach the fields he found that the tales he had heard were exaggerated; one did not just reach in a stream and pick up nuggets as big as a hen's egg. To get gold a man sometimes had to stand eight hours a day in waist-high icy water and pan perhaps only enough gold to keep him alive. And if he made a modest pile he would probably have to spend it all on food; $6 for half a dozen eggs, $100 for a small barrel of flour. . . .

A few weeks after Marshall's discovery, the joint Army and Navy commanders at Monterey agreed that Washington should be notified immediately of the great strike. It was decided that two picked men should leave—one

Gold mining in California. *A daguerreotype made about 1854 by R. H. Vance.*

was to take an overland route, the other, a water one.

The Army selected a Lieutenant Loeser; the Navy, Lieutenant Edward Fitzgerald Beale, one of the unsung heroes of the American West. Beale was summoned, given a canvas bag with some nuggets and dust, and told to start for Washington and not to come back if he arrived and found his Army counterpart waiting for him.

Oddly enough, Lieutenant Loeser was ordered to travel by water; Beale, the sailor, was to ride across the continent on horseback. Beale was the first to arrive in Washington, after completing a virtually impossible trip across Mexico to Vera Cruz, thence to Mobile, and from Mobile to Washington by stage. He had encountered every kind of hazard, peril and attack from outlaws, storms, floods. News of his journey had preceded him and he was given "ovations" wherever he stopped. In Washington he was introduced to the members of the Senate, who gave him a rousing reception.

While Beale gave the Senate the golden word, thousands of "companies" were being organized across the nation. For example, the New York *Tribune* ran a column of advertisements under "California."

> "Via Panama. A company of a hundred men is now forming to proceed to the Gold Regions and will forthwith dispatch an agent to charter a vessel to the Pacific side to convey the company to San Francisco. The Company will leave New York by the 10th of February. For particulars inquire at 121 Water Street, upstairs."

The New Year turned and Senator Jefferson Davis publicly endorsed the southwestern route starting from Fort Smith, Arkansas, as the best one to the gold fields. Posters soon appeared—all put out by the enterprising merchants of Fort Smith—guaranteeing that a company could reach Monterey 60 days after leaving Fort Smith.

Lieutenant Edward Fitzgerald Beale, disguised as a Mexican, carrying the dispatches to Washington which reported the California gold strike.

The Sardine claim. *Photo by R. H. Vance.*

Certificate of John S. Ellis, 1850.

Masthead of the California edition of the New York *Tribune*, October 20, 1854.

The wagons soon creaked into Fort Smith, loaded up with supplies, then moved out along the road leading to the Choctaw and Shawnee villages and down the South Canadian. It was just beyond Shady Creek and the abandoned Comanche camp that they encountered El Llano Estacado—the great "Staked Plains." From then on the journey was monotonous until the wagons reached La Cuesta Valley. Here the old Santa Fe Trail, coming down from Bent's Fort, crossed the Arkansas route. It wasn't long before they saw the spires of Santa Fe and the first (820-mile) leg of the trip was over. There was still a great distance to go before they reached the gold fields.

At Guadaloupe Pass, the gold-seekers found that, like the emigrants far to the north, they had to lower their wagons by ropes. Then water had to be hoarded for the dry trip to the valley of Santa Cruz. Tucson was the first sign of civilization and the breathing-place before the companies set out for the Gila Valley. From there some of the foolhardy tried to take a short cut known as the "Jornada de las Estrellas," only to die in the frightful heat which shrank the wooden wagon parts and forced the men and women to make the trip on foot. Few made it.

For those trapped in the desert there was little hope. The few wells were soon fouled by the many wagons and dead cattle. The temperature was usually 110° and the air was stagnant and foul with the stench of decaying animal flesh.

But despite the hardships and the tales of terrible suffering that were sent back to New York, the gold fever continued to mount. When new strikes were reported the companies increased in size. Now there was another great factor to make the country face west, an even stronger and more compelling lure than the Promised Land of Oregon had been. Now almost all the West, not only the Northwest, was opening up.

Those who reached San Francisco found it a bedlam of shacks, tents, a few buildings, rotting ships and signs in Chinese, French, English, Spanish and German. Dust swirled along the unpaved streets. Violence and death were commonplace. The gold-seekers of 1849 and 1850

found the town was bossed by a tough band of thieves and killers from New York's Bowery known as the "Hounds." They hid out in the dingy saloons and clapboard houses along Pacific Street called "Sydney Town." With the gold dust rolling in, the gambling centers boomed day and night.

By 1850 great changes were taking place in the fields. Wooden flumes which carry water from mountain streams to the sluices were being constructed. River-bed mining, in which whole streams were diverted from their natural course so the bed could be examined for gold, was being introduced. The changes were costly, and much capital was needed for the operations. Now it was the day of gold companies, and the individual with the pan and shovel was rapidly disappearing.

There were still the wild alarums and excursions. It got so that anybody could start a rumor that would result in whole camps, towns or even cities being completely evacuated. Many were the wildest of tales, but the gold-hungry miners never bothered to evaluate them.

In addition to hoaxes, fire and flood added to the hardships of the prospectors. In March, 1852, Sacramento was flooded, and on November 2 and 3 of that same year the city was also gutted by a fire which resulted in the loss of $10,000,000.

San Francisco was almost wiped out in a similar holocaust. When rumors blamed the gangs in Sydney Town, the *Alta Californian* urged the formation of a Vigilante Committee. A small army of the city's leading merchants and professional men agreed that the newspaper was right and at a meeting formed a large group. Under the direction of editor Edward Gilbert, companies of armed men patrolled the streets, staged raids and cleaned up the city.

By 1855, however, much of the lawlessness and wild living had vanished, although there were still bear fights and dog fights and the gambling houses still operated in San Francisco. There were now dozens of churches and schools. There were even wooden sidewalks and Sarony, Archer and Company were distributing lithographs in full color to advertise their fine dressing cases, canes and gents' hats.

Sacramento Street, 1856.

Fort Vigilance, 1856.

Montgomery Block, 1856.

Battery Street, 1856.

Charles Schreyvogel: Painter of the American West

THE three great nineteenth-century artists of the American frontier West are Frederic Remington, Charles Marion Russell, and Charles Schreyvogel. The first two are well known but only within the past several years has Schreyvogel's superb paintings of the Indian Wars become popular with the general public. A number of books and articles have been written about Remington and Russell but curiously little has appeared about the gentle artist from Hoboken, New Jersey, who many believe, including this writer, was the superior artist of the trio and whose works are more historically correct.

When I was researching his life and times in the 1950s and 1960s for my biography *The Life and Art of Charles Schreyvogel, Painter-Historian of the Indian-Fighting Army of the American West*, published in 1969 and now long out of print, I could locate only sixty-two of his major works registered in the files of the Copyright Office in Washington, D.C. This scarcity underscored his determination not to paint merely for reproduction.

Schreyvogel's dedication to his art was awesome. Even when he and his wife were reduced to living on pennies, he refused to accept commissions for illustrating as did Remington. When he was asked why, he replied: "No mechanical process yet devised can do strict justice to the original colors of the artist."

Unlike the flamboyant Remington, Schreyvogel was a shy man who avoided public attention and was content to live almost anonymously in the then rural waterfront town of Hoboken. Ironically, most of his major works were painted on the roof of his narrow row house on Hoboken's Garden Street. As he said, the Palisades that faced him reminded him of the Western buttes.

In December 1899 Schreyvogel first gained recognition when his painting *My Bunkie*, depicting a trooper leaning over to rescue his bunk mate who had been unhorsed during a running fight with the Indians, won the prestigious Thomas B. Clark Award, "the art trophy of the year" as the New York *Herald* described it.

Schreyvogel, penniless and discouraged, had put the painting on the floor with the other entries but had not left his name and address. It was only through a story in the *Herald* that he was finally located.

Crowds lined up to see *My Bunkie*, the hit of the 1899–1900 National Academy of Design Exhibition held in the American Fine Arts Gallery on West 57th Street, New York City. From then on Schreyvogel was recognized as one of the great artists of the American frontier.

His works brilliantly capture the Indian Wars on the plains; the frightened, rearing horses, the howling warriors charging with rifles and lances held high as the desperate troopers fight to save the lives of the immigrants they are protecting and their own lives. Although his scenes are breathless, Schreyvogel seems curiously detached, an objective observer who has caught on canvas in one bright brilliant moment all that could have been seen by a broad sweep of the eye.

One of the astounding authenticated stories I uncovered in researching his life was that many of the Indians in his paintings are actually the face and body of his young neighbor Storie Schultze, a celebrated athlete of Hoboken's Stevens Institute. Storie, a blond third-generation German-American with high cheekbones and penetrating blue eyes, was eerily transposed into a fighting chief once he climbed to Schreyvogel's roof and donned the war bonnet and buckskins the artist had collected on his many trips to the West.

The scarcity and brilliance of Schreyvogel's work have now made them choice items in the art world. For the revision of this book, this writer sought out friends of Schreyvogel and owners of his paintings whom he had contacted years before. Sadly, many had passed away, like Carl Willenborg of Hoboken, who had owned the last collection of major Schreyvogel paintings, known the artist, and owned his house on Garden Street where he had done his paintings on the roof and where his studio was crowded with priceless Indian artifacts. Some paintings owned by individuals and copied by this writer for Schreyvogel's biography had been sold, vanished into private collections, or had disappeared.

MY BUNKIE

CUSTER'S DEMAND

FIGHT FOR WATER

ATTACK AT DAWN

SAVING THE MAIL

PROTECTING THE EMIGRANTS

GOING INTO ACTION

SURROUNDED

HARD-PUSHED

THE END

FIGHTING SCOUTS (EVEN CHANCE)

DOOMED

U. S. CAVALRY HUNTING BUFFALO

THE SCOUT

INDIAN PROFILE

The original painting *My Bunkie* is in the collection of the Metropolitan Museum of Art; *Custer's Demand, Fight for Water, Attack at Dawn, Surrounded, The End, Fighting Scouts—Even Chance, The Scout,* and *Indian Profile* are in the Thomas Gilcrease Institute of American History and Art, Tulsa, Oklahoma; *Saving the Mail* was donated by Mrs. Sandford Brown in memory of her husband to the Charles Schreyvogel Memorial Studio, National Cowboy Hall of Fame and Western Heritage Center, Oklahoma City, Oklahoma; *Protecting the Immigrants*, the collection of J. Robinson Silver, Jr.; *Going into Action*, formerly owned by Mr. and Mrs. Archie Carothers, now in the Charles Schreyvogel Memorial Studio, National Cowboy Hall of Fame and Western Heritage Center; *Hard Pushed* is in the R. W. Norton Art Gallery, Shreveport, Louisiana; both *The Duel* and *Doomed* were donated in 1977 by the family of the late Carl Willenborg, Jr., to Stevens Institute of Technology, Hoboken, New Jersey.

Communications

Uncle Sam's Camels

IN the 1850's a unique attempt to provide for transportation needs in the plains country was made by the Camel Brigade, one of the most fascinating episodes in western frontier history.

In 1853, when Jefferson Davis became President Pierce's Secretary of War, one of his first acts was to draw up plans for a United States Army Camel Corps. He pointed out that the "dromedary" would be excellent for "transportation with troops moving rapidly across the country ... for military expresses ... for reconnaissance ..." The camel had many obvious advantages: the ability to thrive in arid lands, great strength—200 camels could do the work of 1,000 horses and a camel could carry a 1,000-pound load—superior durability under all conditions.

Congress failed to act, but the idea of such a corps caught the public imagination. In 1855 Congress made an appropriation for the purchase of camels for military service. Edward Fitzgerald Beale, who had brought Congress the news of the California gold strike, was chosen as the commander of the Camel Corps. Naval Lieutenant —later Admiral—David Dixon Porter and Major Wayne, an early champion of the Camel Corps, were in charge of the Purchasing Commission. Porter was given command of the transport ship, the *Supply*, Wayne the business end of the expedition.

In July the pair sailed to Tunis, where they bought a camel for experimental purposes. When the Bey of Tunis heard of their mission he presented them with two more. The three were loaded on the *Supply*, with Wayne refusing to split hairs on what is a camel and what is a dromedary. (Actually the two-hump animal is a camel, the one-hump kind a dromedary.)

"I shall distinguish them from each other by the qualification of the countries from which they are said to have originally come—Bactria and Arabia. I shall call the two-humped camel the Bactrian Camel and the one-humped camel the Arabian Camel," wrote Wayne.

The expedition continued via Malta, Smyrna, Salonika and Constantinople to Balaklava, then the focal point in the Crimean War, to find out how the British liked their camel corps. Along the front they found that a corps of camels could make as much as 70 miles in 12 hours. In addition, the animals could be made to kneel in a square, "forming, as it were, a base of operation from which others operated as infantry. . . ."

More than a thousand men crouching behind this wall

A rare daguerreotype of a camel at Drum Barracks, 1865.

of animals could effectively hold off an attacking force, Wayne stated. The next stop for the *Supply* was Alexandria, which they reached in December, 1855.

Granted a special permit, the officers bought nine animals. In January, 1856, they sailed for Smyrna, where they purchased another shipment.

On the morning of February 15, 1855, with a fresh breeze filling her sails, the *Supply* set sail for America with its strange cargo of 39 camels.

After a terrible journey of three months the *Supply* limped into Indianola, Texas, a small port 120 miles south of Galveston, on May 14, 1856. Wayne and Porter had done their job well—only one camel had died, while two had been born.

While Wayne proceeded to San Antonio, Porter was ordered by Washington to return at once to Asia Minor for a second load of camels. Wayne's brief trip, at least in part, supported the theory that the camel could be used successfully on the arid frontier. After a journey of two weeks in steaming heat the camels were as fresh as when they had started.

A permanent camp called Camp Verde was established at Green Valley, sixty miles northwest of San Antonio, but before the Camel Corps really could be absorbed into the service, the administration changed. President Buchanan's Secretary of War, John B. Floyd, ordered a military reconnaissance made of a wagon road from Fort Defiance to the Thirty-Fifth Parallel on the Colorado River. The purpose of the expedition, Floyd announced, was not only to find a new road to California, but also to test the fitness of the camel as a beast of burden in the southwestern plains.

Beale set out upon the 4,000-mile round-trip journey in May, 1857, leading a strange and unusual caravan, which included 25 camels. During the journey, lasting some nine months, the camels were subjected to every kind of test and experience. They survived nobly and the expedition was a success. After receiving Beale's report, Secretary Floyd announced in 1858: "The entire adaptation of camels to military operations on the plains may now be taken as demonstrated."

Floyd tried to get Congress to buy more camels but failed. The Civil War then administered a death-blow to this unique experiment. After various attempts to use the camels—to transfer freight and for other purposes—the Army finally disposed of them at public auction.

Stages, the Pony Express and the Singing Wire

Speedy communication came to the western plains, suddenly and dramatically. On September 15, 1858, John Butterfield, who had made such a success with his stage-coach line in Utica, New York, established his famous Butterfield Overland Stagecoach line, and a letter could now be delivered across 2,800 miles of wilderness and through hostile country for a dollar.

In his initial trip he used 100 coaches, 2,000 horses, 500 mules and 750 men, including 150 drivers. Before he was finished in 1861, when the government withdrew the line because of the outbreak of the Civil War, Butterfield had buried 111 Americans and 56 Mexicans, to deliver that mail.

Not only did the Apaches plunder and raid the stations strewn across the plains and deserts, but road agents—refugees from the California Vigilante Committee—held up the coaches and near Tucson "did a thriving business." Yet it is remarkable to consider that despite the enemies,

red and white, and the swollen rivers, sandstorms, blizzards and other torments of nature, it is on record that the stage was late only three times.

In Tucson, when the high, clear notes of the driver's horn and then the thunder of the galloping hoofs of the teams were heard, "we always consulted our watches; a man could set his timepiece by the Butterfield Line..."

In 1860 the Pony Express cut the traveling time to nine days, and before this romantic chapter in our West had ended, plans were being made to extend a telegraph line across the vast plains and mountains. In 1860 Congress passed a law extending the "electric telegraph," to link the Atlantic coast with the Pacific. Bids were taken with the proviso that the line had to be linked by July 31, 1862. Another stipulation was that a ten-word message between Brownsville, Nebraska, and San Francisco should not cost more than three dollars.

Hiram Sibley of New York, president of Western Union, won the bid and dispatched his general manager, J. H. Wade, to California by steamer via the Isthmus of Darien. He also sent Edward Creighton to survey a route to California.

On November 18, 1860, Creighton left Omaha by stage and soon arrived in Salt Lake City, where he interested Brigham Young in the project. He then rode a mule to California, making the route as he went along. Meanwhile, Wade had forced the smaller California telegraph companies to consolidate with the California State Telegraph Company to establish the one company, the Overland Telegraph Company.

Creighton was now handed the task of building the line. When he started, the western line had already been extended to within 400 miles of Salt Lake City. He set his first pole in July at Julesburg, Colorado. Creighton did not spare expense in equipping his company. He had 75 strong

NEW YORK HERALD, FRIDAY, NOVEMBER 19, 1858.

THE GREAT OVERLAND MAIL.

Conclusion of the Description of the Butterfield Route.

The Road Through Tucson, Fort Yuma and Fort Tejon, to San Francisco.

The Colorado River, Deserts, Plains and Mountain Passes.

Condensed Table of Time, Rate of Speed, and Distances.

INCIDENTS BY THE WAY.

JOTTINGS FROM A WAGON SEAT, &c., &c., &c.

SPECIAL CORRESPONDENCE OF THE NEW YORK HERALD.

John Butterfield.

From the New York *Herald's* account of the Overland Mail route, November 19, 1858.

Hiram Sibley.

wagons, a small tent city, cooking stoves and the best cooks. A large herd of milk cows was driven ahead of each day's route. And the food, as Creighton boasted, "was the best that could be conveyed across the plains and the mountains." Hundreds of oxen and mules were used to bring the materials up the line. Scores of wagons carried up to 4,500 pounds of wire. One of Creighton's obstacles was the vast stretch of treeless plains. Sometimes poles had to be carried 240 miles.

At first the Indians did not bother the lines. There are numerous legends as to why, but Henry M. Porter, who was part of Creighton's team, told in his autobiography that once the Sioux burned down some poles 12 miles west of Fort Kearney. A telegrapher from an "outer" station sent out word to the fort, and the cavalry rode up before the Indians left the spot. From that incident—and other similar ones—the Plains tribes came to believe there was something supernatural about the "Singing Wire."

During the Civil War, ranchmen were hired to keep testing the wires which were cut by Confederate agents trying to stir up the tribes. The line was of extreme importance when the Civil War broke out and during the Indian Wars. There is no doubt that without the telegraph, conquering the West would have taken many more years.

A Pony Express rider exchanges greetings with a crew putting up telegraph poles while Indian warriors watch. *From a painting by W. H. Jackson.*

Slavery and the Civil War in the West

THE great political contest between the free-state and slave-state forces had its impact on the developing West, and was a delaying factor in the formal organization of territories and states. Texas applied for admission to the Union in 1836 but did not gain acceptance until December, 1845, chiefly because of the slavery issue and the threatened disturbance of the delicate balance between free and slave states. Most notable was the case of "Bleeding Kansas."

The Kansas-Nebraska Act in 1854 established the territories of Kansas and Nebraska and provided that the popular vote of the citizens of each territory would decide whether it should be "free" or "slave." The sentiment in Nebraska was clearly "free," but Kansas became the scene of a bloody contest between pro-slavery and anti-slavery fighters. It was a time of bitterness and terror, demonstrating that the enmity and hatred had gone too far and that only the force of arms—actual war—could resolve the issue. Kansas was established as a free state early in 1861, not many weeks before the Civil War broke out.

The white man's Civil War was a godsend to the Plains tribes. The Army posts were stripped or abandoned or else became stepchildren of the War Department, places for the convalescent, the old and the low-grade, raw recruit from the East. These green troops were easily terrified and made to retreat by the sight of a thousand howling, painted Indians beating drums, whirling rattles or screeching their wild cries. In the end the situation became so bad that Rebel prisoners—"galvanized Yankees," as their fellows contemptuously called them—were induced to join the Union Army to fight the Indians.

The newspapers of the period gave a vivid picture of conditions along the frontier after Lincoln called his countrymen to arms. On August 10, 1861, the *Arizonian* reported that a large band of Apaches, possibly more than a hundred bucks, attacked the town of Tubac, riding boldly into the streets to drive off the town's stock and killing anyone they could find on the streets.

The writer for the *Arizonian* then went on: "We are hemmed in on all sides by the unrelenting Apache . . . since the withdrawal of the Overland Mail and the garrison troops the chances against life have reached the maximum height. Within but six months nine-tenths of the whole male population have been killed off, and every ranch, farm and mine in the country have been abandoned in consequence. . . ."

But if the Apaches were raiding it was not without cause. Mangas Colorados, the great Apache chief, had been murdered "while escaping arrest." Cochise, straight and strong as an arrow shaft, took his place. He was savage in his retaliation.

Cochise captured several white settlers as hostages but the exchange never came off. The Apaches killed the helpless men. Within a few hours after their butchered bodies were found the three Apaches were stiffening in the evening wind.

Cochise was relentless. He seemed to specialize in the most hideous tortures. Prisoners were planted in sand hills and wild honey poured on their heads. The Apaches squatted on their haunches to watch the men die. Others were tied to wagon-wheels and burned. Some were sliced into pieces and still others dragged to death at the end of rope.

Left, Cochise's wife. *Photo probably by Camillus Fly. Right*, Little Crow. *Photo probably by Martin's Gallery.*

Left, Little Crow's son. *Photo by Upton. Right*, Standing Buffalo, Sioux chief in the New Ulm massacre.

Little Crow's War

Indian war came to Minnesota with a stunning swiftness in August 1862, after four Sioux warriors from the Rice encampment on the Minnesota River killed five settlers, one a fifteen-year-old girl, at Acton in Meeker County. The massacre apparently was touched off by one buck who sneeringly challenged his friends to prove they were not afraid of the white men by joining him in killing them.

When they reached their camp, one of them cried out to his fellow warriors to get guns, "because there is a war with the whites and we have begun it."

Soon drums were beating. In the settlements along the river men and women continued with their prayer meetings, cooking, eating or enjoying the warm, starshot night while Red Middle Voice, the Rice Creek chief, hurried downriver to the village of his nephew, Shakopee. The night was still young when runners summoned the other principal chiefs, Wabasha, Big Eagle, Mankato, and Traveling Hail to a war council at the home of Little Crow, best known of the chiefs of the Lower Sioux bands.

Two weeks before the murders, Little Crow had been defeated as the head speaker of his tribe. It was a stunning blow and he had been brooding about what role he would play in the future affairs of his people.

At first Little Crow called Red Middle Voice a fool, predicting that the horse soldiers would soon appear to take the four young killers into custody but he was shouted down by the younger chiefs who reviewed their growing fears of dwindling land, the influx of settlers, the number of towns and villages—and the trader who had advised them to "eat grass" when he cut off their credit although they had told him their families were hungry.

It was a tragic story that would be played and replayed for many years in the American West. Other chiefs like Little Crow would face their embittered warriors only to be shouted down when they suggested caution or reconciliation. It is better to die on our feet than on our knees was the grim reply. It is still a mystery why Little Crow finally agreed to lead his warriors in a war against the whites. He had always been friendly to the settlers and had adapted their dress and life-style by the time the outbreak began. He was either intimidated or had taken the opportunity to regain his lost leadership.

Dawn was just breaking when the first bands of painted warriors streamed toward the Redwood Agency to attack the stores, mill, and homes. Before the echoes of the last shots had died away both the Redwood and Lower Agency were in flames, a number of men and women had been slaughtered, and the first survivors were fleeing to Fort Ridgely. When the body of Andrew Myrick the trader was found, a tuft of grass had been pushed into his mouth . . .

An incredible bloodbath followed. Men, women, and children were burned, disemboweled, and cut to pieces. Homes were looted, horses stolen, cattle butchered. The warriors seemed to have gone mad; in most cases the chiefs were helpless, even stunned at the ferocity of their men. Little Paul, an Upper Agency chief, bitterly excoriated his warriors when they returned triumphantly waving scalps.

"I hear some of you loud and boasting you have killed women and children," he shouted. "That is not brave, it is cowardly. Go fight the soldiers! You dare not! When you see their army coming on the plains you will throw down your arms and fly in one direction and your women in another and this winter you will starve."

Other chiefs like Mankato and Little Crow talked of storming Fort Ridgely instead of murdering women and children but Red Middle Voice and Shakopee continued to send their warriors against the unarmed settlements. The looting and killing soon spread to the Upper Agency where warehouses were pillaged and families wiped out. But a few chiefs in that section of the reservation refused to join the war and held back their warriors, advising them that if they wanted to kill whites they should join the murderers in the Lower Agency where Redwood had been wiped out.

Some wounded settlers made their way to safety after incredible hardships. One man, Peter Patoile, wounded in both lungs, crawled and staggered nearly two hundred miles living on roots and berries to reach a tiny settlement on the Mississippi. Miraculously his severe wounds stopped bleeding during his awesome journey. There were also tales of heroism and devotion among the Sioux for their white friends. John Otherday, a full-blooded Wahpeton, led a large group of men, women, and children to safety, as the warehouses of Yellow Medicine were being burned and looted.

Little Crow's war spread, fugitives began to jam into Fort Ridgely—a fort only by its name. Instead of the stout walls of a Western post, it was simply a collection of wooden warehouses and two stone buildings, one a barracks, the other a commissary. Ridgely was thirteen miles southeast of Redwood and the only fortification in the area. The Commander, Captain John Marsh, knew little of Indian fighting.

When the first survivors arrived Marsh sent a terse message to his second in command, Lieutenant Timothy Sheehan, who was patrolling the reservation: "The Indians are raising hell!"

General H. H. Sibley. *Photo by J. W. Campbell.*

A Brown County, Minnesota, pioneering family, typical of those massacred by Little Crow's Sioux warriors in the 1862 uprising.

Leaving a young officer in charge, Marsh led forty-six troopers in a sweep to determine exactly what was happening. Near the Redwood Agency ferry he walked into an ambush. Marsh was drowned leading his men across the river; late that night the bloody, shaken survivors of his command stumbled into Ridgely. Behind at the ferry were twenty-five dead soldiers and Indian interpreter Patrick Quinn, who died in the first volley. As the situation became more crucial, Private William Sturgis, mounted on the fort's best horse, left for Fort Snelling, one hundred and sixty miles away over rough trails covered by bands of warriors seeking scalps. If Sturgis was killed or captured and a large body of reinforcements did not appear, the entire valley and thousands of its inhabitants could be butchered.

Within the next few days Lieutenant Sheehan and his men returned to the fort to be joined by the Renville Rangers, a group of fifty volunteers who had been on their way to Snelling when they heard the news of the outbreak.

New Ulm, the largest settlement on the reservation and sixteen miles from the fort, was the next target of the Sioux. When that failed, they tried to storm Ridgely.

For five hours the small force of defenders kept up a steady fire with howitzers raking a ravine where Little Crow's warriors crouched. Finally, angry and disappointed, the Sioux chief ordered his men to pull back. They had suffered losses, left without loot, and had not even reached the outer fortifications.

Lieutenant Sheehan knew the Sioux would strike again. He had wells dug, water buckets scattered about, water tanks replenished, the parade grounds cleared, howitzers planted in four corners of the fort, and ammunition distributed to every man.

The second attack began a few days later. Eight hundred painted braves, singing their death songs, swept across the plains with the two hundred defenders looking down their rifle barrels, waiting for a target. By noon the ravines leading to the fort were packed with warriors. The strategy of Little Crow was simple; they would overwhelm the fort by human waves.

The attack began with howls and war chants as the air was filled with whistling fire arrows and bullets. Fortunately it had rained the night before and the arrows failed to catch the damp shingles. The charge of the warriors was blunted by the steady musket fire from windows and fire holes. Southwest of the fort haystacks were put to the torch and under the billowing smoke bands of Sioux reached the stables, three hundred yards from the post's headquarters. Howitzers, the dread "wagon guns," cut down the wild charges. Then a twenty-four pounder was wheeled next to a howitzer. Wheel to wheel the guns boomed, their iron hail tearing to pieces a column of Indians under Mankato moving up as reinforcements. As one soldier recalled, the booming of the guns echoed up the valley like crashing thunder sending the warriors fleeing in all directions. After six hours of the fiercest fighting of the Indian Wars, the Sioux broke off their attack. There was only one casualty at the fort and several wounded. Little Crow, who had been stunned by a nearby crash of a howitzer ball, was carried off the field and Mankato led their forces back across the river.

They next struck at New Ulm, strung along the southside of the Minnesota River in the lowest part of the valley. Bluffs covered with trees and brush made a perfect cover for an attack. Wagons, logs, and dirt mounds had been erected in the business section since the last attack, and the citizens of New Ulm waited tensely behind their crude barricade as columns of smoke from burning farmhouses and fields told of the advance of Little Crow's Indian army.

The Sioux, about six hundred warriors, raced down the slightly sloping prairie, spread out like a fan and charged, whooping, shouting, and waving guns and bows. Sharpshooters in a windmill took a deadly toll but for a time it was house-to-house combat. The battle went on all day and night with part of New Ulm in flames. Finally the chiefs realized their game was up and they pulled back up the valley. Thirty-seven civilians had died in the frontier town, two hundred homes were in ashes, and at least sixty were wounded.

Private William Sturgis, who had ridden all night through the hostile territory, had finally reached Fort Snelling. Word was flashed to Governor Alexander Ramsey who ordered troops sent to the area under former

Refugees from the New Ulm massacre pause for dinner on the prairie. *Photo taken by one of the party.*

Governor Henry Hastings Sibley.

Sibley led his slow-moving column to the relief of the hard-pressed defenders of Birch Coulee who had fought the Sioux from behind barricades of wagons and dead horses.

The Indian army, now suffering internal feuds, tried a surprise attack on Sibley's camp at Woods Lake but it misfired and the warriors were scattered. It was then that the chiefs began to parley with Sibley for peace. When Sibley first demanded that the prisoners be turned over to him, ninety-one whites and a hundred and fifty half-breeds were delivered to what was called Camp Release.

Troops now began to round up scattered bands of Sioux who were led in leg-irons to log jails. Surrenders and captures soon swelled the prison population to over 2,000 men, women, and children. Sibley set up what was described at various times as a "Military Commission," "Military Court," and a "Military Tribunal." About a month after it began hearings, the court had convicted and sentenced three hundred and six Sioux warriors to be hanged.

Lincoln, undoubtedly aware of how the Confederacy would exploit the execution of three hundred prisoners and the subsequent worldwide reverberations, demanded that he be given a complete record of the trials.

As winter closed in, a long column of Indian prisoners were moved to new quarters at Fort Lincoln on the banks of the Minnesota River, southwest of Mankato. The warriors, their women and children, shuffled past the blackened fields with the still unburied dead, down the main street of New Ulm where jeering, crying women attacked the column with rocks, scalding water, scissors, hoes, and pitchforks.

Finally word was received from Washington: thirty-nine prisoners would be executed on the large square scaffold built on the riverbank. Before they marched out of the stockade, one more was saved, and thirty-eight Sioux warriors mounted the steps to receive a white muslin cap and stand under the dangling rope. Three rolling drumbeats sounded over the Indians' death chant as the rope was cut and they plunged to their death. The bodies were buried in a common grave on the riverbank only to be dug up by medical students.

Little Crow was later killed near Hutchinson by a farmer and his son out hunting. The other chiefs and warriors not captured, or who refused to surrender, fled to Canada or joined other tribes of Sioux in the West. Only a few returned to their homeland.

The Sand Creek Massacre

In Colorado Territory, Denver and the smaller settlements had been under Indian attack almost since the first shell had exploded at Fort Sumter. By 1862 more than 50 men, women and children had been killed by the Indians. It was almost suicide to move beyond the city limits. Most of the families were placed in a stout blockade on Blake Street with a few men on guard.

One of Colorado's most noted soldiers in the period was John Milton Chivington, whose military genius and fearlessness had destroyed the Confederate supply base

Execution of the 35 Sioux.

Colonel Samuel H. Tappan.

Black Kettle, (*front row, second from left*) and Cheyenne sub-chiefs.

in the battle of Santa Fe on March 27, 1862, many times called "The Gettysburg of the Southwest."

The base was located four miles west of the summit of Glorieta Pass. In order to reach the camp Chivington had his men make leather ropes, 125 feet long, with which they made the descent along the eastern ridge of Apache Canyon. A hazardous enough feat in daylight, in the darkness it was hair-raising. After the command had reached safety, Chivington led his men in a complete surprise attack. Haystacks, ammunition dumps, food and corn cribs along with more than a hundred mules were destroyed.

As Oriskany was the turning-point for the Battle of Saratoga, this was the pivot on which swung the Confederate defeat. Had the Confederates been successful in securing the gold fields of Colorado, Arizona, California and Nevada it is doubtful if the war would have ended at Appomattox. But bickering marred the Union victory. Colonel Slough, commander of the expedition, resigned and Chivington took his place. He was passed over Lieutenant Colonel Sam Tappan, who would prove to be his bitterest enemy.

In November, 1862, Chivington was successful in getting his command converted into cavalry. With his men now in the saddle, Chivington was constantly fighting the raiding Cheyennes, Arapahos, Kiowas and Sioux.

By 1864 nearly every rancher had been burned out or killed along the South Platte. One valley of hay was completely burned. Freighters refused to make the hazardous trips and Denver was cut off from provisions. In 1863 flour was so scarce it sold for $45 a sack. Conditions became so bad the mail was stopped.

Then in 1864 the emotions of the territory rose to a boiling hatred for the red men when the Hungate family, who lived 30 miles east of Denver, was horribly massacred. Eighty bullet holes were found in the mutilated body of Hungate. His wife and tortured children were found tied together in the well. Governor Evans telegraphed a plea

to Washington for help, but as in every war the frontier was told to look to itself. One or more murdered families could not be counted when whole armies were locked in decisive battles.

With Denver practically helpless, the Indians stepped up their raids. Even large settlements were placed under heavy attack. Finally, in desperation, Evans issued a general order that any citizen of the territory could hunt down the hostiles and kill them. He also received belated permission from the War Department to raise a volunteer battalion for an enlistment period of a hundred days.

The newly recruited command was stationed at Fort Weld under Chivington. In the summer of 1864 Black Kettle, chief of the Cheyennes, proposed an exchange of prisoners at Fort Lyons, Colorado Territory. The council was held at Fort Weld rather than Fort Lyons in the fall of that year. Black Kettle, Bull Bear, Chief of the Dog Soldiers, and Neva, another field chief, attended. The council was a failure and the chiefs left in a sullen mood. However, Black Kettle insisted he wanted peace and led his people to a camp on the Big South Bend of Sand Creek, some 30 miles northeast of Fort Lyons. To prove he was peaceful he raised an American flag over it.

While the meeting was going on, the Plains tribes were launching attacks of such strength against the western Army garrisons that General Curtis at Leavenworth sent an urgent message to Chivington suggesting counter-offensives..."I want no peace till the Indians suffer more," he wrote.

Chivington was placed in command of an expedition to Sand Creek which was supposed to open up communications cut off by the redskins' war. At Fort Lyons his men were joined by the First Colorado Cavalry under Major Scott Anthony. The next day they set out for the Indian camp.

On November 29 they halted a mile from the camp, and a detachment was sent on ahead to cut off the pony herd from the camp's warriors. The official order was not to fire unless fired upon. It was a ridiculous order; what Indian is going to stay calm while a white man cuts loose his pony herd?

The inevitable happened. An Indian saw the soldiers at the herd and fired, knocking the bluecoat out of his saddle. The entire command was soon firing. Two howitzers were brought into action and the camp, with an American flag flying, was put under bombardment. Between 600 and 700 Indians, including women and children, were killed before the uneven battle ended. The fight was promptly called a "massacre." Chivington was put on trial and resigned his commission in 1865 to go into the freighting business. He died in 1894.

The "Sand Creek Massacre" is as controversial in western history as Little Big Horn. To read the report of the *Congressional Investigation of the Chivington Massacre*, published in 1867, is to lose oneself in a maze of charges and counter-charges. In the end the reader who has finished the 700 pages of fine print comes to only one conclusion: Black Kettle's people were killed at the hands of Chivington's soldiers.

Chivington, a stiff, proud man, had made many enemies who were ready to use the "massacre" to disgrace him. Among them was Samuel F. Tappan, who never forgave Chivington for being promoted over his head. Tappan, a former Washington newspaper correspondent, fed the eastern press with some wild tales, all of which painted Chivington as the blackest of villains.

Although Chivington may have been wrong in trying to neutralize a camp of savages by cutting loose their horses and not expecting them to retaliate, one must consider the temper of the times. Every man in his command had suffered in some way at the hands of the marauding tribes. When they rode into Black Kettle's camp, the Hungate massacre must have loomed large in their minds.

And although Black Kettle was under the protection of the American flag, he was not exactly a "peaceful" Indian. This was underscored by the fresh scalps of men, women and children found on the bodies of his warriors. Certainly the sight of saddle blankets fringed with women's hair as found in Black Kettle's camp didn't make Chivington's troopers look with mercy on the Indians they were slaughtering.

On the other hand, there were the ugly rumors that the volunteers were all gold-field prospectors who feared they were about to be called East to fight in the war and had deliberately touched off the battle to start an Indian war.

Other reports have Chivington ordering the massacre out of pure hatred for the Indians he had been fighting against so hard and for so long.

In 1864, about the time of the Sand Creek massacre, the Confederacy ordered that a high council of the western tribes be held. In one of the most dramatic and little-known episodes of the Civil War in the West, a young Creek warrior, Tuk-a-Ba-Tche-Miko, was sent as an emissary by the tribes still at peace to as many tribes in the Southwest as possible to induce them to attend a grand council. For weeks on horseback and on foot, he journeyed north to the country of the Osages and the Pawnees, then southwest to the Iowas, Kickapoos and Pottawatomies, then on to the Wichitas, Kiowas, Comanches and Apaches, then north to the Southern Cheyennes and Arapahoes. He crossed the Panhandle of Texas to meet the Navajos, Mescalero Apaches, Northern Cheyennes and Unkpapas, the Teton and Yankton Sioux. After each meeting he would send back a group of small notched sticks which represented the bands and their numbers. On May 1, 1865, the council was finally held on the Washita River. Captain T. M. Scott, Assistant Adjutant General, C. S. A., reported that 20,000 Indians, one of the largest councils ever to be held in the Southwest, answered the Confederates' call. They did not know of Appomattox.

The council agreed to stop raiding and to maintain peace on the frontier. In the main, there was peace in the Southwest for many years, with only occasional raids and atrocities stirring up the old hatred and bitterness.

The Sand Creek massacre. The American flag hoisted by Black Kettle can be seen (*right center*).

Transportation:
From the Horse to the Iron Horse

THE horse was, of course, the principal means of transportation in the West until the advent of "The Iron Horse"—the railroad. But other animals were used to a considerable extent—mules, burros, oxen, dogs—and, on water, clipper ships and river packets.

There was a wide variety of vehicles of which the stagecoach and the covered wagon were the most publicized. Indians, scouts, trappers, emigrants and settlers made their vehicles to meet their needs and to fit in with the nature of the country. As a result, a number of distinctive types were developed, designed specifically to achieve a

A bull-boat made of buffalo hide. *Photo by S. J. Morrow.*

particular purpose or to overcome a difficult condition— rough roads, weather hazards, heavy loads.

"Trains" were common, notably for emigrant travel but also for freighting. They were more economical— fewer guides and guards were needed to escort 50 wagons moving together than for the same number traveling separately or in small groups. They were more convenient and more likely to be self-sufficient. In a large train almost every possible item of equipment, almost every possibly useful article could be carried, whereas an individual wagon or small group would have to cut down its load to the barest necessities. Trains were safer—not only because a large group was less vulnerable to attack from Indians but also because in a large group of people almost every kind of medical and mechanical help and skill was available. And finally it was pleasanter and more sociable to travel in a large company than in a small one.

Because so many of the pictures in other sections of this book show means and methods of transportation only a selection is presented here.

Dog and horse travois. *Photos by General John T. Pitman and J. Anderson.*

The essential beast of burden. *Photo by Alexander Martin.*

A Mormon wagon-train.

Freighters meet on the plains. *Photo by Dan Dutro.*

Red River carts. These were made without metal parts. *Photo by Whitney.*

The last large bull train to the Black Hills. *Photo by Grabill.*

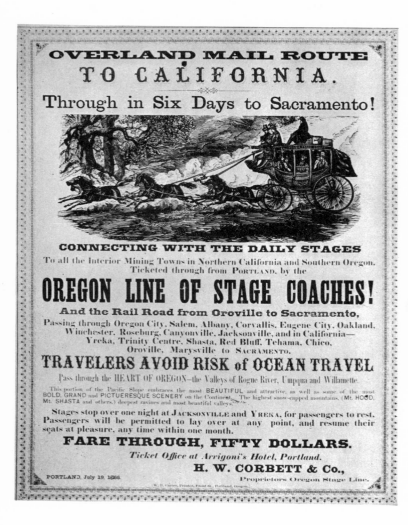

A river packet in the 1870's.

Poster advertising the Oregon Line of stage-coaches and railroad, dated July 19, 1866.

Halliday's Express at Smoky Hill River, 1855.

Heavy freight was transported by freight teams, by river packet or around the Horn by clippers or other vessels. Light or valuable freight, including gold, was sent by "express," privately owned fast transportation. The express companies, such as Wells Fargo, occupied an important role in the resistance to and the fight against outlaws and hostile Indians. They had to protect their valuable shipments and therefore maintained an effective guard and security system and also employed detective agencies, Pinkerton's and others, to track down bandits.

Mail, usually carried by a contractor, went the best and fastest way, which might be by pony, stagecoach, wagon or ship.

The Railroads

While the Civil War fostered the activity of hostile Indians, it also stimulated and speeded railroad-building in the West.

For years efforts had been made to arouse Congress to the need of a transcontinental railroad. Some short railroads had been built in the West before the Civil War, notably the Sacramento Valley line in 1855. But a transcontinental railroad was obviously an enormous project that required not only the government's license and authority but also government financing and privileges.

The great leader of the movement for the Pacific Railroad, the man who organized the committees, raised the money and planned the campaign for the legislation was Theodore Dehone Judah, a visionary sometimes called Crazy Judah, a true hero of the West who is almost unknown now. Almost singlehanded, he pushed the Pacific Railroad Act through Congress. He had failed to win the legislation at several sessions of Congress, but when the War broke out his task was easier and on July 1, 1862, President Lincoln signed the Pacific Railroad Act.

This act provided for the building and operating of a railway between the Missouri River and Sacramento, California. Two companies were given the contracts, the grants and the financing for its construction: the Central Pacific and the Union Pacific. Judah had organized the Central Pacific with four merchants, later to be known

Theodore D. Judah.

as the Big Four, as investors: Leland Stanford, Charles Crocker, Mark Hopkins, Collis P. Huntington. The Central Pacific actually was organized only to build a railroad from Sacramento across the Rockies through the Donner Pass to the silver cities of Nevada. Judah planned that eventually the Central Pacific would build the transcontinental railroad, but he did not tell the merchants that. Just the same they have been given credit for the great vision that was really Judah's. But Judah died in 1863, after having split with his associates, and he was rather promptly forgotten. The Big Four and the fortunes they made from the Central Pacific (now part of the Southern Pacific) had a major influence in the next fifty years of western history.

The other company, named the Union Pacific, was incorporated by the Pacific Railroad Act. The two companies were to build simultaneously, Central starting from the West, Union from the East. For each mile built the railroad would get a loan of $16,000 to $48,000, depending on the difficulty of construction in the specific area, and a grant of ten alternate sections of land on both sides of the railroad.

With such rich rewards, and with the further incentive of extra loans and extra lands for every extra mile it built, each railroad set about energetically and efficiently to outbuild the other. To augment the labor supply the Union Pacific brought west many Irishmen from New

Charles Crocker.

Mark Hopkins.

Leland Stanford.

Collis P. Huntington.

Omaha, N. T., from Capitol Hill. *This and the other photographs on this page were taken by John Carbutt in 1866.*

T. Durant and Union Pacific department heads.

The Platte River opposite Platte City.

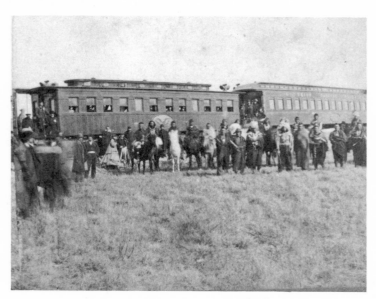

Pawnee warriors in front of Union Pacific palace cars.

Carmichael's graders' camp at North Bitter Creek Valley.

A Union Pacific construction train, 1868.

Representatives of the press at the Union Pacific excursion to the 100th Meridian, 1866. *Photo by John Carbutt.*

#1, General Sherman. This wood-burner, first locomotive on the Union Pacific, was brought to Omaha by steamboat in 1865.

York and from Ireland. The Central found it very advantageous to use Chinese laborers, bringing them to the work camps from San Francisco and even from China.

The competition was keen and ruthless—and wasteful. Since no meeting-point of the two lines had been established, the companies kept on building after they had reached a point where they could have joined. Many miles of parallel railroad were built until the meeting-point was fixed at Promontory Point near Ogden, Utah, where the famous Last Spike, completing the transcontinental railroad and connecting the Union Pacific and the Central Pacific, was driven on May 10, 1869. It had taken only a little more than five years to build the great artery.

During the course of construction across Indian lands there was some trouble with the tribes, notably the Sioux. But many of the Union Pacific men were ex-soldiers, and all were supplied with firearms. There were many raids and fights, but their nature was rather more that of harassment than battles.

Even before the transcontinental railroad was completed, the two companies instituted nationwide campaigns to promote emigration to the territory. Popula-

tion, with its commerce, industry and traffic, is, of course, the lifeblood of any railroad. But also the two companies had large holdings of real estate to sell and one element helped the other. The more land sales, the more traffic—the more traffic, the more the land was worth. Every possible promotion and circulation device was used not only in the East and Middle West but in Europe as well, and all sorts of inducements were made, including special "emigrant trains" at fantastically low fares.

Now the tide of emigration rolled west in great swells. This time it covered the land that had been hopped over by the Oregon Trailers and the gold-seekers. Now it was not only the Pacific Coast that won new population, but also the Northern Plains and all the country between the Missouri and the Pacific.

What was natural in this mass emigration, especially that resulting from European advertising, was the "national" or "foreign colony" character of it. Scandinavians would settle in one area—notably Minnesota, Germans in another—notably Wisconsin, and so on. There was hardly a European country that did not have a "colony" somewhere in the West. In time all these Europeans

The Golden Spike ceremony at Promontory Point, Utah, May 10, 1869. At the meeting of the Central Pacific (*left*) and the Union Pacific (*right*) the last spike, a golden one, was driven, the transcontinental railroad was a fact, and the locomotives were christened with wine. Montague, chief engineer of the Central Pacific, shakes hands with Grenville M. Dodge, chief engineer of the Union Pacific. *Photo by C. R. Savage.*

The Golden Spike. The names of the officers of the two companies are inscribed on one side. Other inscriptions read: "The Pacific Railroad—ground broken January 8, 1863, and completed May 8, 1869," and "May God continue the unity of our Country, as this Railroad unites the two great Oceans of the world."

became assimilated as Americans, but they still retained many of the traditions and folkways of the mother country, and in turn American culture took over and absorbed many of them.

As other main railroads—notably the James J. Hill rail empire, including the Great Northern, the Northern Pacific and the Burlington—were built in the West, the process of stimulating land sales and new emigration was repeated again and again, and the population multiplied. The West was well on its way to filling in and growing up, delayed only by the hazards of the wild Indians and the wild bad men.

James J. Hill. *From a painting by Alfonso Muller-Ury.*

From a brochure of the Chicago, Kansas and Nebraska Railway, St. Joseph and Iowa Railroad Co., Lessee—the Rock Island Route, 1888.

An early palace car.

The Utah Northern bridge across the Snake River. In the background is a toll bridge, and farther back are the original machine shops of the railroad. Formerly known as Eagle Rock, this is now the town of Idaho Falls.

[81]

An Englishman's View of an Emigrant Train

(From an unpublished diary of an Englishman who toured the West in 1876)

September 28, 1876. Arrived at Ogden about 8, where we exchanged from the Central Pacific to the Union Pacific. Left Ogden in a sleeper at 10. Passed several emigrant trains. Emigrants pay half the usual fare, and they are crowded about and treated by the officials like wild beasts. Both the Union and Central Pacific Railway trains rarely travel faster than 17-18 miles per hour, and as they have no competition they are renowned for being the most exorbitant, rude and disagreeable companies in America.

Laying ties and rails. *Photo by Alexander Gardner.*

First train into Boise, Idaho, September 12, 1887.

Central Pacific train on Long Ravine Bridge. *Photo by Thomas Houseworth & Co.*

Royal Gorge, Grand Canyon of the Arkansas. *Photo by W. H. Jackson.*

Snow sheds on the Central Pacific Railroad, near Donner Pass. *Photo by C. R. Bierstadt.*

The summit of Frémont Pass on the Colorado Railroad. *Photo by W. H. Jackson.*

Marshall Pass. *Photo by W. H. Jackson.*

Hanging Rock. Pike's Peak Railroad. *Photo by J. G. Hiesland.*

The Indian Wars

Government Management of Indian Affairs

THE Civil War and postwar troubles with the Indians focused attention on the national policy toward Indians, caused a re-examination of the methods of dealing with them and the establishment of a new system.

As early as 1775 the Continental Congress set up departments of Indian affairs to deal with the various tribes. The first formal treaty between the United States and an Indian tribe was made in 1778 with the Delawares. This policy of making separate treaties with the different tribes, each considered a nation, continued for about 90 years during which time some 360 treaties were made. Though some of these were respected and effective, on the whole they overlapped each other, were generally little understood and even less observed.

In 1789 the United States government assumed charge of the Indians and Congress ordered the War Department to administer Indian affairs. In 1793 the President was authorized to appoint agents to live among the Indians, help them, win their friendship and supply them with animals, tools, merchandise and money. Some of these agents were in control of tribes, some in charge of districts, where they set up headquarters known as agencies with full staffs and with Indians as policemen of the area.

Parallel with the administrative agent system in the early years was the factor system to control trade with the Indians and to protect them from being cheated by ruthless traders. Trading posts or "factories" were established at various frontier centers of Indian population, each with a superintendent of Indian trade in charge.

Kit Carson, famous scout, and the oath of office he took on his appointment as Brevet Brigadier General in the Army, January 4, 1866. *Photo by Mathew Brady.*

These factories supplied all sorts of merchandise to the Indians in exchange for furs, without profit. The government supplied the original capital which was replenished when the furs were sold.

When reputable and responsible private companies like the American Fur Company came into the field, the government withdrew, and in 1822 Congress ended the factor system.

In 1834 Congress passed a law establishing the Department of Indian Affairs under the War Department, providing for rules and regulations to govern the Indians and defining the powers of the various officers.

In 1849 the Department was transferred as a Bureau to the newly established Department of the Interior where it has remained except during crises or Indian wars when an area or a reservation might be placed temporarily in the Army's charge.

After the Civil War two important revisions were made in Indian policy:

Reservations: It was decided to get the Indians, by treaty or by force, to stop roaming and to live permanently on selected reservations of land which would be their own property. From the earliest days some such reservations had been established by treaties, but there had not been an active reservation policy. But in 1868 the reservation plan was pursued vigorously and within 20 years or so all tribal Indians were on reservations. A source of great trouble, as will be explained in later chapters, was the encroachment of the whites on the Indian lands, the breaking of the treaties and the lack of permanence of the reservations.

Wards of the Nation: In 1869 President Grant, at the suggestion of General Sheridan, embarked on a peace policy toward the Indians. No longer would the Indians be considered as members of a tribe or nation to be dealt with through their tribes or nations. Rather the Indians became direct wards of the United States and treaty-making with tribes or nations was abolished.

The Postwar Army

The treaty had been signed in Appomattox's white clapboard house. Lee's weary troops moved homeward for spring plowing, while the men in blue returned to the cities of the North. At first a great stillness fell over the bruised and bleeding land; then it was followed by a national restlessness, a feeling of discontent with familiar places and things.

As happens after almost all wars, many of the returning

A photograph taken at Fort Laramie, 1868, at the time when Red Cloud and his warriors met Sherman and his officers to arrange a peace treaty. *Left to right:* A. H. Terry, W. S. Harney, W. T. Sherman, a Sioux squaw, N. S. Taylor, S. F. Tappan, A. C. Augur.

General George Crook. *Photo by Mathew Brady.*

General Nelson A. Miles.

soldiers found it hard to fit in with the old way of life at home. They missed the excitement, the violence and the adventure. In the South, for many there was no old way to fit into. Homes had been destroyed, property looted and, above all, they had to knuckle under to a government that wasn't their own.

The exodus of ex-Confederates was great. There was a steady stream of them westward, and each year for a while there was an increasing number who had GTT ("gone to Texas"). But there were plenty of Northerners, too, who pulled up stakes and made their way to the new country in the West to seek their fortune and a new way of life.

In the beginning there were four transcontinental routes: southward over the ancient Santa Fe Trail; westward over the Kansas Trail to Denver, westward on the Oregon Trail to Nebraska and Salt Lake City to Oregon or the gold fields of California; northwestward on the Bozeman Trail through Wyoming to Montana. The Union Pacific was building along the Oregon Trail and the Kansas Pacific along the Kansas Trail to Denver. With the railroads operating only short distances, the only method of travel was the horse and the familiar prairie schooner.

In 1866 public sentiment for Army protection against the Indians mounted. Editorial writers in leading papers of the nation and the politicians began calling upon the government to furnish an army that could provide security for the settlers on the frontier.

But an army that could stand up against the aroused Plains tribes had to be sizable, tough, mobile. Now, after Appomattox, there were only 26,000 on the Army rolls. War casualties had taken their toll and they had not been replaced. Unlike that for drafted recruits there had been no bounty for the Regular Army man during the War Between the States.

After the gallant Army of Northern Virginia passed into history, replacements began to move back into the Regular Army. Men in gray and blue who could not return to the good life after four years of war—misfits, bored Easterners who wanted adventure, "galvanized" Yankees, drunkards, thieves and murderers—filled the ranks. Southern officers, who by law could not hold a commission, became top sergeants, corporals and even members of the regiment band. In the Regular Army, non-commissioned officers who had won battlefield promotion for heroic conduct stepped back down to their old rank.

Before the Indian wars would end America would have its own Foreign Legion—the toughest, hardest-riding cavalry in history. It would outfight and outride the greatest horsemen of the plains, including the Comanches.

Like the Foreign Legion, it was an army composed of men of many nationalities: Irish, German, French, Italian, Jewish. Negroes, many fresh from the slave quarters of southern cotton fields, flocked to the cavalry. Because of the thick, furry buffalo robes they wore in the winter, the Sioux called them "Buffalo Soldiers." In Montana and Nebraska General Carpenter's colored regiment was called "Carpenter's Brunettes." The all-Negro 10th Cavalry was one of the best in the West.

Indians themselves were also a part of the army fighting the Indians. Every regiment had its own company of scouts—Pawnees, Crows, Shoshones and Rees (Arikaras), all minority tribes who hated the powerful Sioux. When the Sioux were conquered some of the warriors turned on their own people and donned the blue. In Crook's campaigns against the Apaches some of his best scouts were Apaches.

The general-in-chief of the postwar Army was General Ulysses S. Grant, with William Tecumseh Sherman as General of the Army and Chief of the Mississippi Department. Under their command the army marched and fought. Among its more famous Field Commanders were: Terry, Custer, Crook, Gibbon, Mackenzie, Miles, Howard, Merritt, Carpenter and the rest. Hard-riding Phil Sheridan also played a major role in the war of the plains.

Some of the high-ranking officers were tyrants and drunkards, but the majority were sensitive, intelligent and well-educated. The troopers were mounted on excellent horses, tough western mustangs. The artillerymen were a small group who cared for their howitzers with as much care as they gave their horses. They were always treated with a great deal of respect by the new recruits after they had experienced their first fight with the Sioux. They soon learned that the sharp slam of the howitzer and the whir of the shell over their heads from the reinforcements coming over the rise was the most welcome sound in the world. The Plains tribes feared the guns and usually scattered when they opened up. Accompanying the troops were the mule-skinners or bull-whackers, civilians who could flick a fly off a mule's ear with their long whips.

The posts were reminiscent of the forts in the Mohawk

Signing the treaty at Fort Laramie, 1868. General Sherman is shown second on the right of the right-hand pole.

Brown's Hotel, Fort Laramie, 1868. *Photo probably by Alexander Gardner.*

The old Mormon fort at Bridger in ruins.

Lieutenant Colonel Baker and officers at Fort Ellis, Montana Territory, 1871.
Photo by William H. Jackson.

Soldiers' barracks at Fort Hays, Kansas, 1873.

U. S. Cavalry, early 1870's.

At Fort Maginnis, Montana Territory.

A company of the Fifth U. S. Infantry, Montana, 1878.

Fort Sill, Indian Territory, 1876. *Photo by W. P. Bliss.*

A pack outfit at Fort Custer, 1878.

General Miles and staff, Tongue River, Montana, 1877. This photograph was
taken just before mounting, for the expedition against Sitting Bull and Crazy Horse.
The temperature was 20° below zero. Miles is in the center.

Valley during the Revolution. Square, built of untrimmed logs, the tops pointed with axes, they included officers' barracks—usually log cabins—and log barracks for the enlisted men. Other buildings usually included a guard-house, storehouse, quartermaster's headquarters, hospital and corral. Outside the quadrangle were the quarters for the married men, dubbed "Sudsville" because the women usually augmented their husbands' pay by taking in washing. There was also the sutler's store, which was a combination officers' club, enlisted men's canteen and general store.

There were always women on the post, wives and daughters of officers and men. They were a clannish, gossipy lot divided by feuds and jealousy, but united the moment their men moved out. It was then that their long wait began. It ended when they heard the bugles in the distance or listened with pounding hearts to the report of the weary dispatch rider that most of the troop had been exterminated.

The war with the red men was not a war of great battles of large masses of men meeting head on. It was a succession of sorties, ambushes, sieges and short and savage attacks in which stealth and cunning were demanded of its leaders. It was a war of no quarter, although the "do-gooders in the East" were constantly writing letters to the editors of big dailies denouncing the cavalry for needlessly killing the poor, bewildered red man.

From 1866 to 1875 more than 200 pitched battles would be fought, with the Army outnumbered in all of them. From 1882 to 1887 the Army was at constant war with the Apaches. One regiment participated in 97 field actions.

What Easterners failed to realize was that this foe was terrible, relentless and as dangerous as an aroused rattlesnake. Actually, no one could blame him; the Plains Indians knew they were fighting a war of survival, for land that had been theirs for centuries. What they were really fighting to maintain was an age that was vanishing like woodsmoke in the wind. The westward movement had started; it was moving like a juggernaut from the cities of the East. It could not be stopped.

It is not within the purpose of this book to detail all the Indian battles, but some of the more important engagements are described to indicate the nature and the scope of the conflict.

Officer's tent (B Company, Seventh Infantry), typical of the frontier in 1880.

The Sixth U. S. Cavalry training horses at Fort Bayard, New Mexico.

Target practice on the range.

First U. S. Infantry Band at Fort Grant, 1882.

Company B, 25th Infantry (Carpenter's Brunettes) at Fort Snelling, 1883.

Camp of the Sixth Cavalry, near Fort Fetterman, during the rustlers' war.

Camp of the Fifth Infantry in Yellowstone Valley, Montana, during the campaign against the Sioux.

B Company, Whipple Barracks, 1880's.

The great saga of the Indian Wars began in 1866 when the government commissioners at Fort Laramie negotiated with the Sioux and the Northern Cheyennes for the right of emigrants to pass through the land which had been ceded to the Indians by the Harney-Sanborn Treaty of 1865. It was at this meeting that Red Cloud, the Sioux chief, denounced Brigadier General Henry B. Carrington as the "White Eagle" who was attempting to steal the Indians' land by force. After a violent speech he left the meeting to take the warpath.

The one concession the Army wanted from the Sioux was the unhindered construction of military posts to protect the Bozeman Trail. The Brulé Sioux under Spotted Tail and Standing Elk favored the concession. The older chiefs under Red Cloud, who feared that one concession would only lead to another and yet another, fought to the last against the posts. But the Army was determined to build the posts. No Indians were going to stop them.

In May, 1866, General Carrington, with a force of some 700 men, fully equipped, and guided by Jim Bridger, the mountain man, left for Kearny in Nebraska to establish a new post called the Mountain District. Included in the equipment were the saws and materials for two sawmills to be used in preparing the lumber for the new forts.

At the time there was only one garrison in the area, known as Fort Reno, some 160 miles from Laramie. The latter fort was manned mostly by "galvanized Yankees." Carrington was ordered to march there, then move to a point some 40 miles northward and establish another post on the Bozeman Trail between the Big Horn Mountains and Powder River. The War Department's reasoning was that such a post could command the valley used by the

General Henry B. Carrington.

tribes. A subsequent order had Carrington establish two more posts, one on the Big Horn, the other on the Yellowstone.

Carrington was one of the Army's finest frontier officers. A graduate of Yale, a scientist, Ohio's Civil War Adjutant General, and vigorous foe of the Copperheads, he was also the author of an impressive work on George Washington.

Carrington's force reached Reno in mid-June. A month later he established the command on the Big Piney Creek, about four miles from the Big Horn Range. The air was soon filled with the sound of axes, hammers and saws, while on Big Piney Island, seven miles away, the assembled

Spotted Tail.

Red Cloud. *Photo by D. F. Barry.*

sawmill was trimming the logs. Carrington knew he was under constant surveillance by the Sioux scouts, so he established observation posts on nearby Pilot and Sullivan hills. The small garrison was constantly harassed by Sioux war parties. Stragglers were found scalped and mutilated.

The work on the fort continued through the long, hot summer. It was a rectangle, 600 x 800 feet, with a stockade of pine logs eight feet high with a loophole in every fourth log. Enfilading blockhouses were erected on diagonal corners with portholes for the cannons. Besides the barracks there were also officers' quarters and warehouses. Outside the fort itself was a log stockade surrounding the corral in which the livestock, hay and wagons were kept. In the center of the parade was a tall flagpole, planed and smoothed by the regiment's carpenter.

In August Carrington dispatched Captain Kinney with two companies 90 miles to the northwest to erect a second post, which eventually was called Fort C. F. Smith. In design it was Kearny in miniature. Carrington refused to build the third; there just weren't enough men left.

The main fort was finished in September. General W. B. Hazen, who inspected the garrison, called it the "best I have seen outside the one built by the Hudson's Bay Company in British America." It had been built at the staggering price of 150 men and officers killed and scalped, the wounding of 20 more and the capture of 700 animals against a backdrop of constant vigilance, both day and night.

The armed groups that made the round trips to the sawmills never made a trip without fighting off the swift-raiding Sioux. Five out of seven days the bugler sounded the alert upon a signal from Pilot Hill.

On December 6 the wood train was attacked by Indians in full force, and Captain William J. Fetterman was dispatched with a relief force. The Indians, however, instead of fleeing, turned on Fetterman with a wild ferocity. The raw troops broke and fled, but the ground infantry stood firm. The cavalry, with Carrington himself in the lead, swept over a hill to clash with the Indians; a wild melee followed and the troops finally drove off the redskins. Two days later President Johnson was assuring Congress that now all was peaceful in the West. . . .

But of course the raids continued. Then disturbing news filtered through the log gates that 3,000 bucks were encamped on the Powder River, whetting their scalping knives.

Despite the raw recruits and too few bullets the young officers at that frontier fort possessed an arrogance that was hair-curling. Fetterman was constantly begging Carrington to lead an attack on the main Indian camp, swearing that with "eighty men I can walk through the Sioux camp."

On December 18 the wood train was attacked again and Fetterman got his chance. Upon his plea of seniority Carrington reluctantly gave him the command with strict orders to drive off the attackers but on no condition to chase them across Lodge Trail Ridge.

Fetterman, however, did follow the redskins beyond the ridge and fell into ambush. To rescue him Carrington stripped the post of almost every man, arming his prisoners, cooks and civilians.

Captain Ten Eyck, who had been sent in relief, brought back sad news that afternoon. In his wagons were the bodies of 49 of Fetterman's men, but 32 were still unaccounted for. All the bodies were bristling with arrows; the corpses had been horribly mutilated and in some cases decapitated after shocking tortures. One-fourth of the command was buried secretly that night.

The next day Carrington rode out to recover the rest

Captain Fetterman.

Captain Ten Eyck.

of Fetterman's command. The officer left behind in command of a skeleton army was ordered to raise a white lantern if all was well and a red one if the fort was under attack.

By noon Carrington came to the scene of the battle and found the rest of the bodies, mutilated like the others. One officer had 120 arrows in his body. That night there was a raging blizzard and the temperature dropped to 30° below. Carrington knew that the Sioux were confined to their lodges by the storm, but he also knew he had to get help for his gravely depleted garrison. On his return to the fort he called for volunteers to ride to Laramie for help, and a civilian scout named John Phillips stepped forward and was accepted for the mission.

Phillips, called "Portugee," was given Carrington's own horse, a magnificent Kentucky jumper. At dawn Phillips reached Fort Reno, but it had no telegraph nor was there enough manpower to dispatch a force to Kearny. Portugee rode on through the snow. A few hours out of Reno he was spotted by a force of Indians but outrode them. At daybreak he reached Horseshoe Station and a wire was sent to Laramie. Acting on a hunch that the wires might be down and Laramie would not receive the message, Portugee insisted on riding on. (He was right—the message never got through.)

At Laramie that night a sentry shouted a command as a horse stumbled out of the storm. It crumpled to its knees, dying. The rider slid off, faltered, then staggered forward.

"Courier from Kearny. . . . Important dispatches. . . ."

Men jumped forward to support him, but he waved them away and handed the dispatches to the commanding officer. Then his tremendous stamina and will-power broke. He started to fall, but gentle hands lowered him to the floor and a doctor came on the run.

Portugee Phil had finished one of the most thrilling rides in western history. In three days and nights he had ridden 236 miles through a raging blizzard and through the lines of one of the largest Indian forces in the West. Within a few hours the First Battalion of the 18th Infantry moved out of Laramie.

The news of Fetterman's massacre aroused the nation to a great fever of anger and criticism. Carrington was the Army's scapegoat and was relieved of his command. He was ordered forthwith to transfer himself and his men to Fort Casper.

The one constructive thing that the sad frontier affair brought about was the erection of another fort between Laramie and Reno. It was called Fort Fetterman to honor the rash young officer. The War Department did not see fit to disclose that such a post, built with reinforcements, had been urged by Carrington many months before the fatal battle.

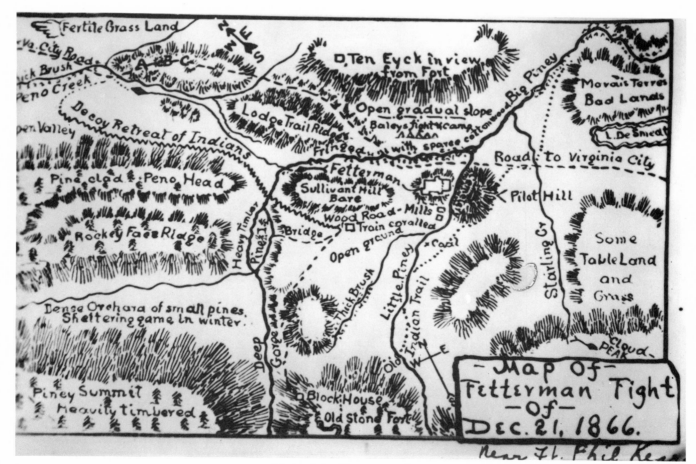

Map of the Fetterman fight.

"Today We Must Fight for Our Lives."

After Carrington departed, Fort Kearny was under constant siege by the Sioux riding with Red Cloud, now the unanimous choice of the bucks as their leader. To go on a logging expedition was to invite almost certain death.

In August Red Cloud, weary of skirmishing and small patrol battles, decided once and for all to come to grips with the issue; he would launch a major attack on Kearny or die in the attempt. In August, 1867, he gathered about him 3,000 braves, the flower of the Sioux Nation, and began an advance on the garrison.

As his ponies moved forward, Captain James W. Powell, a hero of Chickamauga, had arrived at Piney Island with a small party to guard the log-cutting operations at the sawmill. He ordered the wagon bodies that were used in hauling the logs to be arranged in a wide oval. Two-inch holes were drilled into the sides of the wagons. The spaces between the wagons were filled with bags of hay and wheat and stacks of soft pine which would stop a bullet and not cast off flying splinters.

On August 2, Red Cloud's warriors attacked the saw-mill camp as the first step of his strategy to wipe out Kearny. The loggers retreated to the wagon oval after Powell, in a bold sortie, had drawn the Indian cavalry to himself, then retreated to the wagons without loss of a man.

After burning the camp the Sioux attacked the wagon-fort. It was 32 against 3,000. Fortunately, the soldiers were well armed; the best shots had the most rifles. One old Indian fighter had eight rifles beside him, while a poorer shot was assigned to do nothing but keep them loaded.

Red Cloud first sent his best horsemen forward, while behind them on their horses sat the impassive chiefs—Unkpapas, Miniconjous, Ogalalas, Brulés, and the Northern Cheyennes.

Crouched in the wagon-bodies, the troopers, loggers and scouts caught their targets in their sights and waited for Powell's shot, the signal for all to fire. The young officer had made no speeches and had given few instructions. He had said only, "Today we must fight for our lives."

The raiders were now 100 feet away . . . now 50. Powell's rifle cracked, a buck spun out of his saddle and the whole oval belched flame and smoke. That solid sheet of steel from the most rapid firing the Indians had ever encountered stopped them cold. As their comrades fell out of saddles or slumped over, they retreated quickly, leaving behind the writhing wounded and the screaming horses. When Powell counted noses he found his command had been reduced to 28.

"Look to your posts, gentlemen," he said. "They will be back."

This time they returned on foot, wriggling through the grass. Again there was a vast silence from inside the wagon-fort as the Indians poured into it a merciless fire. When they thought they had wiped out most of the defenders, they charged. Again the wagons belched flame as wave after wave crumpled within feet of the wagons. Again they broke and retreated.

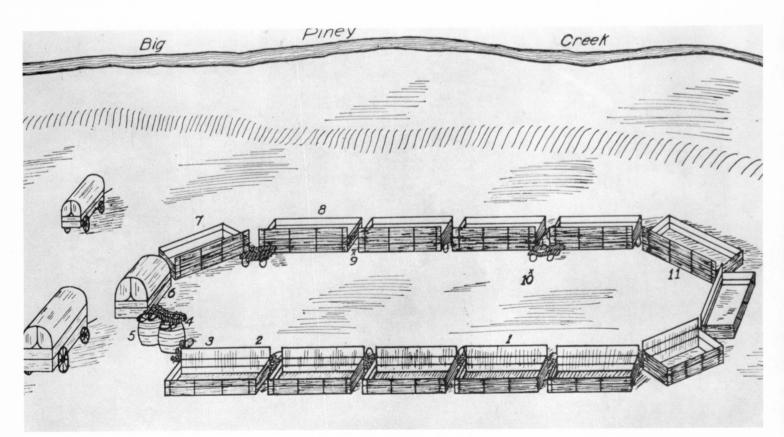

The Wagon Box fight.

Forsyth's fight on the Republican River. *From a painting by Frederic Remington.*

Three times Red Cloud's warriors charged and each time retreated with heavy casualties. Finally he had enough and ordered a full retreat. It wasn't until a year after the battle that Powell learned he and his men had killed 1,137 of Red Cloud's warriors.

In the fall of 1868 a new treaty was made with the Sioux, and Fort Kearny was abandoned. The Indians promptly burned it as the camp of "the bad medicine fight of the white men."

A second classic siege of white men by Indians took place in 1868 when the gallant Major George Alexander "Sandy" Forsyth and 28 men fought off an army of Sioux at Beecher's Island on the Arickaree Fork of the Republican River in eastern Colorado.

The braves, under Roman Nose, hit Forsyth's forces when the troopers were resting their horses on the bank of the river. In the center of the river was a sandy island, smooth as a plate, 20 yards wide and 60 yards long. Due to a drought, the river bed was dry and hardened by the sun. However, on either side of the island, a creek less than a foot deep ran over the rocks and gravel.

The alarm was given as the advance party of redskins, blowing whistles, whirling rattles and beating drums, rode down the slope trying to stampede the trooper's horses. While his men poured a heavy fire into the advancing horsemen, Forsyth ordered a retreat to the tiny island. There they frantically dug shallow firing pits with hands,

cups and pots. Roman Nose himself led the first charge of 500 warriors, the pick of the combined tribes, while his main army fired down from the slopes into the crouching men on the island. The surgeon was killed, Lieutenant Beecher, second in command, badly wounded, and Forsyth was hit in the leg, thigh and head. But, with his own blood filling his tiny firing pit, Forsyth ordered his men to hold their fire until he gave the order.

It was the wagon-box scrap all over. At 50 feet the valley shook with the blast of the rifles and revolvers. Volley after volley tore holes in the ranks of the braves. Roman Nose himself was knocked off his saddle and riddled with bullets. The charge broke and they retreated.

At two o'clock and at six they charged again—only to be repulsed. When night came Forsyth counted his casualties; his command was now reduced to 23. Among the dead was young Beecher, whose name would be given to the island.

That night Forsyth sent out two troopers to crawl through the Indian lines and reach Fort Wallace, a hundred miles away. At dawn the fighting resumed and for five days more the island was under attack, with the men chewing the putrid meat of the dead animals. Forsyth's wounds were gangrenous, and he seemed doomed when help was sighted. It was an ambulance, the vanguard of a force from Fort Wallace. The two scouts had slipped through the lines of the Sioux.

When Colonel Louis H. Carpenter, the officer commanding the relief expedition, rode up he found Forsyth, his rifle across his lap and his revolver nearby, calmly reading a copy of *Oliver Twist*. Later Forsyth said he knew he would break down at the sight of his friend and therefore had taken the worn copy from his saddle bag and made a pretense at reading.

Forsyth was burning with fever. Although the surgeon said he had to amputate at once to save his life, the young officer refused. It took four days to get to Wallace, four days of hell in the bouncing, jolting ambulance. It would take more than two years before his wounds healed completely.

On the trip back General Carpenter's "Brunettes" reported a large movement of Sioux on Beaver Creek, and this word was dispatched to General Sheridan at Fort Hays, Kansas. Brevet-Major General Eugene A. Carr and the Fifth Cavalry joined Carpenter's Tenth at Wallace and moved out three weeks after the rescue of Forsyth's men.

Carpenter's scouts found the Indians, who turned and attacked. Like Powell, the general formed his wagons in a double column, six on one side, five on the other with mules inward, and met the charges with devastating rifle fire from seven-shooter Spencers.

The battle lasted eight hours, with the Indians suffering heavy losses. Finally they retreated. On their way back to Wallace, Carpenter and his men rode through tough Sheridan City, terminus of the Union Pacific, and the men who

Colonel Louis H. Carpenter.

ran out of the saloons gave the troops a "rousing welcome."

In the winter of 1868 Lt. Colonel George Armstrong Custer, the frontier's glory-hunter, leading the famous Seventh, four companies of foot soldiers and the Nineteenth Kansas Volunteer Cavalry, attacked the Cheyenne under Black Kettle in the valley of a small river in the Indian Territory called Washita.

The troopers fell on the village to the accompaniment

Roman Nose leading the charge against Forsyth. *From a painting by Charles Schreyvogel.*

George Armstrong Custer.

[98]

of their regiment's tune, "Garry Owen." It was a massacre, with Black Kettle among the dead. The remainder of the united Kiowas, Arapahoes, Cheyenne "dog soldiers" and reportedly even some wandering Apaches counterattacked. Led by the Kiowa Santana and Black Kettle's successor, Little Rock, they almost had Custer's back to the wall when fresh ammunition arrived. The troops managed to drive off the Indians, following which Custer burned the village and shot more than 700 Indian ponies.

A year later General Carr, leading the Fifth and with the flamboyant Buffalo Bill as his scout, defeated Tall Bull at Summit Springs, Colorado.

Sitting Bull, the Sioux's medicine man, and Crazy Horse, probably the ablest war chief in western history, now had taken a position in the Valley of the Big Horn near Powder River. Forts and federal agencies for Indians encircled them. The Missouri was on the east and north; on the south were the military posts along the Union Pacific, to the west were the mountains. Three expeditions were to be launched against the Indians simultaneously; one was to march eastward from Montana, another was to advance northward from southern Nebraska and a third was to strike west from Fort Abraham Lincoln.

Only one expedition got off, that led by General Joseph Reynolds, who captured Crazy Horse's village, but retreated ignominiously when the Indians counter-attacked. It was not until years later that the Army proved effective against Sitting Bull and Crazy Horse.

Santana (White Bear), the Kiowa sub-chief, wearing the uniform given him by General F. S. Babcock at the time of the signing of the treaty at Medicine Lodge, Kansas, in October, 1867.

The "People"

The wiliest, the cruelest and perhaps the toughest enemy the cavalry ever encountered was the Chiricahua Apache. They made up for their lack of numbers by a fierce hatred of the white man and an almost fanatical kind of courage. During the Civil War they ravaged the Arizona Territory many times, driving the settlers back into the larger towns. Even Tucson was menaced.

After the reorganization of the Regular Army, General George Crook was given the task of subduing "People," as they called themselves. Crook insisted from the beginning that an offensive campaign was the only way to dislodge the tribes from their *rancherias* in the mountain strongholds. In 1871 his methods began to produce results. In the spring of that year Eskiminzin and his band left the mountains and surrendered to the Army at Fort Grant. The burly Indian said simply, "We are tired of fighting."

The citizens of nearby Tucson, who had felt the brunt of the Indian raids in the bleak years of the war, were aroused. On April 28, 1871, a mob raided the Indian camp in Pantano Wash, east of Tucson, and massacred 108 Apaches, mostly women and children. The leaders of the mob were later tried and acquitted.

In Christmas week, 1872, a patrol sent out by Crook bivouacked in a small canyon near Cottonwood Creek. An Apache scout, Nantaje, had reported that there was a large body of Apaches in a big cave on Salt River nearby, that they must march at night; if they were seen in daylight, not a man would return alive. Major Brown, in command, gave the orders and at dusk the column set out.

An advance scout reported that the Apaches, just back from raiding the settlements on the Gila, were dancing in the large cave. The soldiers crept from rock to rock.

Major General Eugene A. Carr.

Soon the *rancheria* was completely surrounded. At a signal from Brown a deadly fire poured into the cave. The canyon shook with sound. From the cave came screams and cries. After a time Brown ordered a pause in the firing. An interpreter called for unconditional surrender, but the answer was defiant; the Apaches were ready to fight to the death.

The lines were ordered to aim at the roof of the cave so the bullets would ricochet into the huddled Indians behind their ramparts. The strategy worked. Warriors attempted to rush forward, only to be cut down.

Another command to stop firing was issued. In a lull the dust and the black powder smoke hung in the air. Then from the cave rose the death chant. Brown reluctantly gave his order. Rifles crashed in solid volleys until there was no answering fire from the cave.

The troops moved forward cautiously, but soon it developed that out of the entire band only 12 women and small children, some badly wounded, were alive. Seventy-six men and boys had been killed in the battle.

Crook's offensive warfare was too much for the Apaches. On April 27, 1873, the last band surrendered at Camp Verde.

Cato, a Chiricahua chief.

General Crook with two Apache scouts. *Left,* Dutchie; *right,* Alchise. *Probably a photo by Camillus Fly.*

Gold in the Black Hills

In 1873 and 1874, two large expeditions were sent out for the purpose of exploring the sacred Black Hills of the Dakotas. The first, in 1873, was under the command of General Stanley. Custer and his Seventh were included.

The following year, Tom Custer, General Custer's brother, captured Rain-in-the-Face at Standing Rock Agency, 20 miles from Fort Abraham Lincoln. But the chief escaped from the jailhouse with a civilian prisoner. He swore he would someday eat Tom Custer's heart.

His revenge was just over the rim of the next hill. . . .

The following year the second Black Hills expedition, this time under George Custer, set out from Fort Lincoln. It was a long train of a thousand troopers and scientists.

Although the Black Hills, sacred to the Sioux, were in the center of their nation, Custer was not discovered. His force skirted the Black Buttes of Wyoming, continued across the valley, and camped near Inyan Kara.

Custer and his staff climbed to the peak, then marched on to nearby "Floral Valley."

He wrote: "Our march was amid flowers of the most exquisite colors and perfume." But Custer found something more important than wild flowers; there was gold in the Black Hills.

Captain Tom Custer.

The Custer family at home, 1874. George Custer is standing at the piano; his sister, Mrs. Calhoun, is playing, "I'm Waiting, My Darling, for Thee"; Mrs. Custer is fourth from the left; Tom Custer's head shows at the right as he leans forward.

Rain-in-the-Face. Taken at Fort Yates.

fearless, resourceful and experienced frontiersman, was elected "trail boss" of the expedition.

Christmas week, 1874, the party camped near the present site of Custer City and on French Creek, where gold had been found. A large stockade and a fort were built and the party settled down for some mining and hunting, but in April, cavalry from Fort Laramie found the party and escorted them out of the hille.

Other parties tried to slip into the Hills after the Gordon Party. One wagon train was found and burned by the troops.

However, it was impossible for the cavalry to hold back the flood of gold-mad men. In the next year the Hills were open and Deadwood was founded. And from the rims of their sacred Hills the Sioux and Cheyennes looked down at the mushrooming gold towns with bitterness.

Shortly after Custer made his report, Charles Collins, editor of the Sioux City (Iowa) *Times,* went to Chicago for the purpose of outfitting an expedition to prospect and mine. But he had no sooner reached Chicago and stated his intentions when Lieutenant Sheridan issued an order forbidding anyone to go into the hills until proper treaties were made with the Sioux. Although Collins was stopped, he went back to Sioux City and started to organize a new company "on the quiet."

On October 6, 1874, 26 men and one woman set out for a secret trip to the Black Hills. For deception, the lead wagon was labeled "O'Neil's Colony"—a homesteading colony on the Elkhorn River, Nebraska. John Gordon, a

Some members of the Gordon Stockade party.

A reconstruction of the Gordon Stockade.

POST RETURN of *Troop composing "Black Hill Expedition"*, commanded by

PRESENT.	ABSENT.

Lieut Colonel G. A. Custer *7*ᵗʰ *Cavalry*, **for the month of** *August*

PRESENT AND ABSENT.			ALTERATIONS SINCE LAST MONTHLY RETURN.		MEMORANDA.
	ENLISTED MEN.		GAIN.	LOSS.	HORSES. PIECES

OFFICIAL COMMUNICATIONS RECEIVED DURING THE MONTH.

[See Army Regulations as to the mode of obtaining missing orders.]

NOTE 4.—Communications will be acknowledged in the following order: 1st, "Letters;" 2d, "General Orders;" 3d, "Special Orders" from the A. G. OFFICE; 4th, "Letters;" 5th, "General Orders;" 6th, "Special Orders" from HD. QRS. OF THE ARMY; 7th, "Letters;" 8th, "General Orders;" 9th, "Special Orders" from DIV. HD. QRS.; 10th, "Letters;" 11th, "General Orders;" and 12th, "Special Orders" from DEPT HD. QRS. All orders will be arranged according to their numbers, and without reference to the date when they are received at the post.

DATE.	WHENCE ISSUED.	WHEN RECEIVED.	PURPORT.
August 2ᵈ 1874			Companies C⁰ & K 7ᵗʰ Cav. accompanied by a Detachment of Engineers left the main camp for the purpose of exploring the North Fork of the Cheyenne River. The prospectors accompanying the expedition found gold this morning.
August 3ᵈ 1874			Companies A. E. L. H. G⁰ M. 7ᵗʰ Cav. and scientific party left main camp for the purpose of exploring the South Fork of the Cheyenne River. Chas Reynolds a guide in employ of the Government left Cheyenne River with the mail for Fort Laramie
August 5ᵗʰ 1874			The detachment returned from exploring the North and South forks of the Cheyenne River.
August 14ᵗʰ 1874			Traveled down the hills into the open prairies and arrived near the base of "Bear Butte"
August 15ᵗʰ 1874			Six Indian Scouts left Camp for Fort Lincoln with the mail.
August 16ᵗʰ 1874			Indians intercepted by our Scouts who sent word that six (6) bands of hostile Sioux were encamped on the east side of the Little Missouri waiting to attack this command.
August 17ᵗʰ 1874 to 25ᵗʰ "			Traveled over a burnt prairie. Grass found in isolated places.
August 30ᵗʰ 1874			Arrived at Fort A. Lincoln D.T.

G.A. Custer
Brevet Major General U.S. Army,
Commanding the Post.

[stamp] SEPT 10 1874 ADJUTANT GEN'L'S OFFICE

Part of Custer's field report for the month of August, 1874. Note the laconic statement of August 2: "The prospectors accompanying the expedition found gold this morning."

The Hostiles Strike Back

LIKE most great war plans, the three pronged strategy devised by Lieutenant General Philip Sheridan looked perfect on paper. Brigadier General George Crook, commanding the Department of the Platte, would move up the Bozeman Trail north into Indian Territory; General John Gibbon, commanding the "Montana Column," would leave Fort Shaw and descend the Yellowstone to keep the tribes from escaping while General Alfred H. Terry, leading a column of 950 troopers, infantrymen, and Gatling guns, would meet Gibbon's advance forces in early June.

All three commands would close the trap about the Sioux and Cheyenne who had refused to return to their reservations. The three columns would rendezvous somewhere on the Big Horn or Little Big Horn.

There was one great flaw in Sheridan's plans: he had neglected to include the charismatic leadership and courage of Crazy Horse, the great Sioux chief.

On May 29, 1876, Crook led his army of slightly more than a thousand men out of Fort Fetterman on the south bank of the North Platte River after being joined by other troops from Fort Russell. There were cavalrymen, infantrymen, 120 wagons, and over a thousand mules. Later Crow and Shoshone scouts swelled the column to about thirteen hundred fighting men.

In early June the column reached Fort Kearny, then pushed on to the junction of Prairie Dog Creek and the Tongue River. On the ninth the first contact was made with a small party of Cheyenne. Crook, "bristling for a fight," moved north to camp near the headwaters of the

Sitting Bull. *Photo by D. F. Barry.*

General Custer and Colonel Ludlow with a grizzly bear they killed during the Black Hills Expedition of 1874-75. *Photo by W. H. Illingworth.*

Rosebud despite the objection of Plenty Coups. The Crow chief warned "Three Stars" that the bivouac was vulnerable because the Sioux and Cheyenne could attack from the high ground.

Crook, who was sure no Indians could stand up against his troopers but not sure of the size of the enemy confronting him, ignored the warning.

Unknown to Crook, scouts sent out by Crazy Horse had been reconnoitering the column. On the morning of the seventeenth the Sioux chief stationed his men on the high ground of the Valley of the Rosebud. First there was contact between scouts of both sides; Crook was taken by surprise and had it not been for the courageous stand of Plenty Coups and his men, Crook's column could have been wiped out.

The battle raged on both sides of the Rosebud for the morning and part of the afternoon until Crazy Horse pulled back his warriors, satisfied that he had defeated Three Stars. At first the Eastern newspapers hailed the engagement as a victory but Washington knew Crook had been defeated; Crazy Horse still held the field, had not been driven back to the reservation, and had prevented Crook from fulfilling his mission as part of Sheridan's three-pronged strategy. Crook retired to his main camp at Goose Creek at the foot of the Big Horn Mountains, where he remained for weeks waiting for supplies and licking his wounds.

The villages of Crazy Horse echoed with the triumphant chants of his warriors as their squaws dismantled the lodges and packed the ponies. Soon the long columns would head for another battle with the horse soldiers at a place called Little Big Horn.

The subsequent Battle of Little Big Horn and the manner in which George Armstrong Custer died made him one of the most popular of American legends. Probably more has been written about him than any other American military figure, including Washington, Lee, Grant, Sheri-

The bluff where some of Custer's men were driven into the Little Big Horn. *Photo by S. J. Morrow.*

The telegram notifying the Adjutant General of Custer's disaster. Dated June 27, it was received in Chicago July 6, 1876.

Gall, who fought against Custer and told the story of the
Little Big Horn massacre. *Photo by D. F. Barry.*

A letter written by Major Marcus A. Reno in 1885, reporting
the discovery of his own diary, found lying on the grass after
the Custer massacre.

dan, and Sherman. The commentary ranges from wild praise to bitter condemnation. As long as there are amateur and experienced historians of the Western frontier, the Battle of Little Big Horn will be fought and refought with scouts perched on every hill, ready to shoot down any error.

Custer's career was marred by feuds, flamboyant publicity, court-martials, and controversy. To bring off his military plans to subdue the Indians and return the tribes to their reservations, Sheridan had restored Custer to his command after he had been suspended by a court-martial.

Custer led his troops out of Fort Abraham Lincoln to the stirring tune of "Garry Owen." Then as the troops disappeared into the distance, the band struck up "The Girl I Left Behind Me" as wives, soon to be widows, gallantly called out their farewells.

Not too many days later on a warm June afternoon Custer and his command were annihilated in one brief

Major Marcus A. Reno.

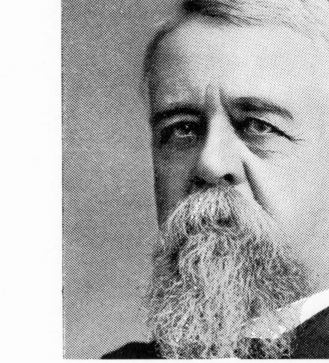

General Alfred H. Terry.

Curly, known to his Crow tribesmen as Ash-ish-ish-e.

General Wesley Merritt.

Red Cloud, Buffalo Bill Cody, American Horse.

hour of fighting, overwhelmed by the largest combined Indian army in the history of the West under the commands of Crazy Horse, Sitting Bull, Gall and Rain-in-the-Face. There was no quarter; when the dust settled Yellow Hair was dead, surrounded by the bodies of his brother, his captains, and his men. On the morning of June 27, 1876, the commands of Terry and Gibbon buried the lost leader and 211 of his troopers who died with him. They also buried fifty-three more of Reno's command, and then started the long, sad journey back with the wounded to the steamboat *Far West*, where on the twenty-first they had all conferred so bravely and full of confidence that they would snap closed Sheridan's trap.

The news of Little Big Horn stunned the nation. Reinforcements and supplies were dispatched to the West with Washington's terse order: bring the war to the Indians. The first blood was scored by Colonel Wesley Merritt, who stopped a thousand Cheyenne at War Bonnet Creek in South Dakota. Here William F. Cody, famed as Buffalo Bill, fought a duel to the death with the Cheyenne chief Yellow Hand, another controversial incident in frontier history.

When Merritt joined Crook the combined forces moved against the Cheyenne and Sioux in a bitter march in which Crook and his men were forced to eat their horses. Amer-

ican Horse and his warriors were penned in a gully under a deadly fire until the dying chief, biting on a piece of wood to hold back his moans of pain, surrendered on condition the lives of his men were spared. The troopers who remembered Little Big Horn wanted no white flag but Crook agreed and the warriors turned in their rifles.

The afternoon was dragging on when a force of Sioux under Crazy Horse appeared in an attempt to rescue American Horse and his men. This time Crook's troopers brought the fight to the enemy as Washington had ordered. As the air purpled, Crazy Horse pulled his warriors back to leave Crook the field.

Supplies came in from Deadwood, and the stubborn Crook planned his winter campaign. Colonel Ronald S. Mackenzie swooped down on Dull Knife's Cheyenne village on Crazy Woman's fork of the Powder River, and drove out the warriors and burned the tepees. In January 1877 General Nelson Miles led his foot cavalry, as tough as any that served under Stonewall Jackson in the Civil War, on a forced march after Crazy Horse, to finally corner him in the valley of the Tongue River.

The Indians poured down a murderous fire from snowy Wolf Mountain but two field guns sent shells hurtling against the tops of the cliffs. While the guns crashed, a frontal attack was made with troopers gaining the top and

American Horse. His buckskin shirt is trimmed with scalps.

Dull Knife.

engaging the warriors in hand-to-hand combat. Under cover of a snowstorm the Sioux retreated up the valley. Tribal feuds and jealousy over the popularity of Crazy Horse and defeats after Little Big Horn split the Indians' united front; each chief led his followers from the main camp. Scattered bands were picked up by the soldiers or surrendered. Among the last was Crazy Horse.

After he had been persuaded that a council would be held the next day, he was escorted to a log building by soldiers and Sioux chiefs now allied with the whites. Only when he saw his fellow warriors in leg-irons and the setting sun pouring through the barred windows did the Sioux chief realize he was being put into a guardhouse. He jumped back and flashed a knife. The bitterness, envy, and jealousy of the other chiefs erupted violently in that small room. Little Big Man grabbed Crazy Horse about the middle and imprisoned his arms but the muscular Sioux broke free and slashed his captor's arm. The other chiefs held him while a guard, Private William Gentles, thrust his bayonet into the body of the struggling chief. He died the following day.

The combined power of the Sioux and Cheyenne had been broken. A fragile peace came to the frontier; it would soon be shattered.

Captain Jack Crawford (x on hat), the scout poet who served with Merritt, shown in the Black Hills, 1876. *Photo by S. J. Morrow.*

To the great father, in the council house of the people,

Red Wing, from the Dakota country of the Black hills, one of the Sioux, conining from the upper hunting grounds of the good Spirit, makes this appeal in behalf of his red brothers.

pale face, and the glory of father Grant, will surround his life, like the glory of the sun at noon day heat.

Red Wing, Sioux, through hand of white maiden

A letter written by Chief Red Wing of the Sioux, "through hand of white maiden" to the President of the United States, "Father Grant."

To the great father in the council house of the people;

Red Wing, from the Dakota country of the Black hills, one of the Sioux, coming from the upper hunting grounds of the good Spirit, makes this appeal in behalf of his red brothers.

Many, many moons ago, the tribes of the Red man was visited by a council of palefaces, who bartered for their fine land, and sent the red man way towards the setting sun, but the blankets, and the shooting irons that the paleface gave, were soon used, and the redskin had no way to live but, as he had before the white man came, (on the chase, seeking game).

The red man settled in his new territory (in one little spot of the great country that the good Spirit gave to the Indian moons before the paleface knew of it), but he had no peace, the white man, eager for more land, more game, eager to drive the red man off, came; our lodges were destroyed, our council fires broken up and the red children of the plains were scattered like the leaves of the forest.

The Indian, burning from his wrongs, made fierce by the treatment of the whites, rushed upon the palefaces; and not making distinction, scalped and tomahawked all he found, believing every paleface to be treacherous and mean, unfit to live in the vast country which the great Manota gave to his children, where they live in their lodges free children of the forest and the lake, and so, he scalped the whites, as snakes, believing that the smile of the Great Spirit, shone on them in the beams of the morning sun, for it.

But, Red Wing no come to tell of this, Red Wing come to whisper to the great father of the white people, of the treaty he made (some time ago) with the Red man when he made the reservation of the Black hills country to the Sioux.

Not yet, has the Summer sun shone, or the winter snow fell, eight times since the treaty was made by Chief Sherman, and other chiefs on the great sachem's side, and the chiefs of the Sioux on the Red man's. Not yet have the leaves of the forest fallen eight times, since the provision ("No persons, except such officers, agents, or employees of the Government as may be authorized to enter on Indian reservation territory, in discharge of the dutys

enjoined by law, shall ever be permitted to pass over, settle upon, or reside in this territory," and, "the honor of the government of the United States is pledged to keep it." treaty.

When this treaty was made by big chiefs sent out by strong Sachem at Washington, Sioux, expect white man keep it, but no, squads of palefaces come, search the country, want to drive red man away, and seize the country, what, Redskin do, if he drove from Dakota, where go? Paleface drove game from other parts of country, Red man no want starve, no want see paleface take lodge and blankets from papoose, go further West, he find the sun setting there, no go south, it no be his home. And so he get fierce, he sharpening his tomahawk, he fixing shooting irons, he get ready to steal on palefaces, when moon hides her face and the stars grow dim. And Red Wing calls upon the great father to prevent the bloodshed of the whites, and the extermination of the Indians, to preserve his treaty, to allow no one to settle in Sioux territory who no belong there.

Red Wing come way east to white maiden to ask mighty father to look after his red children, he has granted heap big sum for the red man's use, heap wampum, but white man greedy, he give red man poor blankets, rusty shooting irons, damp powder, bad beef, musty flour, take wampum big Sachem say for Indian, and spect Indian be satisfied.

Indian no satisfied, he calls of great Spirit to help him, Great Spirit hear, and sends Red Wing to the father at the council house to ask father, to see to red children, to send out brave, good palefaces to distribute stores to Sioux, and Cheyennes and Arapahoes and others. Send chiefs to look after the wants of the red children, send out talking sheet over the country forbidding white man invade Black hills in search of shiners, send words to chiefs at forts no to allow braves to fire on redskins.

This what Red Wing want, this what great Spirit want, the good father at Washington to make his council a council of Peace, want him to protect Red man, then the Indian troubles will subside, and the Red man will pass away, quite and natural from his lodges, to the hunting ground of Manota beyond the setting sun, leaving the country to the paleface, and the glory of father Grant will surround his life like the glory of the sun at noon day heat.

Red Wing, Sioux, through hand of white maiden

Red War in the Lava Beds

While the bluecoats were fighting the Sioux and Cheyennes on the western plains, the United States was engaged in one of its most costly wars—fought in the lava beds of Oregon—during the winter of 1872-73. Here 50 Modoc Indians under the leadership of Kientpoos, better known as Captain Jack, not only held off a force of cavalry and infantry several times their number but defeated the soldiers time after time.

The Modocs first became a major problem to the military in 1852 when they wiped out an emigrant train near Tule Lake. The entire company was murdered, many subjected to hair-raising tortures. One man, left for dead, managed to escape and tell his story.

A Californian named Ben Wright gathered together a large posse and chased the Modocs, who escaped from them in the lava beds. Wright then sent out word to Schonchin, the Modoc chief, to come in for a peace parley. When they arrived Wright and his party opened fire and killed most of the Indians. After the Civil War a treaty was made with the tribe. Under Schonchin, their chief who had led them in the wagon-train disaster, they settled on the reservation only to find to their dismay that they were quartered with the larger Klamath tribe.

There was much friction and Captain Jack, Hooker Jim and Curly Headed Doctor left the reservation to camp on their old hunting ground, the Lost River Country. The Modocs, a shiftless, transient band, frightened the settlers in the region, who protested to the Army. General Edward S. Canby was ordered to return the Modocs to their reservation, "peaceably if you can, forcibly if you must."

Captain James Jackson and 40 troopers were ordered to round up the Modocs and bring them back to the reservation. On the morning of November 28, 1872, after an all-night ride through a downpour, Jackson arrived at the Indians' camp and, in his own words, "jumped" it.

The Indians surrendered, but Jack stayed in his tepee. When Jackson demanded that the Indians surrender their weapons Scar Face Charley, who had seen his father hanged by the white man, refused. Others joined him. When an officer and some men tried to take away their rifles, the battle started. Meanwhile, across the river some civilian volunteers had opened fire on Hooker Jim's camp only to be driven off. When the smoke cleared Captain Jack and the remnants of his people had disappeared in the hills, leaving 15 warriors, women and children dead on the field.

He retreated to the lava beds, where he was joined by Hooker Jim, who had killed 17 settlers on the way. The combined tribes counted 50 warriors and a large number of women and children.

Detachments of the First Cavalry and Twenty-First Infantry, along with units from the Oregon and California Militia, were sent out to bring back the Indians, who were now boasting they could hold off a thousand troops in

Captain Jack of the Modocs.

Shacknasty Jim, Hooker Jim, Steamboat Frank, Judge John Fairchild.

the rugged lava beds. They made good their boast as they moved like shadows among the ridges and cross-passages which they knew as well as the backs of their own hands.

The soldiers stumbled from ridge to ridge, their shoes cut to pieces by the flint-sharp rocks. From out of nowhere rifles cracked, men dropped. Volleys would be turned against the spot from where the shot had come, but when the troops charged they found only emptiness. After a fruitless campaign the army's commander returned to his base with one-fourth of his command killed or wounded. He said he would need a command of a thousand men armed with artillery and mortars to blow the small band of Modocs out of their hiding places.

The First Cavalry was put into the field; reinforcements brought the command to the thousand mark. Artillery was also included, and General Canby himself took to the field. First he tried peace negotiations, promising to put the Modocs on Angel Island in San Francisco Harbor until they could choose another reservation, but this the Indians refused. It was Lost River country—or nothing. Captain Jack wanted to settle on his own terms, but his warriors called for all-out war. In one of their councils legend has the warriors putting a woman's shawl on Jack's shoulders to show their contempt. This action brought Jack to his feet. "If you want war you shall have it," he cried angrily.

The first step which they thought would make the white man withdraw was to agree to a peace meeting with the white man's commissioners, then murder the

Toby Riddle, the Modoc wife of Frank Riddle.

commissioners, who besides Canby included Colonel Gillem, the Reverend Dr. Eleazar Thomas, a Methodist minister well known to the Modocs, H. B. Meacham, a former Indian agent, and another agent, L. S. Dyer. Riddle, a squaw man who had married a Modoc woman, urged Canby to call off the meeting. He said he was sure Jack could not be trusted.

On the lookout for an attack in the lava beds.

On the morning of April 11, 1873, Canby and his party met Captain Jack and his warriors in the large peace tent. Riddle, the squaw man, felt so strongly about the council that before he agreed to act as interpreter he made the commissioners accompany him to the bedside of Colonel Gillem, who had been taken ill, and at the sick bed made a violent protest against holding the council. But Canby, who was not swayed, ordered it held.

The council was brief and tense. The Indians were insolent and savage. It was clear they meant trouble but, unruffled, Canby continued the council. Suddenly Captain Jack shouted an order and each Indian in the tent who apparently had been assigned a victim opened fire. Canby was shot in the face by Jack, while Boston Charlie shot Dr. Thomas as he was kneeling. Dyer and Riddle, who at the last minute had slipped derringers in their pockets, escaped with the Indians after them. Hooker Jim was about to grab Dyer when he turned and fired his revolver. The surprised Indians, seeing their intended victims were now armed, broke off the chase after firing several rounds.

The Indians stripped the bodies of Canby and Thomas and Boston Charlie prepared to scalp them. He had slit the scalp of the wounded Meacham when Riddle's Indian wife cried, "Soldiers are coming," and the Modocs fled.

Colonel Jefferson C. Davis with officers during the Modoc campaign.

The cowardly murder of General Canby aroused the Army; it was clear that Jack and his people had to be dug out of the lava beds even at bayonet point. On the 14th Colonel Gillem left his sick bed to lead a large force in an attack against the beds. Mortars zeroed Jack's stronghold with a curious effect. One shell failed to explode and one curious Indian tried to pull out the plug with his teeth; result: seven dead Modocs. Realizing that the mortars had made his position untenable, Jack retreated back in the maze of crevices and underground passages in the beds.

On April 21 a party of soldiers and Warm Springs Indians set out after them. They were ambushed and many of the soldiers panicked, leaving behind most of the command. When the Modocs had slipped away 22 soldiers and officers were dead and 18 wounded. Not one of the 20 warriors had suffered a scratch.

Colonel Jefferson C. Davis (the Union officer, not the Confederacy's President), commander of the Department of Columbia, was finally given command and ordered to close the shameful campaign at once. Davis, a strict disciplinarian, reorganized his troops, gave them new provisions and weapons and, adopting the Modocs' own tactics, began to tighten a cordon around the lava-bed area.

A Modoc War correspondent, McKay of the San Francisco *Bulletin*, in the lava beds.

The Indians had split into two parties, one under Jack, the other under Hooker. They were now suffering from lack of water, supplies and ammunition. There was also friction in their councils, and finally it was agreed to leave the beds.

On May 10 the Indians, united into one command, launched an attack on the camp of the Fourth Artillery, mounted for this campaign. The surprise was at first successful, but the troops rallied to give the Modocs their first clear-cut defeat in addition to capturing their mules and ammunition.

They now fled from the beds, and Colonel Davis ordered a vigorous pursuit. One large band of 100 families was captured, and Davis offered them their lives if they would disclose the hideout of Captain Jack and Hooker Jim.

A redskin Judas led the troops to where his comrades were hiding. Jack and Hooker Jim were at last taken into custody and Davis prepared to hang them. Washington officials, however, stopped him after a discussion of the legality of the execution. A trial was ordered and Hooker Jim, Bogus Charley and Shacknasty Jim became government witnesses. Jack, without benefit of defense counsel, made a long speech defending himself, but the evidence that he had committed cold-blooded murder was too strong. He was found guilty and sentenced to hang along with Schonchin John, Black Jim and Boston Charlie. Two of their co-defendants had their sentences commuted to life imprisonment by President Grant. The quartet was hanged at ten o'clock on the morning of October 3, 1873, in full sight of their people.

Just before he was executed a chaplain came to comfort Jack with the advice that he was going to a far, far better land. Jack looked thoughtful. "You say, Mr. Preacher, that the place I am going to is a nice place. Do you like this place you call Heaven?"

After the preacher added a glowing description of Heaven, Jack nodded and said with an impassive face, "I tell you what I will do. I'll give you twenty-five head of ponies if you take my place. As you say, Heaven is such a nice place. Because I do not like to go right now."

There were no takers and the four walked the steps to the gallows.

After the hangings, while Jack's preserved body was taken on a tour of the East, the remainder of his tribe was transferred to a small reservation near Baxter Springs, Kansas. The Army totaled up its casualties with a red face; the Modocs had lost 14 dead in the campaign, four hanged and one suicide. The soldiers and white settlers' casualties were 168, of whom 83 were killed. The cost of the campaign was estimated at a half-million dollars.

The Western Scene in Photographs

ONE of the first photographers to penetrate the West was S. N. Carvalho, who accompanied Frémont on his 1852 expedition. But Carvalho's plates were all, or almost all, lost to posterity in a fire. Carvalho sent his plates to Mathew Brady for processing and Brady returned them to Frémont, who sent them to Mrs. Frémont for safekeeping in their home. The Frémont home burned down and all the plates in it were destroyed. But in the Brady studio a plate was found showing an Indian village (reproduced on page 47). It could not have been Brady's or any other eastern photographer's, and many experts, including Paul Vanderbilt, formerly of the Library of Congress Prints and Photographs Division, believe the daguerreotype could have been made by Carvalho.

In the fifties Robert H. Vance made many excellent plates of the California gold-fields, scenes in Oregon, Washington, Colorado and probably Nevada. Alexander Gardner, one of Brady's wartime assistants, made a number of fine western photographs after the War.

But it was Tim O'Sullivan, another Brady battlefield assistant, who was the great photographer of the West. In 1866 and again in 1867 and 1869 he went out as official photographer of the U. S. Engineer Department's Geological Exploration of the 40th Parallel, led by Clarence King. In this, and in the Wheeler Expeditions of 1871, 1873 and 1874 O'Sullivan photographed everything of possible interest. He even contrived an ingenious magnesium flare arrangement for the first photographs of underground mining scenes ever made.

The roster of famous photographers of the West is long and honorable: William H. Jackson, John Hillers, L. A. Huffman, D. F. Barry, Charles R. Savage, C. C. Pierce, A. J. Russell, John Carbutt, S. J. Morrow, Camillus Fly, W. P. Bliss and many others. There were also innumerable local commercial photographers.

But until the development of halftone engraving in the 1880's none of these photographs could be reproduced economically for magazine or book publication. Many did achieve wide circulation in the form of stereoscopic views, which had been made enormously popular by Mathew Brady and Edward Anthony. These were double-prints pasted on cardboard and viewed through a stereoscopic lens to achieve three-dimensional effects.

The sale of stereoscopic "Rocky Mountain Views," "California Scenes" and a host of other such pictures was tremendous and served to stimulate interest in the West.

Probably because they were a convenient 4" x 7" size and backed by cardboard, a great quantity of these views, including many by O'Sullivan and Jackson, have been preserved. But the great wealth of original photographs of the 1865-1890 period of the West has been lost. Only a few collections exist and, as explained in the foreword, a number of these were "lucky finds."

In addition to the photographs shown in the following pages, many other examples of the work of these famous photographers are included in their appropriate sections. The picture on this page was taken on the Wheeler Expedition of 1871. The pictures on the following 14 pages were taken by O'Sullivan on the King Expedition.

Pack mule, pack and packers. A facsimile of a stereoscopic view card. *Photo by Tim O'Sullivan.*

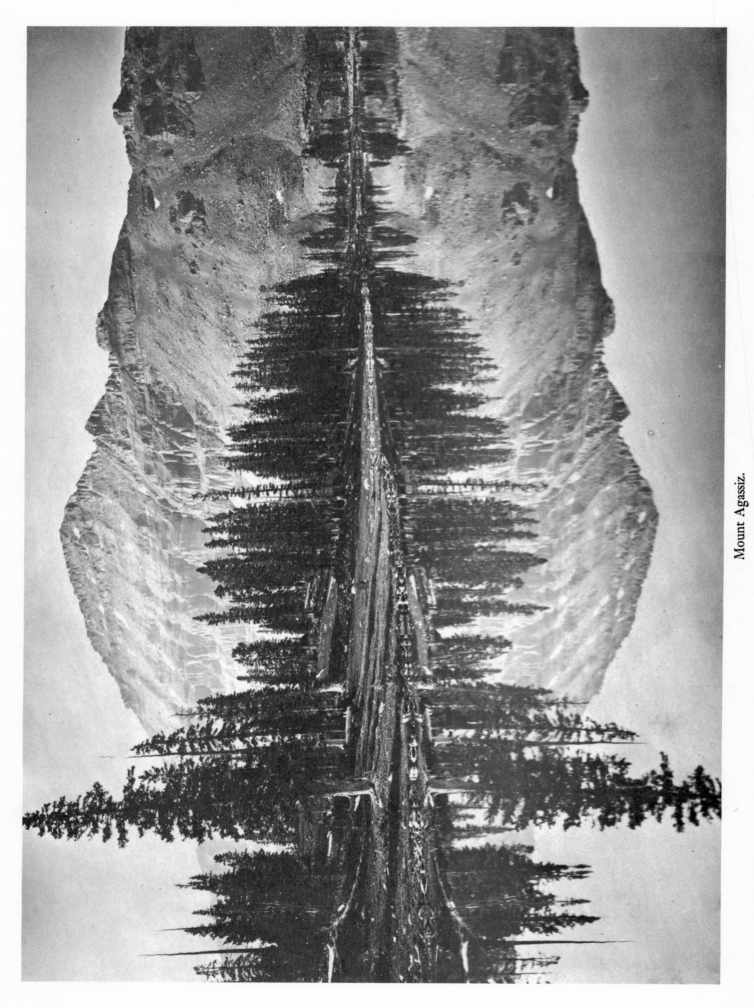

Mount Agassiz.

View on the Snake River.

Shoshone Indians.

Paiute Indians, Pyramid Lake.

Officers' quarters, Fort Ruby.

Company quarters, Fort Ruby.

On the Central Pacific Railroad. Wall and snow sheds east of Summit between tunnels 7 and 8.

Livermore Pass, Central Pacific Railroad.

Donner Lake.

Eastern portal of Summit Tunnel, showing old wagon road east of Donner Pass.

Virginia City, Nevada.

The Virginia Mines, showing the Curtis Shaft (*top left.*) The other three pictures are underground views, the first photographs ever taken in a mine by magnesium light.

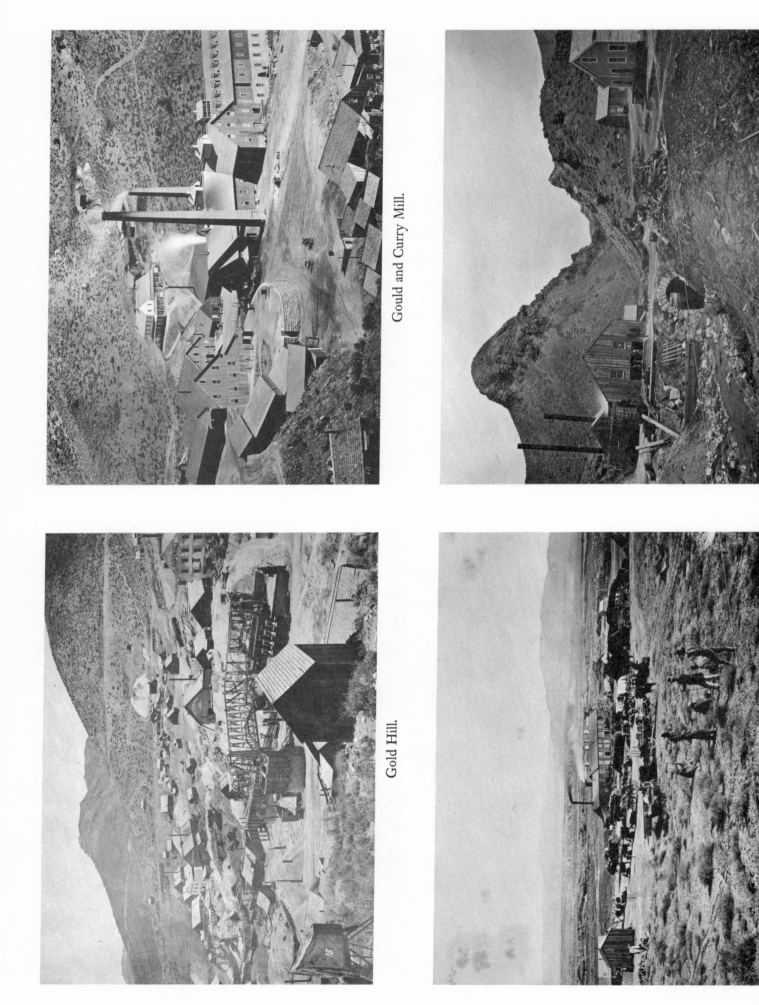

Gould and Curry Mill.

Sugar Loaf, near Virginia City.

Gold Hill.

Montezuma Works at Oreana, Nevada.

Pyramid Lake, Nevada.

Alkali lake, near Ragtown.

Shoshone Falls, Idaho.

Humboldt Hot Springs, Nevada.

Steamboat Springs, Nevada.

Sand dune, near Sand Springs.

Astronomical observatory.

Headquarters U. S. Geological Exploration, 40th Parallel.

King's camp, near Salt Lake City.

On the Truckee River.

Ridge of Trinity Mountains, Nevada.

City of Rocks, Idaho.

Uintah Mountains, head of Bear River, Utah.

Summit of East Humboldt, Nevada.

Pyramid Lake island (lime tufa).

Cottonwood Canyon, Wasatch Range.

Sawmill in Cottonwood Canyon, Wasatch Range.

Glacial lake, East Humboldt Mountains.

Uintah Mountains, Utah.

Big Bend, Truckee River.

Austin, Nevada.

Wasatch Mountains, east of Salt Lake City. Camp Douglass on the left.

ROBERT H. VANCE

Vance, called the "Mathew Brady of the Gold Rush," was one of the earliest photographers of the West, an expert at large-scale views. He operated a studio in San Francisco in the 1850's and made many pictures of the gold camps and of San Francisco.

The view from Poverty Bar to Oregon Bar.

Forest Hill, under the Hill.

Garland's Mill, Placer County.

A. J. RUSSELL

Russell (whose name is sometimes spelled Russel) worked for Brady early in the Civil War. In 1862, at the request of General Haupt, he joined his Railroad Construction Corps as a "special artist." His adventures as a Civil War photographer included being blown up by a shell and landing unhurt, with his camera intact. He went west as a Union Pacific photographer.

Laramie Valley, from Sheephead Mountain.

Malloy's Cut, Sherman Station, Laramie Range.

Dial Rock, Red Buttes, Laramie Plains.

Conglomerate Peaks of Echo.

Serrated rocks of Devil's Slide, Weber Canyon, Utah.

Hanging Rock, Echo City.

Wilhelmina's Pass, showing Devil's Slide at right, Weber Canyon, Utah.

Bitter Creek Valley, near Green River.

C. E. WATKINS

Watkins, originally a New Yorker, went west with the '49ers to the gold fields of California. He was introduced to photography by Robert Vance and took over Vance's gallery in San Francisco in 1854. His photographs of the Yosemite—spelled Yo-Semite at the time —taken in 1861 became nationally known. The plates were taken with his huge homemade camera under the most primitive conditions. All were destroyed in the San Francisco earthquake and fire, including those from which these prints were made.

The Grizzly Giant, 33 feet in diameter, Mariposa Grove, California.

Forest scene, Yosemite.

Yosemite Falls.

River scene, Yosemite.

JOHN K. HILLERS

Hillers, who accompanied the Powell Survey of 1872, was appointed chief photographer after illness had forced the former chief to return to civilization after a few days on the plains. According to Frederic S. Dellenbaugh, whose series on the survey made Hillers' photographs the talk of the country in the 1870's, the photographer descended the unknown Colorado River "in one of the greatest feats of exploration ever executed on this continent."

Ruins of cliff dwellings, Canyon de Chelly.

View in Canyon de Chelly, Arizona, looking west.

Navajo Church.

Uintah Ute scout, western slope of Wasatch Mountains.

Bend in the river.

JOHN CARBUTT

Carbutt's series on the building of the Union Pacific and the famous "Excursion to the 100th Meridian" were personally ordered by T. Durant, vice-president of the railroad. Carbutt accompanied the party which included "two brass bands, two kinds of the most distinguished citizens of America, reporters from practically every important newspaper in the country, a staff of chefs, a French marquis, an English earl, government commissioners and Union Pacific directors." The series is extremely rare.

Engine house and workshops.

Laying the rails—two miles a day.

Landing of the guests for the 100th Meridian excursion.

The way west.

TIM O'SULLIVAN

O'Sullivan is without a doubt the greatest of western photographers. He served his apprenticeship with Mathew B. Brady and was at Gettysburg on the third day. After the King Expeditions he served as official photographer for the Wheeler Expeditions of 1871-74, and took the pictures shown here. He died on Staten Island, January 14, 1883.

The start from Camp Mojave, Arizona. The boat expedition under Lieutenant Wheeler was the first to ascend the Colorado through the Grand Canyon.

Marble Canyon on the Colorado. The cliff is gray, the slope below a brilliant red sandstone.

Mojave Indians.

Northern wall of the Grand Canyon.

Baldy Peak, Colorado, 14,234 feet high.

Navajo squaw and child. Canyon de Chelly, Arizona.

Jicarilla Apache brave, northern New Mexico.

Zuñi Indian braves at their pueblo, New Mexico.

[140]

Navajo squaws weaving blankets, Canyon de Chelly.

Apaches ready for the warpath.

A Ute squaw, northern New Mexico.

Ruins of the Pueblo San Juan, New Mexico.

Roman Catholic Church, Guadaloupe County, Colorado.

One of a group of Pagosa Hot Springs.

Navajo brave with his mother.

Jicarilla Apache brave and his squaw.

Ute braves in "full dress," New Mexico.

WILLIAM HENRY JACKSON

Jackson is one of the best known of all western photographers. When he died in New York City in 1942 he was one of the last of New York's four Civil War veterans. His father was an amateur daguerreotypist and by 1857 young Jackson was his assistant. He was official photographer for the F. V. Hayden Surveys, 1870-1879, and his photographs of that territory, now Yellowstone National Park, were instrumental in the establishment of the park. He retired in 1929, devoted himself to painting scenes of the West, and achieved a notable reputation in that field also.

Grand Canyon of the Arkansas.

Leadville, from Capitol Hill.

Aspen, Colorado.

GENERAL JOHN T. PITMAN

Pitman began photographing western scenes after he entered the Regular Army in 1866. His collection of glass plates, now in the possession of the author, records the life and times on the frontier from Fort Snelling, Fort Abraham Lincoln and the Dakota Territory to the arrival of President Roosevelt's "Great White Fleet" in New York Harbor in 1907-08. Pitman was in charge of the team that developed smokeless powder for the army at Frankfort Arsenal, Philadelphia. Some of his plates include scenes of life at the Arsenal.

Sioux burial platform. Note ropes holding the body to the platform.

Standing Rock Agency. Note the "ant blankets." This was a device copied from the Sioux. The ants destroyed any vermin in a blanket left on the ground.

Bismarck, Dakota Territory, in the 1880's.

On the porch of Custer's house at Fort Abraham Lincoln.

Fort Snelling, Minnesota.

The famous *Helena* of Omaha.

D. F. BARRY

Barry, a superb craftsman among the western photographers, is best known for his gallery of portraits of Indian chiefs and warriors. He began his career in Bismarck, Dakota Territory, in 1875 and was soon known to the Sioux as "Little Shadow Catcher." He persuaded Gall to let him take his picture but the chief returned the next day, threatening to kill Barry if he didn't destroy the plate. Barry hid the plate although Gall drew a knife and went on a rampage in his studio.

Crow Foot, Sitting Bull's son.

Indian Commission at Fort Abraham Lincoln, Dakota Territory, 1889. *Left to right:* General Crook, Governor Fasler, and Major Warner, sitting in front of "Custer's house," which was occupied by Custer in the 1870's.

C. E. WATKINS

In his later years Watkins operated chiefly in the Northwest. His Columbia River series is a rare record of the Oregon-Washington country and his Yellowstone photographs are among the best of that area.

Polar bear, taken at the Columbia River.

Cascades of the Columbia River.

Cascades Canal.

Spokane Falls, Washington Territory.

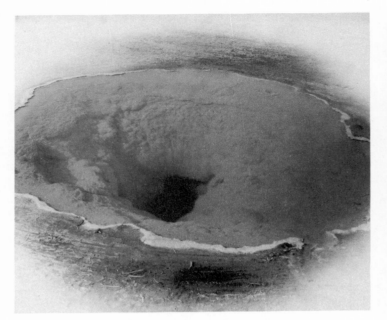

Morning Glory Geyser.

Steam launch, government locks, Cascades.

Golden Gate and bridge, Yellowstone Park.

Salmon wheel boat.

Hell's Half Acre and Five Hole River.

I. W. TABER

San Francisco's Chinatown, its colorful side streets, Seal Rock and early Los Angeles were the favorite subjects of Taber, who became well known in the 1880's for his experiments in lighting and background.

The Golden Gate, from Fort Mason.

The garden of the Santa Barbara Mission.

Lower corridor, Palace Hotel court.

The Three Brothers (4,000 feet).

Table Rock, Glacier Point.

A fallen tree, 300 feet long, Mariposa Grove.

L. A. HUFFMAN

Huffman learned photography as apprentice to his father and began his career as a western photographer with Frank J. Haynes in Moorhead, Minnesota in 1878. He became fort photographer at Fort Keogh, and then opened a studio in Miles City, Montana. He made a fine record of the era, with his excellent photographs of Indians, cowboys, soldiers, buffalo and other wild life. He died in Miles City in 1931.

The chase.

Roped.

Held down.

Examining a dim brand.

CHARLES R. SAVAGE

There is scarcely a schoolboy in America who hasn't studied one of Savage's most famous photographs—the meeting of the transcontinental railroads at Promontory Point, Utah, May 10, 1869. Savage was an Englishman who went west, settling in Nebraska, where he opened a daguerreotype gallery in 1860.

Ute squaws, Utah.

Yucca brevifolia, Mojave Desert.

W. H. ILLINGWORTH

Illingworth, an aggressive and hard-working frontier photographer, was well known in St. Paul, Minnesota. He is famous for his series on the Fisk expedition of 1866 to Montana and for his series on Custer's expedition to the Black Hills.

The Fisk expedition, which escorted emigrants to the Montana gold fields, 1866.

STANLEY J. MORROW

Morrow, believed to have been trained by Mathew Brady, went west in 1870 to open a daguerreotype gallery in Yankton, Dakota Territory. In 1873 he accompanied the General D. S. Stanley Expedition, which protected the construction parties of the Northern Pacific Railroad. He is best known for his photographs of the Crook expedition and the Custer reburial expedition.

The Crook campaign, 1876. A wounded lieutenant being transported by travois.

CAMILLUS S. FLY

The Tombstone, Arizona, photographer who is best known for his series on the peace councils held by General Crook with Geronimo, was also an eyewitness at the famed Battle of the O.K. Corral.

Geronimo, Nachez and Geronimo's son.

Cattle

Cattle trail. *Photo by C. D. Kirkland.*

The Drives North

WHILE the story of cattle in the West began with the *conquistadores* and their introduction of longhorns to the plains, the story of the cattle kingdoms and their fabulous cattle ranches really began after the Civil War.

The first "cow hunts," forerunners of the round-ups, were conducted by men who had returned from the wars to find the land teeming with wild cattle which roamed the plains, much like the wild horses, but in far greater numbers. Cattle could be sold in the beef-hungry North for a fantastic profit. The one problem was how to get the steers to the nearest northern railhead. The answer lay in cattle drives.

Cattle drives were not unique to the Texas frontiersman. The *Tenth Census, Statistics of Agriculture*, paints a vivid picture of those early cattle drives. The report was completed in 1880 by Robert Gordon, a member of the Department of Agriculture, after he had traveled across the West, interviewing scores of pioneering cattlemen and Army officers attached to frontier posts.

Gordon tells of the first cattle drives, some as early as 1837 when cowboys gathered herds ranging in size from 300 to 1,000 in the Nueces and Rio Grande country "and drove them to interior cities for sale."

In 1842, cattle drives were extended to New Orleans with a large herd shipped by Morgan steamer in 1848. The line plied between Galveston, New Orleans and Mobile. However, outlets for the drovers were few and the cattle herds continued to grow larger and larger.

Gordon said "a report" had a drive going north to Missouri in 1842, but the earliest authenticated account of a drive was by a man named Edward Piper in 1846, who took a thousand head to Ohio, "where he fed them and sold them."

One of the most spectacular drives was made, not to the Border States, but to New York City. In 1853, with the nearest railheads on the Mississippi River, Tom Candy Ponting set out for New York with a herd that stretched along the prairie for miles. In the autumn he halted in Illinois to winter and fatten the herd. In the spring he resumed his drive. At Muncie, Indiana, where the trail met a railroad, Ponting decided to put the herd on the "cars"—a brand-new idea in cattle driving. On July 3, 1854, Ponting and his herd reached Bergen Point in Jersey City and were ferried across to the slaughterhouses in Manhattan. The bellowing longhorns caused large crowds to collect, and more than one carriage horse ran away.

Ponting's pioneer method of getting beef to the New York market caught on, and within a few years Texas longhorns were a common sight on the streets. The western cattle drives continued to expand both in the size of the herds and the distances they covered. By 1856 herds were being taken directly to Chicago, Arizona and New Mexico Territories as well as to New York.

Compared, however, to the postwar drives, these early irregular journeys were insignificant. By the time the war had ended and the Texans were back home, the cattle in their state numbered 4,000,000. During the war there had been a few drives for the Confederates, but that was stopped when the Union forces won control of the Mississippi River.

After the war even greater herds of wild cattle ran freely over the state. They were a far cry from today's cattle. The longhorns were tough and short-tempered. As Colonel Dodge wrote in 1876, "Any sportsman on foot would eye with uneasiness the long-horned beasts pawing the earth and tossing their heads in anger at his appearance."

James MacDonald, a Scot, described them as: "Nothing less than Spanish cattle, direct descendants of those unseemly rough, lanky, long-horned animals reared for so long with large herds by the Moors on the Plains of Andalusia." Their meat was "teasingly tough" and they were almost as wild as the buffalo they were soon to replace on the western plains.

These ornery beasts could not be driven by a boy with a stick and a dog as was done on eastern stock farms. Only a physically tough, excellent horseman could do the job. He soon found that to bring a longhorn to the corral he would have to use a rope and a smart horse.

In 1866 the Texas cattleman was not the powerful rancher he would be within a few years; he was usually a cotton or corn farmer as well as a stockman. When he heard of the gold ready to be paid out by the North for beef, he began looking about at the wild herds and began computing figures. On paper he found himself to be a rich man. He lost no time in staging his "cowhunts."

In 1866 more than 200,000 head crossed the Red River

Shipping beef from Montana in the 1880's.

"Rounding 'em up." *Photo by C. D. Kirkland.*

[158]

Putting cattle aboard a steamboat.

and headed for Sedalia, Missouri, then the nearest rail-head to St. Louis. But the drivers found the southwestern roads leading to Sedalia blocked off by former guerrillas and bushwhackers who forced the owners of the cattle to pay bribes. These early trails were scenes of horror where Texans were tied to trees and flogged until they begged to ride back home and leave their herds to the outlaws.

If the Texans showed fight and had enough guns to back them, the outlaws would use other methods mostly to stampede the herd. The bandits would then corral as many of the scattered cattle as possible and hide them. The more brazen agreed to "sell" them back to the original owner at large prices. If the drover didn't have the entire price, the thieves would take as much as the traffic would bear and return some of the herd, keeping and selling the remainder.

In addition to the outlaw bands, the cattlemen found themselves faced with indignant Indian tribes when they entered the Indian Territory. The tribes resorted to the law instead of the gun.

The Five Civilized Tribes, whose wealth lay in their own herds and their rich grazing lands, realized that if they allowed unrestricted grazing, they might find themselves in a land so barren it could not support their own cattle. So they turned to the Indian Act of 1834, which ordered the white men to pay a toll for each head passing across the red man's land.

In 1867 the Cherokee National Council quickly passed a law demanding ten cents for each head. Other tribal councils followed suit, toll gates were erected and Indian representatives held out their hands.

Quarantine laws proved to be another roadblock. The tough longhorns were immune to Spanish fever, but the domestic cattle of Missouri and Kansas could not with-stand the fever, so in 1867 both states passed a law for-

bidding Texas longhorns from entering the states during fall and summer. In addition to the fee-demanding Indians, the outlaws and the quarantine laws, there were the home-steaders, who banded together and forced the drivers to flank their farm lands or settle for the damages done to gardens and fences.

All these obstacles tended to bend the trails further north so that the Texas Panhandle and the eastern part of Colorado became the doorway to the northern ranges. It was a period of trial and error. Some drovers turned to the Missouri-Kansas border toward another railroad east of Sedalia. The trails were rough and the herds usually fin-ished in poor condition. Other cattlemen drove as far as Wyoming, others to Illinois and Iowa.

A "bucker." *Photo by C. D. Kirkland.*

It was the famous Texas drover, J. G. McCoy, who ended the cattlemen's nightmares. A dreamer with a practical bent, McCoy wanted to find a point which would meet the herds coming north and the westward-moving railroads. As he said, "the plan was to establish at some accessible point a depot or market to which a Texas drover could bring his stock unmolested and failing to find a buyer, he could go upon the public highways to any market in the country he wished."

After being turned out of some railway offices, McCoy did sign a contract with the Hannibal and St. Jo Railroad granting favorable rates for shipping cattle from the Missouri River to Chicago.

McCoy now returned to Kansas to pick his spot. He finally found the quiet little town of Abilene in Dickinson County. As McCoy first saw it, the town was a collection of a dozen log huts, covered with dirt for roofing, while the "whole business of the burg was conducted in two small rooms, mere log huts, and of course the inevitable saloon."

But despite its poor appearance, McCoy found what he wanted, a well-watered countryside with grass suitable for the grazing of cattle. McCoy brought in lumber and within 60 days he had pens that could hold thousands of cattle. Meanwhile he sent out a woodsman to scour the plains and tell the drovers what was waiting. After a few weeks of wandering, this man found a herd in the Indian Territory owned by a man named Thompson.

The Texan was suspicious and felt sure this was a trap. But with his hand near his gun and his men ready to go into action, he followed McCoy's man. Before they could reach Abilene, Thompson had sold the herd to some northerner who drove it to Abilene.

Bronco-buster. *Photo by W. G. Walker.*

Another large herd stopped long enough to graze near Abilene and was sold on the spot.

On September 5, 1866, the first herd was shipped to Chicago. Cattlemen from several states shook the town with their celebration.

With the establishment of Abilene as a convenient stockyard and shipping port, the cattle business flourished and an enormous system of cattle ranches developed. The first year 260,000 head were shipped; by 1880 the cowtowns had shipped more than 4,000,000.

Each ranch was a sort of barony, with a spread of thousands of acres in its domain, and in a sort of informal league with its neighboring ranches. For most of the year the cattle roamed the open range—the vast acreage of the area was not fenced off—grazed where they chose and found their own water.

Each steer was branded with the distinctive mark of its ranch owner. These marks were respected by all other honest ranchers, and later on, all brands were registered. But the open range provided opportunity for the cattle thief, "the rustler," who would drive off the cattle, rebrand them, and claim them as his own.

The ranch staff lived in the ranch-house area, which was essentially self-sufficient and consisted of a main house, bunkhouses for the cowboys and the foreman, barns, corrals for the horses, blacksmith shops, and other buildings and equipment in accordance with the size of the ranch.

At round-up time extra hands would be hired by each ranch, and almost the entire crew would go out to the range where they would join the cowboys of the neighboring ranches to round up the steers for the drive to market. Each ranch would obtain possession of the cattle marked with its brand and would brand the calves running with its cows.

Then came the drive north to the cattle shipping point.

The cattle business required a new way of life and especially a new sort of skilled craftsman—the cowboy.

As a result of books, magazine articles and newspaper accounts, ranch life, the "wide open spaces" and especially the cowboy achieved a glamorous, idealized glorification and became a "national institution."

In retrospect the drives north sound thrilling and romantic, but actually it was grueling work that required being in the saddle 15 hours a day, seven days a week. The drovers were usually young, tough ranch hands and excellent horsemen. The ramrod, or trail boss, was older and more experienced. After weeks on the trail, worn by the long hours in the saddle, it is little wonder that the cowboys turned into whooping hellions who sought to hurrah the town with gunfire for relaxation.

The makeup of the outfit consisted of a chuck wagon which carried the food, bedding and tents. From its tailboard, food was served which had been cooked over an open fire. The "big chuck" wagon carried the outfit's supplies, such as branding irons, water barrel, wood for pens, or for firewood. A herd of horses was known as the *remuda* (a word borrowed from the Spanish). The outfit's boss was the horse wrangler, usually a youngster.

Cow horses were well trained. Not only did they help

A Texas cowboy in the 1880's.
Photo by F. Hardesty.

A Montana cowboy in the 1870's.

A rest on the drive.

A Wyoming cattle ranch in the 1880's.

Livery stable, Abilene, 1871.

their owners in roping a steer, but would be "tied" when the reins were let down—ground-hitched. The reason for this training is twofold: the cowboy usually had to leap from his saddle and work fast; secondly, there weren't many places to tie a horse on the plains. Every cow hand furnished his saddle, bridle, saddle blankets, spurs and "hot roll"—his bedding and tarpaulin, a piece of canvas doubled and composed of "quilt or suggans."

The staff of the outfit consisted of a wagon boss, usually foreman of the ranch, cook, hoodlum driver, horse wrangler and the straw boss, who was next in command to the wagon boss.

The *point* of the outfit was the reconnaissance man, who sought out possible Indian ambushes, water and suit-

able grazing country. The least desirable of the posts was the drag rider, the rider at the rear of the herd who swallowed the dust.

The fear of stampede always hung over the outfit. The longhorns were a scary lot, and even the drop of a pan could stir them up and turn them into brawling, runaway herd whose hoofs shook the plains. When a man was caught in a stampede, there was seldom anything left to bury.

The night watch literally rode on tip-toe. He kept his voice down, and to calm the sleeping animals and to defy his own loneliness he would croon like a mother to her young. Thus were born our western ballads.

The most popular trail to the railhead was the Chisholm

San Antonio, 1876.

Martin Garretson measures a longhorn.

Junction City, Kansas, 1876.

Branding on the round-up, Telluride, Colorado. *Photo by W. J. Carpenter.*

Trail, believed to have been laid out by Jesse Chisholm, a legend that has as much controversy about it as Little Big Horn. But whoever found the trail really laid out the Golden Highway of the western frontier. It was level and had plenty of grass and water. The latter was highly important to the success of any drive.

There were numerous other trails that are as important historically. For example, west of the Chisholm were the Panhandle Trail, going to Kansas and Colorado, and the

Looking for a place to land.

Controlling a Stampede
(From *Prose and Poetry of the Livestock Industry*)

BY COLONEL CHARLES GOODNIGHT,
famous Texas pioneer and cattleman

The task of the men was to gain control of the herd and gradually turn the cattle until they were moving in a wide circle. Then, although they might break each other's horns off and crush one another badly, the great danger was past. The well trained night horse needed little guidance and knew that if the herd came his way, all he had to do was to lead. The speed of the herd was terrific, but the position at the head of the stampede was what the trail man desired, for he was in the position to start the herd turning.

In the excitement of a stampede a man was not himself and his horse was not the horse of yesterday. Man and horse were one and the combination accomplished feats that would be utterly impossible under ordinary circumstances. Trained men would be generally found near the *point* at both sides of the herd. When the man on one side saw the herd bending his way, he would fall back and if the work was well done on the other side of the herd, the stampede would gradually come to an end; the strain was removed, the cowboys were the happiest men on earth, and their shouts and laughter could be heard for miles over the prairie. . . .

Cowboys at a corral near Helena, Montana.

Pecos Trail up the Pecos Valley into New Mexico and on to Wyoming and Colorado.

Drives were usually started in the spring when the grass appeared on the plains. The herd did not move like eastern stock but in a long snakelike line. The herd moved out at dawn, with the *point* usually using hand signals, many of which had been adopted from the Plains tribes. An average good day's trek was 15 miles. The first day's mileage was usually twice that in an effort to break the herd from its home-range habits and to tire the confused, protesting steers so that they would not be too much of a problem to the night riders.

Branding a steer. *Photo by C. D. Kirkland.*

One of the most terrifying parts of the drive was the so-called "dry drive," which was simply a drive across a waterless tract of land. For example, a trip across the Llano Estacado, the Staked Plains of Texas, was a dry drive. The 100-mile trip took the herd from the mouth of the South Concho River to the Pecos. In 1855 a survey team headed by Brevet-Captain John Pope of the Topographical Corps was ordered to sink wells across the southern portion of the Staked Plains, but nothing came of it.

Gold strikes helped boost the cattle business. Perhaps a solitary prospector could live off the land, but a community needed beef. In Virginia City the poorest beef was auctioned off at 25 cents a pound in spirited bidding.

News of these prices drifted back to Kansas, Missouri, and Texas. In 1866 Nelson Story came over the Bozeman Trail to Gallatin Valley with a herd of 600 longhorns he had driven up from Dallas. Two years later there were 18,801 cows and calves in and around Virginia City.

When the rails of the Union Pacific began to inch across the plains the buffalo-hunters like Buffalo Bill supplied the crews with buffalo steaks. But the rancher found as ready a market for his steers in the rail camps as he had found in the mining camps and in the emigrant trains.

With the combination of the expanding railroads and the return of the military posts, which alleviated the Indian problem, the cattle industry began to boom. In the

Horse herd. *Photo by C. D. Kirkland.*

The mess wagon. *Photo by C. D. Kirkland.*

Cowboys of the N Bar N ranch on the prairie, during a drive moving 7,000 head of cattle 300 miles. Northwest Montana, late 1880's. *Photo by Dan Dutro.*

beginning the business was haphazard; a drover never knew where he would find a buyer for his herd. It wasn't unusual for a deal to be made around a campfire on the plains and the gold counted on a blanket. By 1870 a Kansas City bank was handling more than $3,000,000 in cattle money.

The country was opening fast, the tribes were being defeated and the ruthless extermination of the buffalo was well under way. The Union Pacific naturally was a booster for the northern ranges. In 1870 the Omaha *Herald* carried a series of letters from a Doctor Latham, a surgeon for the railroad, boasting of the "succulent grasses" that could feed a continent of beef cattle so that the price would come down and the poorest family could live on steaks. The following fall the letters appeared in pamphlet form and gained wide circulation in the East. There also appeared the typical tenderfoot story about the storm-bound freighter who was forced to turn loose his team of oxen to die. Imagine his surprise and joy in the spring to find them well fed, sleek and fat. The wild yarn would be incorporated many times in the prospectus by new cattle companies.

By 1875, ten years after the first steers had splashed across the Red River, the cattle industry was booming beyond McCoy's wildest dreams. The *Rocky Mountain Husbandman*, quoting the Buffalo *Live Stock Journal* in 1875, wrote exuberantly: "Cotton was once king but grass is now. If grass is king, the Rocky Mountain region is its

throne, and fortunate are those who possess it."

The West, with its free "boundless, gateless pasture," was there for the asking. All a man needed to make a fortune in cattle were a few cowboys and a branding iron. By 1881 the Northern Pacific reached the Yellowstone and before long, names that rang like bells in the Indian Wars became routine stops on the timetables.

As Granville Stuart, one of the West's superior cattlemen, put it, "There were 600,000 head on the range that was now devoid of buffalo, with the elk and the antelope indeed scarce. The cowboy had become an institution."

Not all the capital in the booming cattle companies came from American sources. A large part was foreign. The stockmen's boom was the talk of Europe, and before 1880 no less than an estimated 20,000,0000 head of cattle in Texas, Colorado, Missouri, New Mexico and Arkansas were owned by foreigners.

Edinburgh was a Cheyenne in miniature, and as John Clay, an agent for English investors, was to write in the London *Economist:* "Drawing-rooms buzzed with the news of the last of these bonanzas, and staid old gentlemen who didn't know the difference between a steer and a heifer discussed it over their port and nuts." It is amusing to contemplate the doughty Scots, with their mutton-chop whiskers, in the funereal quiet of the best clubs, arguing over rangeland that only recently had known the tread of a moccasin.

Omaha, Nebraska, 1870.

Dodge City, Kansas, 1867.

El Paso, Texas, 1880.

Congress Street, Tucson, Arizona. *Photo by Buchman and Hartwell.*

Painting by Frederic Remington.

The Cowboy

The nature of the work determined the character, behavior, appearance and even the language of the cowboy. It was tough work that required energy and youth. Only the best riders, the most skilled in roping and marksmanship, were hired by the outfits. The cowboy took great pride in these skills, engaged in all sorts of contests—shooting, horse-breaking or bronco-busting, roping—and looked down with contempt at the inept, soft-muscled newcomer whom he called a "tenderfoot."

It was lonely, monotonous work; loquacious men were a rarity. Many of the words he did use were borrowed from the Spanish, who were there and dealing with cattle before him: lariat, remuda, arroyo, mesa, rancho, pueblo, canyon.

His costume was Spanish in origin—the high heels, the chaps, the spurs, the boots, the bandana. But the hat, the five-gallon or ten-gallon Stetson, was American.

Among the many who have depicted the life of the cowboy perhaps the two most famous are Frederic Remington, the great painter of the West, some of whose pictures are shown here, and Theodore Roosevelt, who wrote from long personal experience many books and articles about life on the plains and also took a number of photographs of cowboy activities. A few of these rare pictures are shown here, and serving also as an illustration of ranch life is the following bit of the Rough Rider President's personal history.

The Cowboy Who Became President

The young bespectacled tenderfoot named Teddy Roosevelt had anything but good luck when he went buffalo hunting for the first time in the badlands of Dakota in 1883. First of all, it rained for a week. When it finally cleared he and his guide found the remnants of a herd late in the night. In the moonlight Roosevelt wounded a bull, but when he tried to finish it off the buffalo turned and charged, almost finishing Roosevelt.

In addition the horse bolted and the heavy rifle barrel made a deep gash in his forehead. Miles from their camp on the Little Cannonball, Roosevelt and his guide, Joe Ferris, decided to camp for the night. In the early hours a wolf frightened their horses and they had to search for them in the darkness. When they found the animals at last and rolled up in their blankets, it began to rain.

In the morning they found another herd. Roosevelt crept close, fired and missed. The herd stampeded and his chance to get a "buffer" was gone. The world's most famous hunter never forgot that shot.

The rain continued for several days, a lashing cold rain that numbed both men. They rode all day and spent miserable nights trying to sleep. The first clear day Joe's horse narrowly missed a rattlesnake's fang, and a bluff weakened by the rain broke under them, sending men and horses tumbling down the steep slope. A few hours after they had set out again, Roosevelt's horse stepped into a

A bend in the river (The Little Missouri). *All the pictures in this series, except the last, were taken by Roosevelt in 1882.*

Elkhorn Ranch.

The saddleband in the rope corral.

The midday meal.

gopher hole and made a complete somersault, pitching Roosevelt almost ten feet. While Joe held his breath Roosevelt got up, adjusted his glasses and remounted. They had ridden but a few feet when the earth gave way under Roosevelt's horse and it sank into the gluelike mud up to its withers. After a back-breaking hour they pulled the frightened horse out with lariats.

Joe, the veteran plainsman, began to eye Roosevelt with a sort of awe. At night beside the campfire he was stunned to see "Four Eyes," as he called him, take up a book as if he were in a comfortable living room. It was during this rough hunting trip that Roosevelt casually told Joe that his lungs were bad and that the doctors hadn't given him much more time to live.

They finally returned to the ranch run by Gregor Lang. There Joe Ferris discovered that he was mistaken in thinking the rough days and nights had finally cured the tenderfoot. Rather he had fallen in love with the raw, vast badlands. Roosevelt told Lang that he had made up his mind to run cattle there and wanted him to recommend someone to take charge for him. Lang suggested Bill Merrifield and Silvane Ferris. The next day after a short talk with these two men Roosevelt took out a checkbook, wrote a $14,000 check and he was in the cattle business.

High noon.

Branding calves.

In the corral.

Roosevelt never forgot his years as a ranchman in the Dakotas. As he told Hermann Hagedorn, who wrote the excellent *Roosevelt in the Badlands,* his years on the plains were a "kind of idyll." Someone once said of him that he had "a weakness for murderers," and certainly the future President of the United States met his full quota of desperate men in the wild and woolly town of Little Missouri. There were gunfighters, outlaws, cattle thieves, horse thieves, gamblers and confidence men.

One of the most exciting chapters in his life in the West centers around an outlaw named Red Finnegan. A stocky man with a brick-red complexion, he boasted that he was from 'way up Bitter Creek "and the further up you went the worse people got."

In March, 1886, as Roosevelt prepared to go out on a long-planned hunting trip he found his skiff gone. A torn red mitten, identified as belonging to Finnegan, was found nearby. Footprints showed that Finnegan had been joined by two other men.

Roosevelt boiled at the theft, but since travel by horse was impossible he got his ranch hands to build another boat. In three days the craft was finished. Meanwhile he sent some of his men to Medora to get enough supplies for a two-week journey.

With Wilmot Daw and Bill Sewall, two Maine frontiersmen he had taken to the Badlands, Roosevelt set out in the crude craft down the Little Missouri. The region through which they passed was bleak. The weather was bitter cold, and occasionally the wind stung their faces with particles of ice.

On the third day they rounded a bend and saw Roosevelt's original boat on the bank and the smoke of a cook fire shredded by the wind. They flung off their coats, and while Sewall swung the boat in toward shore Daw and Roosevelt knelt in the bow, rifles ready. They knew Finnegan was "a shooting man" and could pick them off from the bushes.

Gathering the day herd.

Cattle on a sandbar.

Fortunately, he and his companions were out searching for game and had left the boat in the custody of a halfwit who told them Finnegan was accompanied by a halfbreed outlaw and killer.

They disarmed the halfwit and waited. After a short wait they heard the two men coming through the sage-brush. Roosevelt waited until they were within twenty yards, then jumped up.

"Hands up!"

The halfbreed dropped his rifle, but Finnegan went into a crouch as if to get off a hip shot. But Roosevelt stared down the barrel of his shotgun and said calmly, "You thief! Put up your hands."

After they had searched the pair Roosevelt told them, "If you try anything we'll shoot you."

The next day they started downriver but were stopped by a great ice jam which had been moving along the river for days since the thaw had set in.

Their provisions ran out, there was no game in the bleak country and they were reduced to eating unleavened bread mixed with the muddy Little Missouri water.

A few days later Roosevelt set out on foot and found

Elkhorn ranch house.

Ready to start.

a small ranch, where he borrowed a horse which turned out to be a half-broken bronc. After a rough ride he tamed the horse and rode 15 miles to a larger ranch at the edge of the Killdeer Mountains. There he hired a covered wagon, provisions and a rancher, who drove the wagon to the camp on the ice-bound Little Missouri.

The thieves were put into the wagon, and Roosevelt and the driver set out for Dickinson, which had the nearest jail. His journal gives a brief account of the stages of that 300-mile journey:

April 7. Worked down to the C. Diamond Ranch. Two prairie chickens.
April 8. Rode to Killdeer Mountains to arrange for a wagon which I hired.
April 9. Walked the captives to Killdeer Mountains.
April 10. Drove captives in wagon to Captain Brown's ranch.

Captain Brown looked puzzled when Roosevelt drove in. "What I can't understand," he said, "is why you made all this fuss instead of hanging them offhand."

The next night Roosevelt turned the prisoners over to the United States Marshal in Dickinson.

The prisoners.

[175]

Barbed Wire

Joseph Glidden, a dour, thin-lipped farmer, was fascinated by the exhibit in the De Kalb, Illinois, County Fair. He had returned three times to stare at the invention of Henry Rose, a farmer who had a place north of his. It was simply a rail fence topped by a row of sharp spikes.

Back home, Glidden sat on the back porch brooding. Finally he borrowed his wife's coffee grinder and, with the aid of an old grindstone to bend the wire, he made the first practical barbed wire fence. He was granted a patent on November 24, 1874. The patent, number 157,124, is one of the most important in western history.

Barbed wire is as completely American as pumpkin pie or wild turkey. The strands which stretched across the plains of the early West helped to change its history. It bred lawsuits, feuds, violence and murder, but it played a major role in bringing the West to agricultural pre-eminence.

The history actually begins with an angry German farmer who had a fruit grove a few miles north of San Antonio. The longhorns were still roaming at will and were ruining the farmer's fruit crops. He finally built a fence and studded its top with large spikes. Then the next day he took a seat in the nearby tree to see the fun.

The longhorns arrived and for a moment eyed the fence. Then with a roar they charged. They retreated licking their wounds. The jubilant German ran into town and in the saloon told his triumphant tale. He was astounded to see his listeners give him a cold stare and leave. That night a delegation of flint-eyed men with shotguns and six-shooters paid him a call.

"Get that cruel and inhuman fence down, mister, or you'll leave town in a box," was the warning. The fence came down at dawn and it was many years before another barbed fence was erected.

After Glidden began manufacturing the wire a 25-year-old salesman named John W. Gates decided to augment

First piece of double-strand barbed wire. Made in 1874 by Joseph F. Glidden, who used the crank of a grindstone.

Part of the "coffee mill" used by Glidden to form barbs for his first barbed wire.

Poster distributed by Washburn and Moen and I. L. Ellewood about 1877.

his weekly salary of $25 by going west and selling the idea of barbed wire to Texas cattlemen.

In San Antonio they laughed at him as he spread his samples across the bar. Finally he forced them to agree to an experiment. In the town square he built a large corral. The next day 25 of the toughest longhorns in the county were driven into the corral by excited, whooping cowboys. Tails raised, eyes wide, they charged at the fence. It held. They backed off, pawed the ground and charged again. This time they retreated for good. Before nightfall Gates—later famous as "Bet-a-Million" Gates—had more orders than he could fill.

For a long time Texas ranchers had realized that the tough, angular longhorn was not the best of beef cattle. He didn't have the weight, the docility or the low feeding-cost factor that other cattle had. The new wire seemed the answer to their problem. New breeds could be introduced with the assurance that each breed would be controlled (within the wire) and unmixed. At first the cattle barons, who considered the range free, refused to accept the wire. Cowboys with cutters were sent out. Fence wars started and men died, sprawled across the cut wire.

The violence was so great that the Governor of Texas in 1884 summoned a special session of the legislature and passed a law making wire-cutting a felony. The passage of the law ended wire-cutting and now to the grazing herds came the Herefords, Durhams, Shorthorns and Polled Angus Brahmas—all fine breeds.

On one section of the famous King Ranch, the Gertrude Ranch, were errected 1,500 miles of barbed wire. Inside this enclosure was developed one of the world's finest breeds, the Santa Gertrudis, three-eighths Brahma and five-eighths Shorthorn, combining the natural beef qualities of the latter with the hardiness of the Brahma.

The rapid growth of the barbed wire business in the West is underscored by the following table of wire sales from 1874 to 1881:

Year	Pounds Sold
1874	10,000
1875	100,000
1876	840,000
1877	12,863,000
1878	26,655,000
1879	50,337,000
1880	80,500,000
1881	120,000,000

A ton of wire made two miles of staunch three-strand wire. In 1876 the adoption of Bessemer steel created a revolution in the wire business. Now wire could be produced cheaply and the price dropped from 18 to 8 cents a pound. Now even the humblest sodbuster could fence in his quarter.

Curiously, wire also helped to bring law and order to many a wild section of the West. It encouraged land

John W. ("Bet-a-Million") Gates.

Part of the first wire drawing frame, which could produce 2,500 pounds of wire a day. Previous equipment could produce only 50 pounds a day.

investment and improvement. Crops now could be grown and rustling dwindled to a nuisance crime.

The following table sums up the meteoric history of barbed wire:

1874 Joseph Glidden obtains his patent and forms a company in De Kalb, Illinois.
1875 Actual production of barbed wire begins.
1876 Washburn and Moen Company, Worcester, Massachusetts, obtains all patents on the wire, and with the adoption of Bessemer steel produced a cheaper and more durable material.

Windmills

Like barbed wire, windmills played an important part in the development of the American West. Without them the cattle business could not have survived. They appeared on the great plains in the early 1870's when the cattleman was faced with the grave problem of supplying water for his rapidly expanding herds.

The simple fact is that the range land, the Great Plains country—once called the Great American Desert—is very dry, with annual rainfall much nearer the arid desert level of less than 10 inches than the satisfactory level of 30 inches or more that prevails in good farming areas. In addition the natural water-storage conditions are unfavorable. Often, when the rains do come they come in great storms and the water runs off quickly so that not enough is retained. Rivers, streams and springs dry up.

In the West, from the days of the *conquistadores* even until now, water has been the crucial factor, determining the economy, welfare and growth of any section. If sufficient water was available, or could be obtained by well-digging, irrigation or other means the area could support more life, could flourish and grow. Without more water there could not be more life. But there was more life—increasing population and expanding herds—and so besides the search for water there was and is the continuing fight in the dry parts of the West for water. There were constantly scraps, lawsuits, battles and war about the control of water supply, the diversion or damming of streams, the construction of aqueducts, tunnels and reservoirs.

Since the Spanish, men in the West have tried everything including snake dances and prayer to induce rainfall and to increase the supply of water. In the post-Civil War years the artesian well—the word is taken from Artois, France, where it originated—was the talk of the plains. In an artesian well the water, once reached underground, flows to the surface by itself. Cattlemen were wildly enthusiastic when they heard that such wells, ranging in depth to as much as 400 feet, had been drilled in dry Kansas. Large bonuses were offered to drillers. Test drills were made, only to reveal that the condition of the plains earth and its topography made artesian wells virtually impossible. The water could be reached, at one depth or another, but it would not rise to the surface by itself. It would be an ordinary well—ground water that had to be drawn or pumped to the surface. Ordinary wells provided only a scant supply. If it was necessary to go 200 feet down or more to find water (as was the case in most of the Great Plains area) it was just about impossible to obtain a sufficient quantity of water by hand pumping. Power pumps had not yet been perfected and were not a practical solution at that time.

Finally, someone recalled that windmills could be used to pump water. Soon windmills became an important factor and a major industry in the West.

The Aermotor Company of Chicago was one of the

Early western windmill.

The first steel windmill.

pioneering windmill companies. This company made the first iron windmill in the 1880's. It became extremely popular among the cattlemen and before the century had turned, its iron fan was catching the four winds wherever they swept the western plains.

Windmills are still a very important part of western life. In 1957 the Aermotor Company reported sales of 7,000 complete windmill outfits for pumping water, with most of them going to Texas, New Mexico, Nebraska and Arizona.

With the introduction of the windmill came a little-known western figure who, although not so romantic as the cowboy, was just as necessary. This was the itinerant windmill builder. Little if anything has been written about him.

One of the earliest was George Strait, who in 1870 left his home in New York's Tioga County in the rural serenity of Condor, to seek his fortune building windmills on the western plains. He was a faithful correspondent in his letters to his family. They not only describe the trials and tribulations of a pioneer windmill builder but also give an interesting picture of the times.

Most of the letters are addressed from Missouri Valley, Iowa, and cover the years 1874-76. After leaving Condor, Strait built windmills in Nebraska, Omaha and the Dakota Territory. But he finally settled with his wife, Fanny, and two small children in Iowa, "the finest state in the Union." As he said in his first letter, "My only regret is that I did not come out here ten years ago."

He averaged about $200 a month. In one letter he outlined what it cost a family in the way of food. "The best kind of flour costs $1.25 per sack, cornmeal $.75 a pack, good wheat for $.60 a bushel. Pork is $5 a hundred pounds and beef about the same." He added, "Fanny and the children love the land, and they have all the wild duck, geese, prairie chickens they want to eat . . . last night I was lucky and came home with seven wild ducks. . . ."

Writing to his parents on January 3, 1875, he tells them he is so busy erecting windmills that he can't even find time to send them some wild game for the holidays.

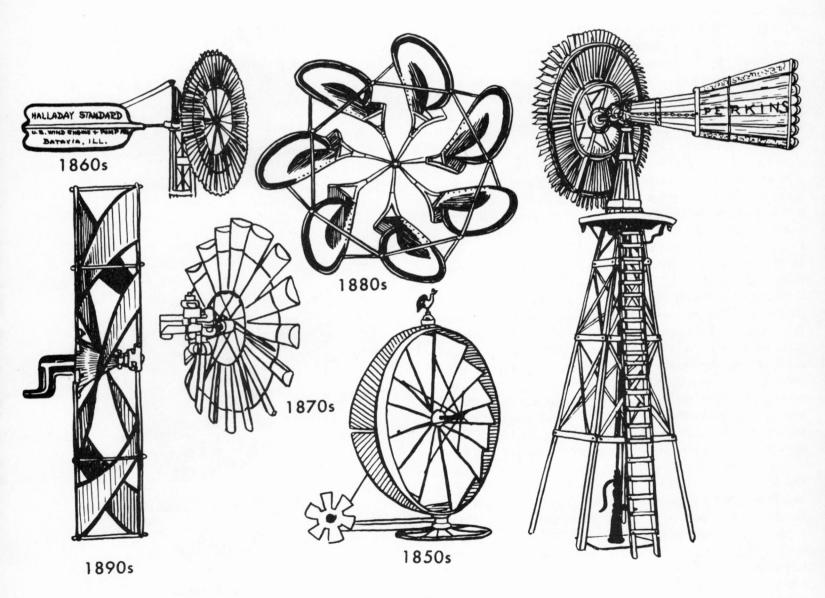

Fifty years of windmill-blade arrangements.

Another type of windmill.

The same day Strait's son wrote in a childish scrawl to "Grandma and Grandpa" that he liked the frontier and observed casually that 275 Cherokees "were around."

On February 14 Strait wrote his parents, giving them "an account of the events of the past weak (sic)." One of the most important, he wrote, was the erection of a windmill "in the timber about twenty miles from here where the Indians are thick. We stayed all day in a little cabin and had to roll up in blankets, and one of the men stayed awake to keep a fire going. We was there one day and one night and they come for us to bring us to put in another water works (windmill). We stayed there one day and one night. We had plenty of wild hog to eat, and there is plenty of wild game. But it was so cold that the Indians kept to their wigwams. Came back Thursday and expect to go out again. Last week clear for my share was $62."

On March 7, 1875, Strait, in writing to his father, described how the cattlemen were virtually standing in line begging him to put in windmills. "This weak (sic) I have three artesian wells to put in and three windmills to erect if Bell (his helper) is well enough to be away from home.

One of the windmills is for a stockyard about one mile out of town. They keep from 2 to 300 head of cattle and I am going to put them up a windmill to pump water for them. I got all the business I can attent to."

Apparently Strait's reputation as a windmill builder was getting around because he described "a man who has been around after me to go out to Montana to put in windmills to pump water for the gold mines. I don't think I shall go there as I have plenty of windmill work here." Then as an afterthought he added, "The Indians are much too ruff (sic) there. There is too much risk to run in such a trip."

His last letter of April 23, 1876, proves beyond any doubt that the Union Pacific was using windmills to draw water for its engines. Strait's home was now in Little Sioux, Iowa, and in his letter to his sister, Elisa, who had been ill, he described how "I have been out on the Sandy Desert on the Union Pacific putting in waterworks for them."

Apparently the railroad had been satisfied with his work and contracted for more mills, for Strait had moved to Little Sioux "to be nearer to my work." Again he points out he has more work than he can attend to.

The End of a Western Era

The first major disaster in the western cattle industry came in 1873 when the eastern banking firm of Jay Cooke & Company suspended payments and closed its doors. A panic swept the nation. Confidence was destroyed. Banks and businessmen from the foremost industrialist to the smallest local merchant were afraid to buy or invest. Prices plummeted. Many factories closed and people were afraid to spend money on anything except absolute necessities. The panic was particularly disastrous to the market for beef. Prices were ridiculously low. A single cattle company lost $180,000 in three weeks. Many others could not even raise the cost of the transportation when they sold their herds.

It took three years for the cattle market to get back on its feet. Finally came the great boom of the golden eighties. Money was plentiful once again. Railroads had criss-crossed the country. The tribes were reduced to the status of beggars. The range was wide and free. Towns were rising and the great tide of immigration from Europe was at its peak.

By 1882 cattle was selling for $35 a head; a profit of 300 per cent could be made. In 1883 a terrible drought swept the West. Thousands of dead cattle littered the over-stocked, dried-out range. Prices went even higher because of the scarcity. But two years later in 1885 when there was no drought and plenty of supply, prices dropped sharply. There was a rush to unload, and beef hit the market at any price.

In 1886 the severest winter in the history of the West struck the plains with unprecedented savagery. Snow was roof-high, the temperature sub-zero. In the fenced areas, steers whose instinct made them move before the storm, found their way blocked by barbed wire. Armies of them died on the ugly strands. People in frontier towns recalled many years later how they had clapped their hands over their ears to drown out the cries of the dying cattle wandering through the snow-choked streets.

In the spring the cattlemen rode slowly across their domain. As the late "Cimarron" George Bolds, once Bat Masterson's deputy, remarked just before his death: "You could weep at the sight of them . . . one outfit near Garden City (Kansas) had a handful left. Some didn't have any ears or tails . . . we couldn't stand it, we had to shoot them."

The dripping of the icicles over the bunkhouse door was the death knell of an era.

Dodge City, snowbound, 1870's.

Homesteads

The Nester

THE cattleman accepted the fickleness of his long-horns, the uncertainty of the weather, the natural danger of the ambushing hostiles, but he did not accept the homesteader, the sodbuster or the "nester" as he contemptuously called him.

In return, the homesteader hated the often tyrannical cattle barons. Their conflict is one of the true dramas of the West. On the side of the cattleman was his long struggle to conquer the land; he usually had an aching wound from an arrowhead or a Cheyenne bullet to prove that he had put his life on the line for his spread. But in the end it was the homesteader who won out. He not only had the law on his side, he also was the forerunner of a new era that could not be halted. It was irony to top irony; the cattleman in his own time had heralded the end of the free life of the Plains tribes. Now it was his turn to face the fact that his day and his time were ending.

The peak of homesteading came at a time when the range was being overcrowded and at a time when the stockmen themselves were divided. The smaller rancher was now bucking the Stockmen's Association that con-

A homesteader's cabin in Colorado.

trolled and regulated the cattle business. The newcomer found it almost impossible to obtain admission to the charmed circle. It was true that any stock grower was eligible for admission, but to be admitted was another question. The investigation committee almost always turned down the new applicant. Rather than risk doing without the many advantages of belonging to the powerful organization, the stranger usually tried to find a less

A homesteader alongside an adobe hut.

[183]

May 19 1855.

Sir:

The bounty land claim of Robert Hayne *No. 8726 filed under the act of 3d March, 1855, for services rendered in the removal of the Cherokee Indians under Capt.* Haywood Weir — Tenn — *United States volunteers, has been examined. As it is shown by documents on file that said company was part of the forces raised under an act of Congress passed May the 23rd, 1836, and served exclusively in the removal of said Indians, with whom no war existed during their enlistment, and as the benefits of the above and all other bounty land acts extend only to those who were called into service* BY THE AUTHORITIES OF A STATE, OR TERRITORY, *and have been paid for the same by the United States, or who served in some one of the several wars in which this country has been engaged since 1790, said claim cannot be allowed.*

A rejection of a bounty land claim.

crowded area where his chances of survival were greater.

To admit more cattle was to endanger the cattle industry, but to allow the homesteader to move onto the open range and interfere with their grazing cattle was to the big ranchers almost unthinkable.

With the introduction of barbed wire, the cattlemen had begun to fence in public domain land, land that belonged to the government and was available to homesteaders only. In the early eighties the situation bordered on the fantastic. Routes of travel were wired off, even mail deliverers complained that they were forced to detour around some cattle king's empire, sometimes at rifle point. Many times homesteaders and small ranchers closed ranks as they watched the encroachments of the big cattle companies.

The San Antonio *Drovers' Journal* in 1884 reported that the Texas governor was forced to ask the legislature to help free the county seat of Jones County, which had been cut off from the rest of the state by cattlemen's wire fences. In 1884 Colonel Goodnight's Red River Ranch had 250 miles of fence. The wire of Goodnight and his neighbors stretched from the western border of the Indian country straight across the Panhandle and clear into New Mexico for 35 miles! In Colorado one cattle company had 40 townships cut off by wire fence, an area of more than a million acres. Signs warned the trespasser what would happen to him.

The homesteader at first tried to ignore the fences, but no sooner would he start housekeeping when he would receive a visit of a dozen or more hard-looking cowhands who gave him just a few hours to clear out. If he didn't obey, he was either shot down or driven out and his cabin and belongings burned.

Settlers started to send in complaints to the Land Bureau in Washington. The Bureau conducted its own investigation and the testimony of the hearings was staggering. In 1883, after an outbreak of violence, the Secretary of the Interior advised the settlers to cut the wire fences on the land they had filed for.

Actually it was no easy matter to sell the eastern farmers the idea of a Utopia in the western plains. For too many years the West had been pictured as a terrible, arid place which couldn't grow an apple. As far back as 1775 Edmund Burke was telling the House of Commons that the Great American Desert was a deadly menace, that it was a desolate land which would breed a race of "English

Application }   Homestead
No. 1.   }   Land Office
                 Brownville N.T. January 1st 1863

I Daniel Freeman of Gage County Nebraska Territory
Do hereby apply to Enter under the Provissions of the
act of Congress aproved May 20th 1862 Entitled; an act
to Secure Homesteads to actual Settlers on the Public Domain
The South half of N.W¼ & NE¼ of N W¼ & S W¼ of NE¼ Sec 26.
in Township four (4) N in Range Five East containing 160 acres
Having filed my Pre Emption Decleration thereto on
the Eighth day of September 1862
                                   Daniel Freeman

                 Land office at.
                     Brownville N.T. January 1st 1863
I Richard F Barret, Register of the Land office do
hereby certify that the above application is For Surveyed
Lands of the Class which the applicant is legally Entitled to Enter
under the Homestead act of May 20th 1862 and that there is No
Prior valid adverse Right to the Same

                           Richard F Barret
                                     Register

A Nebraska homestead application and certification.

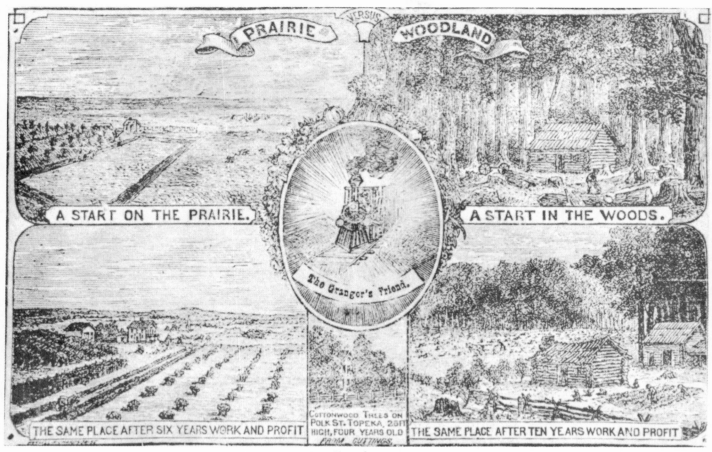

A railroad poster.

Tartars, a fierce and irresistible cavalry, [who would] become masters of your governors and your counsellors."

Early Western explorers brought back the same picture of the West. In 1810 Pike described the West as a vast, treeless wasteland. This was confirmed by Stephen H. Long's expedition of 1823. The terrible experiences of the emigrant trains was further evidence to the East that only sand and sage grass could exist in the West. Even Francis Parkman was convinced that the western plains country was sterile. He wrote: "Sometimes it glared in the sun, an expanse of hot, bare sand; sometimes it was veiled by tall coarse grass. Huge skulls and whitening bones of buffalo were scattered everywhere. . . ."

It was not a picture that would send eastern farmers hurrying west even though they were given a free quarter-section, 160 acres of land.

Subsequent government surveys, principally that of Ferdinand V. Hayden, did not materially change the nation's thinking. Then Charles Dana Wilber, an amateur Nebraska scientist, coined the phrase that was echoed time and again in Washington: "Rain follows the plow." Wilber took to the lecture platform and told large audiences about the fabulous possibilities for the western homesteader.

After the panic of 1873 homesteading began to increase. America recalled Greeley's famous remark, "Go West, Young Man, go forth into the Country." Now the unemployed were being advised that if they "made a farm from Uncle Sam's generous domain, you will crowd nobody, starve nobody. . . ."

However, although the settlers did increase up to the panic of 1887, they never did fulfill the Republican Party's great dream that the West would one day develop into a vast agricultural region. Large grants of land to railroads, failure to enact a realistic land program, speculators and cattlemen's frauds failed to make the homesteading program the success it should have been. From 1862 to 1890 only 372,650 Americans took advantage of the Homestead Act. Actually the Union Pacific sold more land at $5 an acre than was conveyed free under the government's public land program.

Congress passed many acts in an attempt to induce the farmer to go westward. The Land Office sold Congress the idea that if enough trees were planted, rainfall would increase to such an extent that the sage grass country would yield vast fields of crops. The Timber Culture Act was passed in 1873 by which a homesteader, in addition to his original quarter-section of 160 acres, was given another quarter-section to plant 40 acres of trees.

In 1877 Congress, still determined to move the eastern farmer westward, passed another law giving him an additional 640 acres on the condition that he irrigate the whole section within three years. Both acts were far removed from reality. It was big politics and nothing more.

One of the most important reports on the land itself was that submitted to Congress by Major James W. Powell

A homesteader family and their sod-house.

in 1878. In his *Lands of the Arid Regions of the United States* Powell advocated a revolutionary plan to classify the West in such sections as those fit only for pasturage, for minerals, timber and so on. Congress refused to move, but the report did result in the establishment of the United States Geological Survey, whose main purpose was to make such classifications.

In addition Congress created a Commission on Public Lands. The Commission toured the western country, in-terviewing both homesteaders and cattlemen. The Commission's report confirmed Powell's contention that some sort of classification should be made.

By the late seventies the cattleman was still king of the frontier. In 1879 the Land Office reported to Congress that vast tracts of public land were being denied to homesteaders by cattlemen who had fenced them off and that water rights were being granted to the beef men by the worst kind of fraud, conspiracy and bribery.

A sod-house in the Dakota Territory, 1880's. *Photo by General John T. Pitman.*

Finally Congress acted in 1885, passing a law making it a crime for anyone to fence public-domain land. The cattlemen tried to beat this by paying their cowboys to stake out claims along the stream sites. Thus for twenty-five cents an acre, they had exclusive control over the section for three years. At the end of that time, by paying a dollar an acre and running a plow here and there they could retain the land permanently.

In some sections the homesteaders, by weight of numbers, controlled the community. In the late eighties in western Nebraska they boldly killed cattle that wandered on their land. As they became part of the local communities, cattlemen found the tables had turned; in Wyoming they might control the judges and the juries, but in Nebraska it was an all-granger grand jury that was refusing to return a true bill against a farmer accused of wantonly killing some stock.

But no matter how strong their numbers, the homesteader's life was poles apart from the romantic picture painted by the Washington politician and Greeley's editorials.

It was a hard life, a constant battle against the arid land, against drought, grasshoppers and loneliness. Women aged

A half-completed sod-house near Eagle Butte in the Dakotas. The sod will be built up about the walls. *Photo by P. T. Peterson.*

The Life of a Dakota Homesteader

An old friend of the author, Pat McDonough, recalls homesteading with his family at Lantry, midway between Eagle Butte and Dupree in Central South Dakota. The McDonoughs' first home was a sod hut on their quarter.

"Fuel for a fire was a problem," Pat wrote. "There were no trees for miles around. The Sioux sold berries and wood. When we were out of wood we used cow chips, deposits by the wild cattle which roamed the plains near us. There were stock yards down near the railhead, but instead of corraling the cattle, they let them roam for free forage.

"I was five years old at the time and my brother was seven. When we got up at the crack of dawn to walk to school we first climbed a small hill and looked around the land. If there were no cattle in sight we would continue on to the school which was about a mile's walk. If we saw the steers we would return; they were dangerous and would charge when they saw or smelled a human.

"School was a small shack; the class had about a dozen kids.

"Mother used to bake bread for men who were 'batching it' on the claims. They would provide the flour and Mother did the baking while they sat around outside.

"Later my father and uncle and neighbors built a larger house, which was composed of three rooms. Immediately a family of rattlers built a house in one corner. It's an understatement to say it was a hazard walking to the outhouse.

"Our sport was simple and born of the frontier. In the winter we used as a sled a mortar box,

about four feet wide and six feet long, with a couple of boards nailed across for seats.

"We had a handyman by the unlikely name of Arthur Murray, who called my mother chief cook and bottle washer.

" 'I'm the sod-packer,' he would say when we would ask him what he was.

"He never forgot those days. For years while he lived he would send the family cards celebrating certain anniversaries, such as the first day he came to work for us.

"There were plenty of Sioux bucks around. One day Mother got the scare of her life. She turned and there was one big as life.

"All he would do was grunt and say 'minnie.' Mother wanted to give him what he wanted because stuck in his belt was a murderous-looking knife. Finally, by pointing and sign language, she found out all he wanted was water from our pump for his horse.

"We didn't have Mass every Sunday. The priest traveled over a wide area of the frontier. Sometimes he would say Mass in the settlers' homes. I can recall he once said Mass in our house. I also can recall him telling us how he said Mass for the tribes in a tent.

"One thing I can recall of those days was our first house. It was so small we had to put the bed outside in the daytime and the table at night."

in months and many times went mad from the endless space, the great quiet broken only by the high keening winds, by the feeling of desperation and hysteria that settled over them with each dawn.

In the end, after working from dawn to dusk, the homesteaders' reward was a miserable sod hut and crops ravaged by the elements; a dreary present, a hopeless future.

Sheep

Another object of the cattleman's hatred was the western "woolies"—sheep. Like the cow pony and the longhorn, the plains sheep were the product of the Spaniards. They had been raised by the missions and had accompanied the Spanish colonization attempts on the frontier.

Colorado was the principal sheep state along with Montana and Wyoming, all beef territories. In 1880, according to the *Tenth Census Report*, there were 1,820,945 sheep in these states. The woolies also invaded Kansas, Nebraska and the Dakotas, but never in such numbers.

The disastrous winter of 1887, which broke the back of the cattle industry in the West, enabled the sheep business to prosper. Although the cattlemen of the 1880's bitterly opposed the sheep herds on the theory that they cropped the grass too short and killed it, that their smell drove away cattle, and that sheep destroyed young trees, they soon found no alternative but to turn to sheep-herding. By 1890 a large number of former beef men were in the sheep-raising business.

The sheep drives, with all their color and drama, were not so widely publicized as the cattle drives north from Texas. However, there were extensive sheep drives from as far south as California to as far north as Nebraska, or from the Rocky Mountain areas to Kansas. The California drives took several months but the profits were large.

The herds could be easily controlled by one man and well trained dogs whom sheep men valued as much as cowboys did their ponies. When the herd was on the move, the dogs circled its flanks constantly, nipping at the heels of the woolies who refused to stay in line.

Just as the cattle drives had their grub wagons, so did the sheep-herders have their own vehicle. This was a large

A Colorado sheep ranch.

A freighter loaded with wool. Montana in the 1880's.

Sheep-shearing on a Monterey County, California, sheep ranch. *Photo by I. W. Taber.*

wagon with a covering of canvas several layers thick. Inside the wagon were a stove, chairs, tables, and so on. In other words it was a sheep-herder's home on wheels.

The owner of the herds, called the flockmaster, usually stayed in the main camp, which was on land leased either from the railroad or from the county. One of his hands was constantly contacting the moving camps of the herds, bringing supplies, news and orders.

Armed with a staff as he followed his thousands of woolies, his sheep dogs circling the herd, this lonely, usually bearded man could have stepped out of a Biblical picture. When the herd stopped he would rest on a high point gazing out over the feeding animals, watchful always for the wolves.

July was shearing time for the sheepmen. Teams of professional shearers went from ranch to ranch, shearing by hand. After the shearing, the sheep were "dipped" by being driven into a vat containing sulphur and tobacco.

In the 1890's war between the sheepmen and the cattlemen exploded. Cattlemen sent raiders to clean out the sheepmen by killing the sheep, shooting the herders and burning their homes. Men with sacks over their heads, called "gunny sackers," did most of the damage to the sheep camps. In Wyoming the sheepmen fought six years against the raiders, who not only dynamited the camp but stampeded the herds until they ran over cliffs and were smashed on rocks below.

Besides the cattlemen, the prairie wolves and the gunny-sackers, the most feared enemy of all the sheep-herders was the prairie fire. The first sign was the smell of smoke, then the faint, far-off wisps of smoke. Dogs and men would make frantic efforts to save the herds. The frightened animals would mill about, falling and tumbling over each other in utter confusion. Often enough, the shepherd had all he could to save himself and his dogs. He would return the next day to find the plains littered with the blackened bodies of his beloved woolies.

A sheep-herder's "dipping station," Wyoming, 1880.

A sheep-herder's camp, Wyoming, 1880.

The Buffalo's End

THE journals of Coronado's men, the letters, copybooks and reports of the early western trappers and explorers and the journals of the Forty-Niners constantly point up the general wonderment and awe at the great herds of buffalo which roamed the Western Plains.

Ironically, the American buffalo is not a buffalo at all, but rather a bison. Scientists point out that the term "buffalo" should be applied to the water buffalo, the carabao, or African buffalo. But scientists or not, the word, "buffalo" will stand forever in western history.

At the time of the discovery of the American continent the buffalo herds covered one-third of the North American continent. It is generally believed that there were herds north of Great Slave Lake, while to the south they extended into Mexico. To the west they ranged as far as the Blue Mountains of Oregon, and in the East there were abundant herds in Pennsylvania and New York, up to the Canadian border.

The buffalo is the largest and most distinctive game animal on the North American continent. In height a full-grown bull stands five to six feet at the shoulder and weighs about 2,000 pounds. The buffalo differs from the common cattle because it has 14 ribs and a smaller weight of viscera; cattle have 13 ribs, Brahma cattle only 12. The flesh of the buffalo is similar to beef. The hunter always tried to kill a fat, dry heifer or cow, as its flesh was tender and more pleasant than that of the bull. Plainsmen agreed that the hump was the choice part, and that a constant diet of buffalo meat was less tiresome than that of any other animal. Hunters were also of the opinion that a man on a buffalo meat diet seldom missed bread.

The buffalo's coat is dark brown but grows paler towards spring. Trappers' journals tell of rare roan animals, while the white buffalo, which were revered by the Blackfeet and Sioux, occurred about one in two million.

In the spring and summer the buffalo would paw the turf and wallow in the holes to rid himself of vermin and loose hair. The buffalo wallows had the appearance of a large saucer. The buffalo's natural habitat was the treeless plains, and when a tree was discovered by the herds, it would be quickly destroyed by the shaggy hides pressing against the trunk. Hunters called them "rubbing posts."

There have been cases recorded of explorers and trappers finding a large, solitary rock on the plains and a ditch around it worn down to a depth of three feet by the circling beasts who rubbed against its sides.

When the first telegraph poles were strung it was not considered necessary to raise the wires high off the ground.

American bison bull.

A typical buffalo wallow.

Buffalo skulls and bones.

This view changed when the buffalo used the poles as rubbing posts and knocked them over. When the harassed wiremen drove in spikes the buffalo fought among themselves to get near the spiked pole, so that method of stringing wires was soon abandoned.

A calf, usually born from April to June, would follow its mother for about a year, then seek its own way in the world. Its life span was usually about eight years, but Martin Garretson, the famous buffalo expert, reports that in some cases the buffalo lived to an age of fifty years, or more.

The buffalo was a sluggish sort of animal, mild, inoffensive and dull—except when a cow had a calf beside her. So dull were they that hide hunters usually established what they called a "stand"—and methodically wiped out an entire herd. In most cases the lethargic beasts did not stir from the spot but only stared stupidly at their dead or dying mates.

The stampedes were terrifying. Eye-witnesses tell us that it seemed the whole earth was trembling under the pounding of their hoofs. In 1867 a large herd tried to cross the South Platte River when it was low. The leaders were soon stuck in the mud, but those behind just continued to stampede so that in a few hours the entire mile-wide river was black with the bodies of dead or dying buffalo.

The buffalo had herd habits from which it never deviated. When it sought water, the whole herd followed in one mass, then after drinking, rested and returned to the feeding ground. Thus, when the early pioneers were seeking water they simply followed the buffalo trails.

The buffalo's instinct for direction also helped the western pioneers. At all times he followed the line of least resistance so that when the survey teams mapping routes for the railroads followed the trails left by the roaming herds, they could travel for miles without having to improve the grade. The Baltimore and Ohio Railroad, for example, followed the buffalo trail across the mountains to the Ohio River; the Union Pacific up the Platte Valley follows an old buffalo trail all the way from Omaha to the Rocky Mountains.

The estimated peak population of buffalo has been a matter for debate among scientists for years. A conservative estimate would be sixty million.

In Townsend's *Journey Across the Rocky Mountains*, published before the Civil War, he tells how he was awed by the sight of one vast buffalo herd "which covered a whole plain as far as an eye could see." The width of the plain was about eight miles. In 1871 plainsmen reported to Fort Larned that a herd was crossing a plain which was 50 miles long and 25 miles wide. The plain was completely covered.

Although the herds covered the western plains like one great rippling black blanket, they were quickly wiped out of each section as civilization advanced into it, and were just about completely exterminated as soon as the outrunners of civilization reached across the plains. The ex-

Cheyenne squaws dressing and stretching buffalo hides. *Photo by S. J. Morrow.*

termination of these vast herds is a chapter in history which most Americans view with shame and disgust.

In Pennsylvania the last herds were wiped out in 1799; in 1803 the last buffalo was chased out of the city of Buffalo in New York State; by 1820 they were practically extinct east of the Mississippi.

By the time of the Civil War there was a brisk trade in buying and selling buffalo skins for robes, hats and "buffer" overshoes with the hair turned inside. For a pound of cheap sugar a trader could buy from the Indians a buffalo robe worth ten dollars in the Missouri River towns. Tourists from the eastern cities paid fifty dollars for a prime robe; and more if an Indian squaw had decorated it with colored porcupine quills.

By 1870 some firms were selling as many as 250,000 robes. The next year there was a shed in Cheyenne, Wyoming, 170 feet long, 60 feet wide and 30 high, that was bulging at the joints with robes.

Buffalo tongues being cured or smoked by suspending them over a smudge fire.

It was the Union Pacific which split the herds in two—the northern and southern herds. By 1871 the range was overrun with hide-hunters. At one point there were more than 5,000 hunters in the field along with countless pleasure-seekers who simply shot down the great beast, perhaps took his horns and then left the carcass for the lobo wolves who were always harrying the herds.

For a time it seemed the nation had gone on a buffalo-killing spree. In two months, 260,000 buffalo had been slaughtered in one section alone. By 1875 there were so many skins the market fell to about a dollar a skin. When the herds drifted into Texas the hunters followed them, still wantonly killing them off. Near Fort Griffin a four-acre section was once covered with drying hides. By 1878 the southern herd had been wiped out. The few remaining buffalo fled to the Staked Plains, where the last four were shot down in 1889.

Not only the hunters but the government itself was part of the shameful conspiracy to kill off the herds. The Indians were on the warpath and it was commonly accepted that once the herds were wiped out, the red warriors would come back to the reservations. In an open debate in 1876, Congressman James Garrison openly charged that the Secretary of the Interior had told him he would "rejoice," as far as the Indian question was concerned, when the last buffalo had been shot down.

After the hide-hunters had done their bloody task, the bone-scavengers arrived. For 12 miles along the Santa Fe there were mounds of bones 12 feet high and 12 feet wide. The bones brought from $8 to $12 a ton and were shipped east for fertilizer, while buttons and combs were made from the horns. From 1868 to 1881 $2,500,000 was paid out for buffalo bones. It required 100 buffalo to make a ton of bones.

The northern herd soon met the fate of its southern mate. From 1876 to 1882 the hunters ruthlessly wiped out the herd. By 1883 there was one small herd left near the Cannonball River in North Dakota. In September of that year Sitting Bull led his hunters in a winter hunt, killing about a thousand in one day. By the fall of the next year there were no buffalo left.

The passing of the herds was a calamity for the tribes. They were truly the "Indian's cattle," for they provided him with food, shelter and clothing. No part of the beast was wasted; even the hair was braided into reins and the green skins were used as kettles. The hoofs were used to

Buffalo grazing in a National Park preserve.

"The valley was covered with buffalo." *From a drawing by M. S. Garretson.*

glue arrows to the shafts; the horns were made into drinking cups and part of the war bonnet. Even the buffalo chips, the dried excrement, called "prairie coal" by the settlers, were used in fire making. Thus, in the end, not only a species, but a nation had been exterminated.

Many attempts, going back to a James P. Swain of Westchester County, New York, in 1868 have been made to mate wild buffalo and cattle. Swain's attempts were successful and as he reported, the cows gave a surprisingly large amount of sweet milk and "they were so mild even a small boy could herd them."

Efforts were also made to preserve and perpetuate what few buffalo remained. At the turn of the century the total buffalo population in America had dwindled to about 1,000. There was a small herd in Yellowstone Park under federal protection, but poachers killed them off until there were only 20 left. In 1902 Colonel Charles J. Jones, the Kansas frontiersman, widely known as "Buffalo Jones" was appointed warden of the Park by Congress and given an appropriation of $15,000 to buy buffalo and to build up the herd. Twenty-one were purchased from private owners, including Colonel Goodnight. Under the leadership of Dr. William T. Hornaday, director of the New York Zoological Park, a new herd was started in Oklahoma with 15 of the finest pure-blooded buffalo—all from New York's Zoological Society.

In 1905 Dr. Hornaday also organized the American Bison Society. Among the achievements of the Society was the establishment of the Montana Bison Range in 1909 and the Wind Cave Herd of South Dakota in 1913. In 1918 the Society again saved the buffalo from disaster when it managed to suppress a cattlemen's campaign to open the Parks to grazing stock. Through such efforts, the American buffalo population has mounted slowly so that today it numbers approximately 10,000—a figure nearly ten times that of 50 years ago!

A hide-hunter's camp on Evans Creek in the Texas Panhandle, 1874. *Photo by George Robertson.*

Gold and Other Mining

AFTER the great strike at Sutter's Mill the prospector became a permanent western figure. His uniform of battered hat, boots, flannel shirt, pan, shovel and mule became as distinctive as the chaps and spurs of the cowboy. He moved about the West "looking for color" in every gulch, valley or canyon. In the diggings he endured frightful hardships, and there were times when he struck it rich only to sell his precious find for a fraction of its real value.

One of the first strikes after the California find was in Gregory's Gulch in Colorado. In the first week of May, 1859, John H. Gregory and two other men led their burdened mules out of Cherry Creek to look for a claim. They ended on Clear Creek, the present site of Central City. Gregory began washing a pan of dust and got a dollar's worth. The party took a bag of dust valued at about $15 to Denver, and the stampede was on.

1859 was also the year of the news of the fabulous Comstock Lode found in the Virginia Mountains of Nevada, some 20 miles from Reno. It was the richest silver deposit ever found, and there was plenty of gold in the hills also.

The influx of treasure-seekers was enormous and the town of Virginia City, founded the same year, became the boom-town hub of the whole mining camp area. In its early years it was probably the rip-roaringest mining capital of them all, with the biggest and best saloons and bars. By 1860, it even had a newspaper, the celebrated *Territorial Enterprise*, of which Mark Twain was an editor (1863-67). The fame of Virginia City lived on long after the gold and silver petered out. It has been restored now

A prospector with his "staff of life," the water donkey. *Photo by B. W. Kilburn.*

The rush to the Comstock Lode, Virginia City.

to the appearance of its liveliest days and is a tourist center, popular with all visitors to the area.

In 1863 the first big strike was made in Montana. That summer William Fairweather, Robert Vaughan and a small group were prospecting on a creek when Fairweather took his horse across to tie to some trees.

"There's a ledge over there we ought to try to get some money for a little tobacco," he said.

Vaughan returned to the spot with Fairweather. Fairweather dug and Vaughan washed the dirt. While his companion expertly panned the water and dirt Fairweather began scratching a ledge with his knife.

"Looks like I found a scad!" he cried.

"If you have one I have a thousand," Vaughan jubilantly replied.

The first pan contained $2.80 worth of gold. The next pan was worth over a hundred dollars. Day after day they continued to pan the gold, pledging among themselves to keep their find secret. But as at Sutter's Mill, such a secret could not be kept.

Soon one of the maddest gold rushes was taking place, with most of Montana's population hurrying to the gulch which Fairweather had named Alder Gulch from the grove of alder there. In a matter of hours, a new city, also called Virginia City, was born, and in a few years it became the territorial capital.

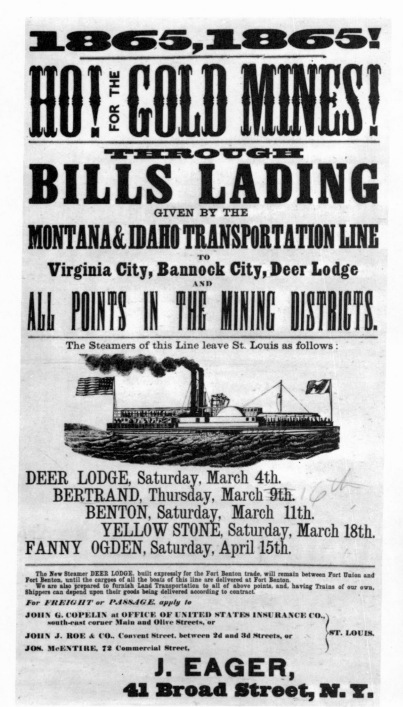

An 1865 broadside.

George Warren, discoverer of the Copper Queen mine. *Photo by Camillus Fly.*

A Black Hills miner guarding the camp. *Photo by S. J. Morrow.*

From a statement of the Carson City mint, February, 1872.

Alder Gulch took on the aspect of an ant-heap, with prospectors virtually crawling over themselves to pan gold. So rich was the color that a poor average for a miner was a hundred dollars a day.

There were many other gold and silver discoveries, many other mining-camp boom-towns, notably Deadwood in the Black Hills of South Dakota, where gold was discovered in 1875, and Tombstone, where rich silver mines were found in 1877. Both of these towns, each founded a year or so after the finds, were notorious as hotbeds of wildness and reckless revelry.

Copper was discovered near Butte, Montana, in 1880, with some rather different consequences from the silver and gold discoveries. Copper mining was a much more mechanized operation than gold or silver mining. Large or well-capitalized companies had to conduct the actual mining and the area became more industrialized and somewhat more orderly than the other mining areas. Also, there was widespread speculation. Worthless lands and even options on worthless land were sold and resold at higher and higher prices. Copper-mining companies were formed with practically no assets, but they continued to sell shares at ever-increasing prices. The boom fever spread over the country, and when the bust came, there was much more money lost in the speculation swindle than was made in copper profits for many years.

As the people moved west, new riches—notably in

Mine entrance, Colorado, 1860's. *Photo by W. H. Jackson.*

Deadwood, South Dakota, 1876. *Photo by S. J. Morrow.*

[197]

Another view of Deadwood, 1876.

Idaho and Colorado, besides the areas already mentioned—were discovered on or under the ground—zinc, iron, coal, borax and many other metals and minerals. Each find drew new population from the East; each had its own peculiar impact on its era. But essentially the two extremes were the gold and silver towns on the wild side and the copper areas on the sober, industrial side. Naturally, the famous gold mines were the ones to capture the interest and imagination of the country. Everyone wanted to know about them. Stories about them found a ready market, and newspapers and magazines published many accounts about them.

In the early rushes there was a great deal of "salting" by fast-talking promoters. To salt a mine, a man would distribute gold dust over a claim. The best method was to load a shotgun with gold dust and fire the load into a hill or mound. In 1859 a group of solemn-faced miners watched Horace Greeley get down on his knees and wash pan after pan of dirt. In the end the famous editor had a small bagful of glittering dust.

Getting to his feet, he said, "Gentlemen, I have worked with my own hands and have seen with my own eyes, and the news of your rich discovery shall go all over the world as far as my paper can carry it."

He was cheered wildly by the gleeful miners, who had carefully salted the mine before Greeley had arrived.

Cabin of the "bottle fiend" of Deadwood, surrounded by kegs full of bottles. *Photo by S. J. Morrow.*

In the West booms rose and fell. In 1863 mere holes in the earth were being sold as mines in Colorado. Naive buyers in the East bought millions of worthless, so-called mines. So great was the transfer of property that the clerk and recorder of Gilpin County was forced to employ an extra staff to assist him in the paper work. In the spring the boom collapsed like a punctured balloon.

The boom towns of the West were as picturesque as they were dirty. At Helena, Last Chance Gulch, Virginia City, Alder Gulch and Bannock on Grasshopper Creek miners lived in holes dug into the sides of the hills or in tents made of anything from canvas to potato sacks. Chair bottoms were of rawhide or rope. Beds were mounds of straw covered by a ragged blanket.

Prices were fantastic. A straw boom cost $5, eggs, $3 apiece—$2 more than in the last days in Confederate Richmond; flour, $25 a sack; water, 50 cents a barrel; peaches 50 cents each.

The saloons were usually large tents which shared barber shop and grocery facilities. Such places were always madhouses of shouting miners trying to attract the attention of the harried clerk, gossiping prospectors with weeks of beard waiting for a chance in the barber's chair and drunken members of the local amateur quartet practicing at the bar. There were many bars but few churches.

Mail service was desired almost as much as whiskey and women. When a camp was set up, riders delivered mail to Fort Laramie for 25 cents a letter. Later the stagecoach would take over, cutting the cost of postage.

Sports were cruel and vicious: bullfights, dogfights and cockfights. Boxing matches ended only when one contender was beaten into insensibility. In 1865 in Virginia

Ready to blast in the West Stewart Mine, Butte, Montana, 1880. *Photo by N. H. Forsythe.*

Shaft scene in a Cripple Creek, Colorado, mine. *Photo by James A. Harlan.*

Placer mining at the Plowman Mine, Idaho City.

City one fight started at eight in the evening and ended at dawn after 185 rounds had been fought. The battle was declared a draw.

As the boom towns became more civilized, traveling circuses and road shows would appear. The New York *Tribune*'s correspondent in 1866 reported that the Virginia City Theatre held 200 customers, a large stove, candles at the footlights and a green cambric drop curtain. The audience was apt to get wild and sometimes the performers also; one night in Tombstone Calamity Jane forgot the villain was only an actor and pegged a shot at him. Fortunately, she missed.

Cemeteries and Boot Hills were established almost as soon as a town was born, but undertakers took their time in arriving. In Denver's second year, six men died in a mine disaster. There was no undertaker, so the women of the town dressed the bodies and the miners buried them. It would be a long time before the formal black hearse would replace the bumping quartz wagon which took the crude pine coffins to the cemetery outside the town limits.

The men were rough in dress and manner, but a great many were highly educated. In 1862, when George Crocker and his party walked 150 miles to Colorado City to attend the Territorial Legislature, he arrived at the House of Representatives with a worn blanket, a six-shooter on his hip, a blue flannel shirt, trousers patched with buckskin, and an old slouch with its rim half gone. He was bearded and gaunt with weariness, but when he was elected Speaker of the House, he made a speech which would have been a credit to a polished diplomat.

Boom towns attracted professional gamblers, men and women and plenty of gunmen and bandits. Games of all kinds went on day and night. Fortunes were won and lost with the flick of a card. Men died in a game of cards, their blood staining the green baize tables.

An advertisement in *Samuel's Directory*, Portland and East Portland, 1874.

Ruins of the old Mexican smelter at Ouray, Colorado. *Photo by C. H. Clark.*

The dance hall was a favorite spot in the mining camps. Here a lonesome miner could buy a ticket for a dollar—the proceeds were usually split down the middle between the dance-hall owner and the girl—and dance around the room a few times. After a gay whirl, the miner could take her to the bar for a drink and, if he wished, arrange to spend some time with her alone.

The rough mining camps underscored the American knack for bringing order where chaos had existed. Before legislators or courts could be elected and established, vigilante committees and miners' courts took care of the swift administration of justice. Veteran miners had an amazing knowledge of mining laws and constitutional privileges, and it was difficult for the law-breaker to defeat justice in those early courtrooms. The majority of votes elected the judge in murder trials, and a jury was chosen from the spectators.

Like the cowboy, the miner left his own vocabulary on the western frontier; diggings, dust, shebang, color, pan out, lead, outfit, and apparently the favorite expression of all—"You bet!"

Timber-r-r!

STANDING side by side with the cowboy on his horse, the prospector with his pan and the painted Indian brave is the bearded logger with his double-bitted axe. He is as much a part of the American West as his companions. And, like the others, he has placed his stamp on our folklore, our ballads and our traditions.

Curiously, the logger paralleled the cattleman in his philosophy of the West. He paid no heed as to who rightly owned the land on which grew the timber he wanted. As far as he was concerned it was all an open range and whoever got there first served himself first.

The first loggers were usually small parties of one or two men who stocked up a canoe with enough provisions to last them a few weeks, then set out to reconnoiter the country for excellent timber sites. When one was found, a camp was made and the axe-men would be sent for.

The loggers spent the winter cutting and trimming the timber and sending it downstream on the ice. As early as the 1850's small logging parties "got out" as much as a

million feet of lumber, using only 15 men and two yoke of oxen. The ice route had to be utilized because there were no roads and the Indian trails were too narrow for the yoke of oxen.

The camps that were established in the West were patterned after the "State of Maine" camp. There was but one building about 40 feet long and elevated two feet from the ground. The roofs were usually of evergreens, the walls of logs.

In a way the building resembled the long-house of the Iroquois in the East. In the center of the room was a large fireplace; above it was a fire hole. Sometimes wooden pine shakes were extended down from the roof to about a foot above the fireplace to act as a sort of funnel to catch the smoke.

The fire was used not only for cooking but for heat and illumination, as there were no windows. Berths were built along the sides of the walls. The loggers slept with their heads toward the wall. Between the logger's feet and

Early western logging camp showing wooden sled. *Photo by Martin's Gallery.*

Driving logs on the St. Croix River, 1870's.

the fire was a broad plank called the "deacon's seat," which he used as a step to get into his bed. Here he sat, dressed and gossiped.

At the end of the building was the pantry, the world of the cook. Here were the rough tables and chairs where the men were fed. Here also was the inevitable grindstone, which was always in use as the loggers ground fine their axes. Other standard items were the water barrel and the bucket used for washing.

Blankets were usually buffalo robes. At night a visitor might think he was in a laundry, with all the heavy woolen socks hanging on lines crisscrossing the room. Sometimes the loggers slept spoon-fashion under a single cover. When one logger got tired of sleeping on one side he would shout "Spoon" and the whole line would turn over.

In the pre-dawn darkness the cook's assistant would walk into the bunkhouse banging on an iron triangle and shouting for all to rise and shine. After a hearty breakfast they would move into the forest.

The logging party was divided into teamsters, who hauled the logs; choppers, who felled the giants of the forests; sawyers, who sawed the logs into sections; and swampers, who prepared the roads. Expert choppers were the heart of the camp. A man who was an expert with his double-bitted tool received as much as $75 a month in the pre-Civil War era.

A log jam on the St. Croix, 1870's. *Photo by M. Nowack.*

A bull team (oxen) on the skidroad. The skid-greaser is getting a new can of grease for the skids. The Douglas fir region on the north bank of the Columbia River, 1895.

A skid road.

In the early days of western logging, many of the Maine methods were used in preparing the logs. One was to "go-devil" the log or drag it whole to the river bank, where it was cut into sections. The double saw soon took the place of the double-bitted axe. With this tool two men always worked together. After a scaler selected a tree, they made a bite on one side with an axe, then started to saw on the other. It was an extremely risky business. Sometimes the tree trunk would split and the cry "Whip the saw!" would ring out. The saw was then turned to the other side and the men began frantically sawing to stop the split.

There was always danger in the felling of the tree. Sometimes the tree did not fall in the direction the loggers intended, or else in falling it hit another tree and the massive trunk would whip about. The first warning that a fall was near was the harsh, ripping sound that grew in intensity. Then the forest would echo with the traditional "Timber-r-r! Down the line. Watch out."

When they heard this cry, the loggers scrambled for safety as the giant of the forest plunged down, making the earth tremble as it hit. Out of the dust and falling leaves would come the sawyers, who first trimmed, then used their two-handed saws in an even rhythm to saw the big trunk into 16-foot sections. The cut loads were then put onto a sled with the aid of heavy chains and oxen. The next step was piling them on the ice for the trip "down-river."

The life of a western logger was hard and lonely. After supper each logger took his turn on the grindstone. Then they would settle down on the deacon's seat for an evening of smoking and telling tall tales. A camp that had a fiddler was considered first-rate. After eating he would take his stance in the middle of the room and begin playing. Sometimes, to relieve the monotony, the loggers would "hurrah." To cowhands this meant shooting up a town or "treeing it"; to loggers, this was an all-male dance. The men who would act the part of the ladies had a bandana tied around one arm. Then they kicked and swung their partners all night to the fiddler's tune.

Sunday was a day of laundering: washing and boiling clothes. In the afternoon card games would be held, or perhaps a new tenderfoot would be sent to beg of the cookie where he could find a "bean-hole."

As the cattle kingdoms expanded in the seventies and eighties, so did the logging camps. It soon became the custom of the larger companies to hire expert timber cruisers, who would go out alone and mark whole tracts of excellent timber to be cut.

Camps now numbered as many as 100 men, who would cut millions of feet of pine during one winter. Now the old Maine camps were gone. In their place were large bunkhouses, cook and pantry buildings and dining rooms. Fresh meat, vegetables and pastry took the place of the old pork and beans. New methods were also introduced, such as the "Michigan Road." This was a system used in Michigan in which a tank wagon would ride up and down the road, dousing it with water to insure a heavy coating of ice when the freeze came.

The number of logs on the river increased so that the lumbermen, like the cattlemen, produced their own brands, which they used to stamp the ends of their logs. Each logger registered his own brand.

One of the most exciting aspects of logging was the "drive" downriver. The pick of the camp put on their heavy caulked boots and overalls and selected their peavey, canthook and pike pole. At the landing they began breaking up the logs and soon were moving downstream. The logs, bouncing and floating at all angles, invariably piled up in a huge, grinding, crushing jam. The drivers would then start seeking the one log that had "frozen" the drive. A skillful driver could find this log and with his pike pull

it free. Then slowly, with a loud, wrenching groan, the jam would disintegrate and the logs would work free.

To prevent a recurrence the drivers would ride the logs, skipping from one to another, poling, pulling and guiding the timber through the rapids, over small waterfalls and along the sluiceways. There were also times when even the most skillful driver could not find the reason for the jam. Then dynamite would be used to break up the jam of twisted timber.

After the timber was cut into sections at the sawmill these also would be floated downriver. But now a "crib" was made of the sawed sections. This was usually a crate-like affair 16 feet wide, 32 feet long and up to 20 inches deep. In the middle and at the end of the crib were huge oars made from a tree trunk. Meals on the crib were prepared on a pile of sand. Just before the Civil War, tents appeared on cribs, later followed by shacks. It usually took a crew of 20 or more tough oarsmen to move the cribs downriver.

The logging crews were a colorful part of the western

A fallen giant redwood, 17½ feet in diameter at the stump, approximately 1,300 years old. Near Fort Bragg, California. *Photo by Frederick.*

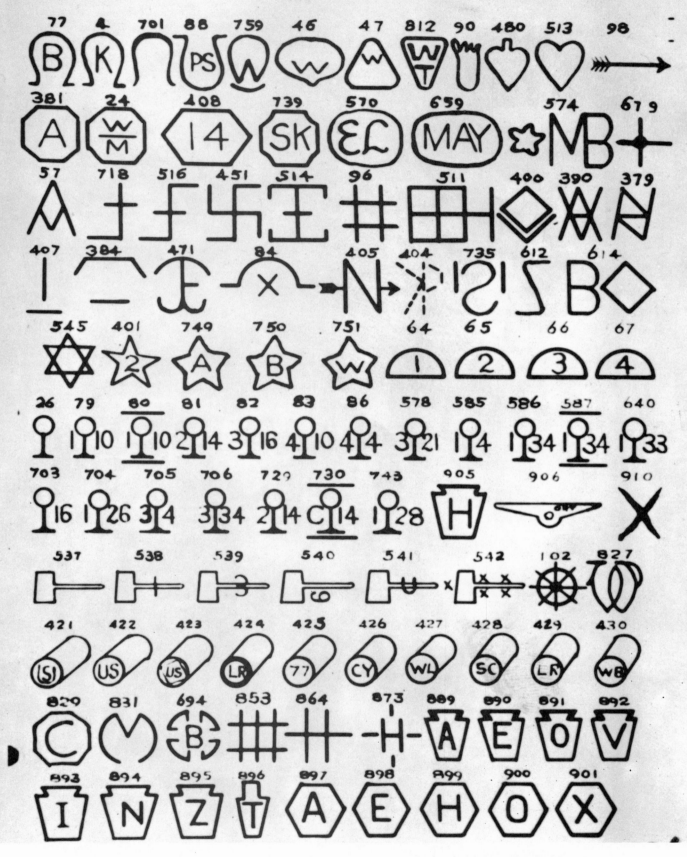

A few of the several thousand company log-brands registered at Olympia, Washington.

Moving logs by horse team.

Moving redwood trunk sections by bull team.

Logs moving downstream.

Moving redwood sections by locomotive.

frontier. After a long, hazardous drive downriver they would "tree" a town as high on payday as any cow outfit after a drive from the Red River country up to Abilene. Huge, powerful men with thick beards, grimy, checkered mackinaws and insatiable thirsts, they often took a steamboat back upstream to the main camp. More than one skipper had to blow for help when his burly passengers decided to challenge each other in a fight on the lower deck—"for the fun of it."

After the Civil War, raft-tugs made their appearance, and soon the western waters were crowded with the tiny, blunt-nosed crafts towing the large rafts.

Puget Sound log-dump. Preparing to roll logs from the pier into the water.

Moving logs by steamboat and raft. These logs are being towed some 1,200 miles, from the Columbia River to San Diego.

Riders of the Outlaw Trail

THE figure of the lean rawboned gunfighter, holsters tied down, advancing slowly along the deserted dusty street of a Western cow town toward another man who silently waits for him, is an accepted part of American folklore. The scene has been played numerous times in books, songs, ballads, always with the gunfighter as the central figure.

His counterpart is the outlaw, that handsome, merry-eyed desperado who robs the rich for the poor and protects the helpless and the weak. He will always be pursued by the sheriff's posse, only to leave them far behind as he and his men ride across the plains to a secret hideout in the hills. Their specific and violent crimes are forgotten, only the pageantry remains.

Since the end of World War II the road agents and the gunfighters of America's Wild West have been claimed by the world. There are Western historical organizations in many European countries; an authentic Western town has been built in France, and in Italy any book on Uomini Disperati is eagerly read.

In reality the gunfighter and the outlaw existed in the Wild West from the founding of the cow towns after the end of the Civil War to the 1890s. By the turn of the century the legendary Wild Bunch, one of the last of the out-law groups, had disbanded with most of its members in Boot Hill, prison, or "on the dodge," as they called it. Butch Cassidy, Harry Longbaugh, the Sundance Kid, and pretty Etta Place were in New York City preparing to leave for South America to introduce outlawry, Western style, to the pampas of South America. Jim Cummins, who had ridden with Jesse James, was living in the Confederate Home, Higginsville, Missouri, and earning his living "breaking colts" for farmers instead of robbing trains and banks.

Richard Fox's pink *Police Gazette* first introduced them in sensational articles and series accompanied by crude woodcuts. The circulation of the *Gazette* was enormous; copies were read in barbershops, saloons, livery stables, bordellos, pool and dance halls until they virtually fell apart. In nearly every article the outlaw and the gunfighter were portrayed as handsome, daring, and fighting the establishment. They were always superb horsemen and expert marksmen. Frank Leslie's *Weekly* and *Harper's*, generally more factual and less garish, also dispatched special correspondents to the Wild West who sent back thrilling stories of stagecoach rides, holdups, Indian attacks, buffalo hunts, railroading, and homesteading. In *Harper's* of July 1867, Theodore Davis, fine Civil War

The Adams Express Company broadside by N. Currier, 1850. Adams, one of the largest public carriers during and after the Civil War, was the favorite target of the outlaw gangs of the Wild West.

from Old Book No.1. Page 104

FRANK. RENO.
Train Robber. Seymour. Ind.

Frank Reno, leader of the outlaw brotherhood, "inventors" of train robbery.

Rare early photograph of Jesse James, who became America's Robin Hood after the Civil War.

combat artist, wrote a stirring account of his stagecoach journey from Atchison, Kansas, to Denver, Colorado, which included an Indian attack.

The saga of Wild Bill Hickok is an excellent example of how these journals helped to mold an American folklore hero out of a frontier bully and a cold-blooded killer. *Harper's New Monthly Magazine* of February 1867 presented Hickok as a hero who had single-handedly killed a band of desperados invading the Rock Creek Overland Stage Depot in Nebraska. It wasn't until 1927 when George V. Hansen, a pioneering settler and Nebraska banker, decided to investigate the legend that the truth was finally uncovered. Hansen, who found the lone survivor of the incident along with unpublished court documents, revealed in the *Nebraska History Magazine* how Hickok had taken part in the cold-blooded killing of three unarmed men who had come to the station to collect a debt owed by the stage company.

Who were these men? Where did they come from? Were they all illiterate psychotic killers? These questions are partially answered by the outlaws and gunfighters themselves. Incredible as it may seem, some took time out from robbing banks and trains or filling Boot Hill to write their autobiographies or to aid a biographer.

For example, John Wesley Hardin, one of the celebrated man killers of the Wild West, endured the horrors of Huntsville Prison in Texas for nineteen years to study to become a lawyer and to write his autobiography. Ben

A seventeen-year-old Jesse James as a guerrilla leader during the Civil War. Note the revolvers.

Thompson, who rivaled Hardin in a skill with a six-shooter and a disregard for life, his own included, assisted his biographer, a respected Texas judge. Tom Horn, hired gun of the cattle barons, finished his autobiography shortly before he was executed for the murder of the fourteen-year-old son of a Wyoming sheepherder. Bat Masterson, who helped to tame Dodge City, later became a columnist on New York's Morning *Telegraph*. During that time he wrote a series of articles on the famous lawmen and gunfighters he had known. Polk Wells, not as well known in the annals of outlawry, described in his autobiography how he had terrorized the Middle Border after the Civil War.

They all had enormous egos. Bob Ford, who killed Jesse James and was immortalized in the well-known ballad as the "dirty little coward who killed Mr. Howard," described in one of his many newspaper interviews how he accompanied Jesse to the Saint Joseph railroad depot to buy three newspapers so Jesse could read stories about himself. At the time the outlaw leader was planning a bank

An account of the wedding of Jesse James and Zerelda Mimms as dictated by Jesse while on his honeymoon to a friend who sent it in to the St. Louis *Dispatch*. It appeared on page one on June 9, 1874.

PITTS

BOB YOUNGER   JIM YOUNGER

COLE YOUNGER

STILES   MILLER

FRANKLIN CO. ENG. CHI

THE ROBBERS—KILLED AND CAPTURED.

Members of the James-Younger band of outlaws, killed and captured after the Northfield bank raid.

robbery, which he promised Ford would put him on page one of the nation's newspapers.

Harvey Logan, the deadly Kid Curry of the frontier, wrote to a friend in Montana after he had made his sensational escape from the Knoxville jail, predicting that his exploits would soon "outshine" those of Harry Tracy, the outlaw and killer then being hunted in the Northwest.

Tom Horn insisted he despised the "yellow journalists" who were covering his murder trial but he still posed for any newspaper photographer who came to the jail.

The posse that captured the Youngers after the Northfield raid in 1876. *Left to right, top row:* Captain W. W. Murphy, Ben M. Rice, C. A. Pomeroy. *Bottom row:* Sheriff James Glispin, G. A. Bradford, Colonel T. L. Vought. Man at extreme right is unidentified.

Probably the biggest egotist of all was Hickok who dressed like a dandy as he patrolled the streets of the rough army posts or cow towns. He never turned down an interview and never failed to fill a naïve reporter with towering lies about his exploits.

Outlaws and gunfighters were seldom the cavaliers of romance. There is no evidence that Jesse James ever held up a landlord to return the mortgage money to a weeping widow with children clutching at her skirt. Jesse had only one philosophy—charity begins at home. Although he was a skilled horseman, he was far from the superb marksman of myth. Once during a bank holdup he fired point blank at a teller and missed. As Dick Liddil, his favorite rider who turned state's evidence, later testified, Jesse fired six shots at a young man who refused to be held up and missed each time.

Few walked up the legendary street to meet their enemy, face to face, gun to gun. Kid Curry patiently waited all night to ambush Jim Winters, a rancher in the Little Rockies section of Montana; Ben Thompson tried to talk the teen-age John Wesley Hardin into killing Hickok for him when Wild Bill was sheriff of Abilene, and Butch Cassidy killed an unarmed teller in South America.

Women were attracted to them. In January 1875, a newspaperman covering the trial in San Jose of California's

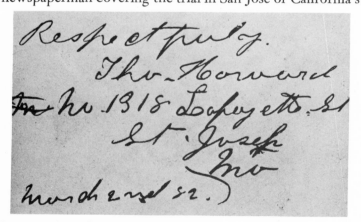

Rare portion of a letter written by Jesse James while hiding out in Saint Joseph, Missouri, under the alias "Tom Howard," from November 1881 until April 3, 1882, when he was killed by Bob Ford, "that dirty little coward."

legendary outlaw leader, Tiburcio Vasquez, indignantly pointed out that the "galleries [of the courtroom] are filled with ladies representing the elite and respectability of the city. . . . Vasquez unblushingly directs his glances at them."

In Knoxville women tried to bribe jailers to deliver their love notes to Kid Curry along with flowers and fine foods. In Cheyenne an attractive schoolteacher tried desperately at the last hour to save Tom Horn from the gallows while John Wesley Hardin's teen-age bride waited faithfully for nineteen years for his release from prison only to die shortly before he was pardoned.

American highwaymen and outlaw bands did not begin in the Wild West. During the American Revolution army commanders in New York State were not only concerned about the British Army in Manhattan or Tory guerrillas but also an outlaw band called "the grays" who indiscriminately raided British and American army posts

Missouri's Governor Thomas Crittenden who led the fight to destroy the James-Younger band. This photograph was taken by Mathew Brady, probably in his Washington studio.

and robbed dispatch riders and civilian travelers. There was also a rustler with the colorful name of Silverheels, and in the savage neutral ground of Westchester the Cowboys, a British guerrilla band, fought the Guides attached to the Americans for the last remaining cows and horses.

There were also the Doanes, celebrated in song and legend, who plundered Bucks County, Pennsylvania, and parts of New Jersey. Three days after Cornwallis's surrender at Yorktown the band swept into Newtown, Pennsylvania, to rob the home of John Hart, county treasurer, of a large amount of silver and paper money. One of the Doane riders, James Fitzpatrick, known to outlaw history as "Sandy Flash," took off on his own to prey on wealthy landowners before he was captured in 1781 and executed in Old Chester, Pennsylvania.

Outlawry later broke out along the Natchez Trace

when Sam Mason, who had been one of George Rogers Clark's men, organized an outlaw band to become the terror of Mississippi. After Mason was killed the fabled Harpe Brothers terrorized settlers moving along the Wilderness Road and later Ohio until they were hunted down and killed.

John Murrel, known as the Great Land Pirate, took their place until he too was captured, with the *Police Gazette* writing and rewriting his life story for many years. The California gold camps were also plagued by outlaws and bandits but it wasn't until after the end of the Civil War that the organized outlaw bands and gunfighters became part of the American legend.

The first were the Reno brothers of Indiana who are credited with "inventing" train robbery. In October 1866 the gang held up the eastbound train of the Ohio and Mississippi Railroad, a broad-gauge line that later became part of the Baltimore and Ohio system. The loot was

Bob Ford with the gun he used to kill Jesse James in Saint Joseph, Missouri, in 1882.

There were five brothers, John, Frank, Simeon, William, and Clinton—the last the only one who refused to become an outlaw. Frank was the leader, John second in command. During the Civil War they had been bounty jumpers; after Appomattox they turned to extortion, bribery, arson, and terrorism to control large sections of Jackson County.

Following a series of robberies the Adams Express Company hired Allan Pinkerton, head of the famous detective agency. He and his operatives eventually broke up the outlaw clan, chasing them into Canada. After London approved their extradition, the Renos were removed to

One of the last photographs taken of Jesse James shortly before he was killed in Saint Joseph, Missouri, by Bob Ford.

about $13,000. One of their most spectacular train robberies took place at the water stop of Northfield, Indiana, Friday night, May 22, 1868, when the outlaw brotherhood stole seventy-nine thousand dollars in gold and government bonds designated for the United States Treasury in Washington. After wounding the conductor and hurling the express messenger out into the darkness from the speeding train, the gang abandoned the train just south of Farmington, below Seymour, Indiana, and fled on horses. It was a train robbery technique that would be used for years by every outlaw band in the West.

The children of Jesse James, Mary and Jesse Edwards James. In honor of his constant defender, John Newman Edwards, Jesse gave Edwards' name to his son. The children were present in the small frame house in Saint Joseph, Missouri, when their father was killed by Bob Ford.

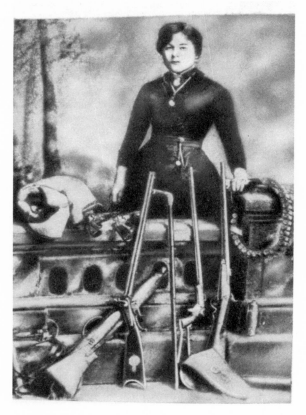

Zerelda (Zee) James with her husband's gun belts and pistols after he was killed in 1882.

A sketch of Jesse James that appeared in New York in Frank Leslie's newspaper shortly after Jesse was killed.

the New Albany, Indiana, jail. Late on the night of December 12, 1868, an army of hooded vigilantes, using a captured train, took over the city with military precision, marched on the jail, and lynched the Renos and their riders in one of the bloodiest scenes in the post–Civil War years.

Curiously, the Renos and their exploits never captured the imagination of the public as would the James-Younger band of outlaws who took their place on the outlaw trail. There is little doubt Jesse James is America's premier outlaw and America's Robin Hood.

The amazing part of the saga of this strange complex man is that while he perfected his techniques of bank and train robberies, he avoided capture for sixteen years. His end came in a fashion to win him national sympathy despite the enormity of his crimes.

Jesse and his men also helped to split the Missouri Democratic party into two factions: pro-Confederate and pro-northern. An example of the division between the two groups is the scene that took place in the state legislature a short time after Jesse had been killed. When a legislator finished reading his proposal that the Missouri lawmen be praised for their long and bitter pursuit of the outlaw, he was greeted with hoots and jeers and a barrage of spittoons.

There is little doubt that Governor Thomas Crittenden's role in persuading the railroads to put up the reward money for the capture of Frank and Jesse James cost him the renomination and shattered any presidential dreams he may have had. William Wallace, the courageous Jack-

son County prosecutor who put Frank James on trial for murder, lost his bid for the congressional, senatorial, and gubernatorial candidacies.

The first inside story of Jesse's leadership was told by Dick Liddil, once his favorite rider, who surrendered when he heard the horns of the hunters loud in his ears and became a state's witness. Six months after Jesse was killed by Ford, Frank James flamboyantly surrendered to Governor Crittenden at the statehouse in Jefferson City. Wallace then indicted him for the murder of a passenger during a train holdup. From the witness stand Liddil vividly described how Jesse would send riders out to alert members of the band that he had plans for a "strike," and how they would meet in the forest to hear their leader outline his strategy for a bank or train robbery.

Liddil also gave the jury an insight into the character of his lost leader. He testified that once Jesse summoned the gang and was leading them to the spot where the robbery was to take place when Jesse suddenly held up his hand and the file of riders came to a halt. Then Jesse announced to his startled followers that the raid was temporarily postponed. When Liddil asked the reason, Jesse James, probably the best-known bandit leader in the world at the time, told his men he had a toothache and wanted to return to Clay County so his mother could treat it!

For the first nine years of his career as a bandit leader, Jesse led his men across the Midwest robbing banks, trains, and stagecoaches. The loot was usually inflated in the headlines; weeks after the robbery the actual amount of money stolen—usually the Adams Express Company was

William Wallace, the courageous Missouri prosecutor who forced Dick Liddil, Jesse's rider, to become an informer, and who later put Frank James on trial for murder. James was acquitted.

the victim—was whittled down. For example, no safe was supposed to have yielded $60,000, but later it was estimated the gang stole around $6,000.

There were other things on Jesse's mind during this time; in between his robberies he was courting his sweetheart, Zerelda Mimms. The story of their love affair is more moving and romantic than anything concocted by Richard Fox's hack writers on the *Police Gazette*. In the spring of 1865 Jesse was wounded while surrendering with his guerrilla band under a white flag. He escaped by shooting one of the horses of the pursuing Yankee cavalrymen. After hiding all night in the woods, bathing his wound with creek water, he managed to drag himself to a field where a man was plowing. The farmer, a Confederate sympathizer, took him to friends who eventually delivered him to his mother in Rulo, Nebraska.

When his wound failed to heal, Jesse begged his mother to bring him back to Clay County to die.

Mrs. Samuel took her son in a wagon to a riverboat that brought them to Harlem, now North Kansas City, where Jesse's uncle, John Mimms, operated a boardinghouse. All summer and fall the young guerrilla fighter was nursed back to health by his pretty cousin, Zerelda Mimms, called Zee by her friends. Before Jesse left for Clay County he and Zee were betrothed.

In the years that followed, Jesse gradually became one of the most wanted men in the country. There had been the Iowa train robbery in July 1873, another at Gad's Hill the following year, the spectacular bank holdups, the savage shootout between the Pinkerton detectives and John and Jim Younger, which had resulted in John's death and the subsequent deaths of a Pinkerton operative and the local lawman he had hired as a guide. Earlier another Pinkerton detective, who had foolishly tried to masquerade as a farmhand looking for work, had also been killed.

In between robbing trains and banks Jesse had faithfully courted Zee, or Josie, as he sometimes called her. It makes a marvelous scene of this nationally hunted man, boots polished and hair trimmed, riding boldly up to his uncle's boardinghouse to spend the evening with Zee, his rifle near at hand and his holstered Navy Colt hidden under his jacket.

Zee is a shadowy figure in the saga of Jesse James. From the few interviews she gave after Jesse's death and from memoirs of those who knew her, she appeared to have been a realist who never viewed her sweetheart as a plumed knight who robbed the rich to help the poor. Zee undoubtedly believed in what a gravedigger would say many years later as he patted down the last shovel of dirt over Jesse's grave: "He was driven to it."

Until that last day in Saint Joseph, when Bob Ford pulled the trigger, Zee never stopped loving Jesse James.

They were finally married in the spring of 1874 in Kansas City and spent their honeymoon in Texas. One day in Galveston they met a friend Jesse knew worked for the Saint Louis *Dispatch;* on the streets of Galveston the nation's most wanted man dictated his own wedding announcement.

On June 9, 1874, the story appeared on page one of the *Dispatch* with the headline: "Captured." The subheads read: "The Celebrated Jesse W. James Taken at Last. His Captor a Woman, Young, Accomplished and Beautiful."

The reporter wrote that Jesse and Zee were waiting for a boat to take them to Mexico, then Vera Cruz, "and from there to take him into the interior to take him to a farm." The reporter also revealed that Frank James and Annie Ralston, daughter of a wealthy county farmer, whom Frank had recently married, were also honeymooning with them. Jesse's dictated wedding announcement reads:

"On the 22nd of April, 1874, I was married to Miss Zerelda Mimms of Kansas City at the home of a friend there. About fifty of our mutual friends were present for

Dick Liddil, one of Jesse's favorite riders, who turned informer and became the state's star witness against Frank James in his murder trial.

Kearney Mo
May 3rd 1911

My Dear Johns:
Your favor of the 27th duly to hand, contents noted. Well say, that at the present time, know of nothing that will prevent me from appearing in drama you have produced, at Suburban theater, the last week in August. I concur in the belief that it will be a success, from the fact, am positive there are many plays being produced at the present time, that are probably not as strong, that are money makers. As to my vigor and activity will let you be the judge, when we meet. Hope this meeting will be in the near future. I see no reason why you cannot run up here, any Saturday night spend Sunday with me, we can talk the details over, and come to amicable understanding, just what I am expected to do.

Any time after next Sunday will suit me to meet you at Kearney. You can leave St Louis via "Burlington" arriving here at 6:30 or 7 A.M. Why I suggest this is for the reason I can not very well leave here, for sometime. You of course know that my Mother died while enroute to Mo from our home in Oklahoma. It was a great loss to me. To feel the living presence of one whose loyalty was beautiful as hers, was a possession, few men ever realize or appreciate in this life. Am maintaining her old home just as she left as nearly as it is possible to do so. Am more than anxious that you should visit here, am positive you will not regret doing so. There is much history attached to this old home, so make it convenient to come, notify me just when you will be here, I am
Yours as Ever
Frank James

Rare, unpublished letter written by Frank James on May 3, 1911, on the death of his mother. After his dramatic surrender to Governor Thomas Crittenden in the fall of 1882, Frank was put on trial for murder but was acquitted. Richard D. Sinchak, who kindly permitted the publication of this letter, part of his large autograph collection, points out Frank had returned to the old James home in Clay County, where he wrote this letter.

the occasion and quite a celebrated Methodist minister performed the ceremony. We have been engaged for nine years and through good and evil report, and not withstanding the lies told about me and the crimes laid at my door, her devotion to me has never wavered for a moment. You can say that both of us married for love, and there cannot be any sort of a doubt about our marriage being a happy one."

Instead of farming in the "interior" of Vera Cruz, Jesse and Zee returned to Missouri. Two years later he led his men into Northfield, Minnesota, where the outraged citizens drove them off with rocks and bullets. Jesse and Frank escaped but the Youngers were captured and sent to Stillwater penitentiary for life terms.

The gang struck again at Blue Cut in Jackson County; this time the safe gave up only $200. But there was a new

Rare photograph of the Dalton brothers when they were cowboys on the Bar X Bar Ranch near what is now Pawnee, Oklahoma.

The members of the Dalton outlaw band dead in a street in Coffeyville, Kansas, after their disastrous bank raid on October 5, 1892.

and aggressive prosecutor now on the scene who vigorously hunted down the train robbers and began putting them in jail.

One by one Prosecutor William Wallace took down their statements and persuaded them to become state's witnesses. His biggest coup was when he talked Dick Liddil into surrendering and agreeing to become a witness against Jesse—whenever the bandit leader would be captured.

Then on Monday morning, April 3, 1882, came the news that not only shocked the state but also the nation: Jesse James had been killed by Bob Ford in the living room of the tiny clapboard house in Saint Joseph where Jesse had lived with Zee and their two children. His alias at the time was "Mr. Howard, a horse dealer."

The surviving Younger brothers were later released but only Cole returned to Missouri; Jim Younger had committed suicide over a frustrated love affair. Frank James, who had been acquitted of murder, died in 1916; Cole passed on the following year.

The Dalton Brothers next appeared, riding for a short time along the Oklahoma frontier, only to end in a blaze of gunfire when they attempted to hold up two banks at the same time in Coffeyville, Kansas, on Friday morning, October 5, 1892. Only Emmett Dalton survived his wounds. After spending some time in prison he was released, married his childhood sweetheart, and went to California where he became a successful contractor. He died in July 1937.

The Southwest also had its bandit leader, Sam Bass, who became part of American folklore. Charlie Siringo, author of one of the classics on cowboy life, described Bass as the "hero of more Texas cowboys than any other bad man."

Tradition pictures Sam as a smiling reckless young leader who remained true to his friends, was gallant with the ladies and free with his stolen gold. In brief, the traditional Robin Hood of the frontier. Behind the myth was an illiterate likable cowboy and teamster who had drifted into the "robbing business," as he called it, to get easy money without working too hard.

Sam and his gang first held up the Deadwood stage in the fall of 1876, then the following year turned to train robbery. They boarded the Union Pacific at Big Springs,

John Rollin Ridge, creator of the Joaquin Murieta legend.

Rare photograph of Tiburcio Vasquez, California's folklore bandit leader, who was executed March 19, 1875, in San Jose after he was granted his last request to inspect his own coffin.

Sam Bass and two of his riders, Jim Murphy on the left and Sebe Barnes on the right. Murphy turned informer and lured Bass into an ambush of Texas Rangers and local lawmen at Round Rock, Texas, in the summer of 1878.

Nebraska, cleaning the express safe of sixty thousand dollars in newly minted coins from the San Francisco mint. The passengers also "contributed" about four hundred dollars in cash along with jewelry and watches.

Sam and his men continued to hold up trains, mostly in Texas, until he was betrayed by Jim Murphy, one of his riders. In the summer of 1878, after an aimless tour of small Texas towns looking for an easy bank to hold up, Sam was lured into Round Rock where an ambush had been set up by Texas Rangers and local lawmen. He was cut down in the gunfire and died a few days later, calling out: "Let me go! . . . The world is bobbing around me."

California also had its legendary outlaw leaders but one, Joaquin Murieta, is fictitious. He was made up in 1854 by John Rollin Ridge (Yellow Bird), son of John Ridge, the Cherokee leader. His *Life and Adventures of Joaquin Murieta, Celebrated California Bandit* sold about seven thousand copies and Ridge, who had written the melodramatic book to pay his bills, assumed he would soon satisfy his creditors. However, when he went to collect his royalties he found the publisher had fled with the profits.

Five years later the California *Police Gazette* rewrote

his book and ran it in ten installments, illustrated by the California artist Charles Christian Nahl. From the series came another paperback and this time sales soared. During and after the Civil War, Ridge's original work was stolen, reworked, and published both in the United States and Europe. Finally the fictitious outlaw's story became history when Hubert Howe Bancroft, whose histories of California are still reference sources, incorporated Murieta into his *California Pastoral: 1769–1848* In 1936 Hollywood discovered the melodramatic tall tale of Murieta, and Warner Baxter played the bandit's role to entertain a nation slowly emerging from the Great Depression.

The other California bandit leader, Tiburcio Vasquez, was real and deadly. He was born in 1835 in Monterey and at fifteen was questioned in the stabbing of a man who died in a dance hall brawl. He turned to horse stealing and rustling and by twenty was in San Quentin. He escaped but soon returned to serve four years.

After his release Vasquez, a slender man who liked to dress like a dandy, formed a band that preyed on stagecoaches, gold camps, and ranches. In 1873 his raid on Tres Pine, Monterey County, misfired. He and his men rode out, their grain sacks bulging with money taken from the

Desolate Hole-in-the-Wall country, headquarters of the Wild Bunch, one of the last of the outlaw bands in the Wild West.

general store, leaving behind three dead men and a small boy brutally clubbed into unconsciousness. Vasquez was finally captured in May 1874 by a posse under Sheriff William Rowland of Los Angeles. He died on the gallows on March 19, 1875, in Santa Clara County. His final request was to see the coffin he had selected. After admiring the satin lining he exclaimed: "I can sleep here forever very well."

The last and largest outlaw band in the Wild West was the Wild Bunch riding out of Wyoming's Hole in the Wall, a barren, lonely valley bordered on all sides with towering red walls. The gang, which first turned to rustling, was born of a depression in the cattle country that followed the disastrous blizzard of 1886–1887. Cattle barons, determined to save their dwindling herds, struck back with killings and lynchings. On April 5, 1892, a cattleman's "army" of hired gunfighters "invaded" Johnson County, Wyoming, and the well-known "Johnson County War" took place between the mercenaries and a makeshift force of rustlers and homesteaders. The cattlemen's army finally surrendered to troops of the Sixth Cavalry from Fort McKinney, near Buffalo, who escorted them to the fort where they were charged with murder. After many court battles they were finally released in January 1893.

Aimless, jobless cowhands then began to drift into Hole in the Wall, fifty miles south of Buffalo and a day's hard ride to Casper.

One of the first rustling gangs was headed by George (Flatnose) Currie. After he was killed while stealing cattle, the leadership of the group was taken over by Harvey (Kid Curry) Logan, one of the most dangerous men on the Western frontier. Later Robert LeRoy Parker, known to the West as Butch Cassidy, joined forces with Kid Curry's band.

After several bank and train robberies, the gang began to fall apart from the increasing pressure of private and

railroad detectives and the improvement of manhunting techniques.

Cassidy, Harry Longbaugh, and Etta Place, an attractive prostitute, journeyed to New York in the spring of 1901 and then on to South America where they terrorized remote gold mines, trains, and banks. Etta returned to the United States to be operated on for appendicitis; Cassidy and the Sundance Kid were killed by a unit of the Bolivia cavalry after they refused to surrender in a small walled barrio in San Vincente.

Harry Longbaugh, alias the Sundance Kid, and Etta Place, photographed in New York City before they left for South America to introduce outlawry, Wild West style, to the pampas. The watch Etta is wearing was bought for her by Longbaugh and Butch Cassidy at Tiffany's while the trio was strolling up Fifth Avenue in 1901. At the time this photograph was taken, Cassidy had returned to the West to take part in the last train robbery staged by the Wild Bunch.

A Gallery of Rare Billy the Kid Photographs

FOR many years Robert N. Mullin, retired oil company executive, has researched the early life of Billy the Kid. He became a close friend and sometimes a collaborator with Colonel Maurice Garland Fulton, who had spent his whole life investigating the Lincoln County War. Mr. Mullin made several important discoveries in the life of America's most famous outlaw; locating and interviewing Chauncey Truesdell, Billy's classmate in Silver City, New Mexico; the Santa Fe marriage certificate of Billy's mother, Catherine, and William Antrim (assisted by

This is one of the rarest of photographs in the history of Western outlawry. It shows Henry McCarty Antrim, later Billy the Kid, America's immortal legend of the Wild West, as a small boy in Silver City, New Mexico Territory, where he grew up, attended the local school, and according to his teacher, Mary Richards, "was no more a problem than any other boy."

his daughter, Mrs. Frances Daseler), and a collection of extraordinary photographs depicting Billy as a young boy growing up in the mining camp of Silver City, New Mexico.

Mr. Mullin found Truesdell, then ninety-two, in Phoenix, Arizona. Although he was frail and permanently confined to bed, the pioneer's mind was still "surprisingly sharp." Among the papers Truesdell displayed was his Silver City public school report cards from 1871 to 1874, the years that Billy the Kid attended the school. As Truesdell told Mullin, everyone in Silver City knew Billy by the name Henry McCarty or Henry Antrim, after his mother married Antrim. Only when a photograph of the dead outlaw was published did the residents of Silver City realize the boy who loved to dance and sing and play end man in a minstrel show at Morrill's Theatre was the West's most celebrated gunfighter and outlaw.

The extremely rare photographs were obtained by Mr. Mullin from Lawrence E. Gay of Lordsburg, New Mexico, who had secured them from the estate of John B. Morrill, proprietor of the Morrill Opera House in Silver City where Billy as a boy loved to take part in amateur plays and minstrels. Billy lived in a log cabin on Main Street, "at the end of the bridge over the big ditch" with his mother, stepfather, and brother Joseph, or "Josie," as he was called. Joseph died in Denver on November 25, 1930. According to his death certificate he had been born about 1854, some five years before the accepted year when Billy was born. Catherine McCarty Antrim, as her neighbors recalled, was a "jolly Irish lady full of life and mischief" who took in boarders to help support her family. Mr. Mullin discovered Billy's boyhood in Silver City was typical of any youth growing up in a frontier mining camp. After his mother's death he went to live with Mr. and Mrs. Del Truesdell and his classmate Chauncey, and waited on tables at the Star Hotel operated by the Truesdells.

In September 1875 Billy was jailed after a kiddish prank in which he hid some laundry taken from a local Chinese man. He refused to reveal the name of the boy who had joined him in the joke and after three days in the Silver City jail escaped by climbing up the inside of a chimney. He fled to Arizona, then on to New Mexico Territory where he would soon become a legend of the Wild West.

The only known authenticated portrait of Catherine McCarty Antrim, mother of Billy the Kid. It was found among the effects of John B. Morrill, owner of the Morrill Opera House, Silver City, New Mexico Territory.

The wooden marker, long vanished, over the grave of Catherine McCarty Antrim, mother of Billy the Kid, who died September 16, 1874. The spelling of her given name and the date of her death were in error.

The Antrim log cabin where Billy grew up in Silver City, located on Main Street "at the end of the bridge over the big ditch."

Main Street, Silver City, New Mexico Territory, in the 1870s as a young Billy the Kid knew it. The street was washed away in the 1895 flood.

The interior of John Morrill's Opera House in Silver City where Billy the Kid worked as a property boy and played in amateur shows.

A typical cast on the stage of Morrill's Opera House in Silver City. Billy the Kid's teacher, Mary Richards, recalled how he loved to dance and sing in the amateur shows put on at the Opera House, sometimes taking the role of a girl. This cast is obviously doing Gilbert and Sullivan's *H.M.S. Pinafore*—note the admiral, sailors, ship's halyards, and the orchestra. At first it was believed Billy was playing a girl's role in this picture, but established facts prove that would have been impossible. *Pinafore* was not introduced until May 25, 1878, and by that time the Kid had killed his first man near Camp Grant, Arizona, and was a fugitive.

John Jones, who loaned Billy his horse after the young wanderer appeared at the Jones ranch. Johnny and Billy remained friends even after Jones joined the opposing side in the Lincoln County War, in which he was killed.

Barbara Jones, known as "Ma'am Jones" and "The Angel of the Pecos," who cared for the starving Billy the Kid when he staggered up to her ranch house near the Seven Rivers in October 1877 after Apaches had captured his partner, Tom O'Keefe, and their horses and supplies. The teen-age pair was crossing the northern section of the Guadalupe Mountains on their way to the Pecos Valley looking for work when Billy left his partner to fill their canteens. He hid when he heard shots and returned to find Apache signs and his partner, horses, guns, and supplies gone. The body of young O'Keefe was never found.

Billy the Kid

BILLY the Kid is America's immortal legend. The story of the smiling, slightly buck-toothed young desperado has been told countless times in novels, histories, ballads, and ballet. Curiously the truth about Billy is more romantic and thrilling than the distorted legends and myths.

His name was not William J. Bonney but Henry Mc-Carty and he was born in New York City, probably on November 23, 1859. There is no documentary evidence to substantiate this date supplied by Pat Garrett in his well-known biography of the young bandit whom he killed.

However, ample evidence to support the claim that the real name of Billy The Kid was Henry McCarty and that he was born in New York City can be found in this writer's *Authentic Wild West: The Gunfighters* (1976). Documents used included the application of Billy's widowed mother for Osage land in Kansas, now in the National Archives, listing her as "Mrs. Catherine McCarty." The civil marriage record of Catherine McCarty and William H. Antrim in the First Presbyterian Church of Sante Fe, names their witnesses as "Henry McCarty" and

his brother, "Joseph McCarty." Antrim's application for a Civil War pension describes his stepson's name as McCarty, whose father "McCarty died in New York City."

The superb research of W. E. Koop in his "Billy The Kid: Trail of a Kansas Legend" reveals that after the death of her husband, Catherine McCarty left New York City to live with her two young sons in Indianapolis. The 1868 City Directory has her living at 199 North East Street, a short distance from the home of Antrim. It was here that the Civil War veteran undoubtedly first fell in love with Billy's mother. In 1870 Catherine moved her brood to Wichita, Kansas. Land records disclose she owned and operated the City Laundry with young Henry and Joseph probably helping her with the washing. Antrim, the records show, lived nearby.

After she was stricken with tuberculosis, Catherine took her sons to the mining camp of Silver City, New Mexico Territory, where she operated a boardinghouse and finally married her presistent suitor, Antrim, in 1873.

Following the death of his mother and a minor brush

Applicant's Affidavit.

U. S. Land Office, Augusta, Ks *March 2.8" 1871* Personally appeared before me, **Andrew Akin,** Register of the Land Office at Augusta, Kansas, *Catherine McCarty* of *Sedgwick* County, State of Kansas, who, upon his oath, says: That he is an applicant to purchase the *North West* quarter of Section *12* in Township No *27* south, of Range *1* east, under the provisions of the Joint Resolution of Congress, approved April 10, 1869, for the disposal of the lands ceded by the Osage Indians, under the 2d Article of the Treaty of September 29, 1865; that he is *a citizen the Head of a family* and a citizen of the United States; and that he has not settled upon and improved said land to sell the same on speculation, but in good faith to appropriate it to his own exclusive use or benefit; and that he has not, directly or indirectly, made any agreement or contract, in any way or manner, with any person or persons whatsoever, by which the title which he may acquire from the government of the United States should inure, in whole or in part, to the benefit of any person except himself.

Witness *A Lainsworth* *Catherine X McCarty* *her Mark*

Sworn to and subscribed the day and year above written.

Andrew Akin Register.

This application filed by Catherine McCarty, mother of Billy the Kid, for purchase of Osage land helps to prove the Kid's real name was McCarty and not Bonney. Her mark also reveals she was illiterate.

Wolleweber and Mrs. J. Peak. Also, March 1st
1873. Mr. William H. Antrim and Mrs. Catherine
McCarty, both of Santa Fé, New Mexico.
Witnesses, Harvy Edwards, Henry McCarty.
Joseph McCarty, Mrs. A. R. McFarland

April 1st 1873.

And Miss Katie McFarland. Given under my
hand and seal, the day and date above written.
D. F. McFarland,
Pastor of Pres. Church Santa Fe
New Mexico.

The marriage record of Billy's mother to William Antrim in March 1873 again
establishes Billy's name as Henry McCarty. His brother, Joseph, listed with Billy
as a witness, died in Denver during the Depression.

with the law, Billy left for Camp Grant, Arizona, where
he killed his first man, F. (Windy) Cahill, the community's bullying blacksmith. Billy was identified by the
Arizona *Citizen* as "Henry Antrim, alias The Kid." A
fugitive from a murder charge, he fled into New Mexico,
narrowly escaping torture and death at the hands of a
marauding band of Apaches who killed his partner.

Billy entered Lincoln County, New Mexico, hired as a
cowboy by a young Englishman, John H. Tunstall, whom
Billy accepted as a father image. The cultured rancher
gave Billy a rifle, a horse, and, more important, friendship.

The savage Lincoln County War that erupted shortly
after the Kid appeared was not a range war between the
powerful forces of John S. Chisum and the smaller ranchers as some writers have depicted, but rather was brought
about by the incredible official corruption existing at the
time in the territory. Tunstall, a brave but rather foolish
man, had joined forces with Alexander McSween, a lawyer, to open a general store to fight the political and commercial monopoly established by the firms of J. J. Dolan
and L. G. Murphy, who had strong ties to the Santa Fe
Ring, a group of corrupt government officials who controlled the territory of New Mexico. Lincoln County's
sheriff, William Brady, once admitted to McSween in a
moment of frustration: "Murphy controls me."

Tension between the two camps increased during the
winter of 1877 and 1878 when the Dolan-Murphy forces,
aided by the Santa Fe Ring, instituted legal proceedings
against McSween.

Billy the Kid at the time was a lighthearted youngster
who laughed a lot, loved to dance, and was popular with
the girls at neighborhood dances. But his friends on the
Tunstall ranch also noticed that his pale blue eyes could
suddenly become cold and hostile when strangers approached the Tunstall spread or when he escorted his employer on the long ride to Lincoln and the Tunstall store.
He had astounded many with his uncanny skill with a
six-shooter.

In February 1878 a band of hired guns caught Billy
and several other cowboys on a lonely trail as they accompanied Tunstall to Lincoln. Billy and the others rode hard
for a group of rocks, as Billy later explained, "to stand
them off," but when they arrived they were shocked to
find their employer had decided to remain behind and
attempt to reason with the gang. Within minutes Billy
and the others watched as Tunstall was cold-bloodedly
shot down.

Tunstall was buried in Lincoln with Billy vowing to kill
every man in that raiding party.

The scene now shifts to Washington for the beginning
of a strange and little-known chapter in the saga of Billy
the Kid. It takes place in the Oval Office of the White
House where Carl Schurz, Lincoln's friend and Secretary
of the Interior, is pleading with President Hayes for permission to send an agent into Lincoln County to uncover
evidence of the widespread official corruption and to obtain eyewitness testimony to the murder of John Tunstall.

Hayes was well acquainted with the murder. As Schurz

talked, he may have recalled the chilling visit of Sir Edward Thornton, Great Britain's Minister to the United States, who demanded that Tunstall's murderer be brought to justice. Earlier John Partridge Tunstall, father of the slain rancher, had appealed directly to his friend, the Marquis of Salisbury in the Foreign Office, asking that his personal letter to Thornton be delivered immediately. In his letter Tunstall insisted that justice be done in the case of his murdered son.

After he received Tunstall's letter, Thornton held a conference with Secretary of State William M. Evarts who in turn pressured the Department of Justice; the promise was made that a "thorough inquiry into the murder" would be conducted by the Territory's District Attorney Thomas Benton Catron. What Evarts did not know at the time was that Catron was a member of the Santa Fe Ring; soon he would become the bitterest enemy of Billy.

The slow-moving international machinery had little effect on the Lincoln County War where survival depended on a man's courage and skill with a gun and not silk-hat diplomacy. Mexican sheepherders were murdered and their herds scattered. Bands of hired guns swept across the county, looting, burning, and killing; one of their victims was a fourteen-year-old boy.

In Washington Hayes quickly agreed with Schurz's suggestion and approved his Secretary of Interior's selection of Frank Warner Angel, a young Jersey City, New Jersey, lawyer.

What is known of Angel is buried in the crumbling files of a Jersey City newspaper but the mounds of documents in the National Archives attest to his personal courage, fierce devotion to the law, and a hatred of official corruption that would last a lifetime.

— I was met by every opposition possible by the United States civil officials and every obstacle thrown in my way by them to prevent a full and complete examination —

An excerpt from the final report of Frank Warner Angel to President Hayes, pointing out the "opposition" he faced in New Mexico while trying to uncover evidence of official corruption as an agent of the White House. At least one prominent rancher in Lincoln County predicted to Hayes that Angel would be murdered before he concluded his investigation.

Excerpt from the statement given to Frank Warner Angel by Godfrey Gauss, cook at the Tunstall ranch, describing how the band of gunmen hired by the Dolan-Murphy forces appeared at the Tunstall ranch. He lists Billy the Kid as present at the time. Gauss would later witness the escape of Billy the Kid from the Lincoln Jail.

The posse was composed of Billy Mathews, George Hindman John Hurley, Jessie Evans, Frank Baker, Jack Long "alias" "Rivers," & George Davis, + O.L. Roberts There was at the Ranch with me, R. A. Widenman R. M. Brewer, John Middleton William Bowey, & F. T. Waite, + McCloskey As the posse approach Mr Widenman went out and called on them to stop, and for Mathews to came over alone, which he did and commenced reading a paper & said he came to attach McSweens property,

Alexander McSween, who, with John Tunstall, led the opposition in Lincoln County against the corrupt Dolan-Murphy forces. He was shot and killed by hired gunmen while fleeing from his burning home in Lincoln in July 1878 with Billy the Kid.

Angel undoubtedly knew the gentle horses who drew the proper carriages and peddlers' carts of his native Brooklyn and Jersey City but certainly he was not prepared for the vast, lonely Lincoln County, where it took a day's ride to travel from one end to the other of John Chisum's ranch; where horses and bouncing buckboards were the only transportation, and a celluloid collar and necktie were seen only at weddings and funerals.

The young lawyer settled down in Lincoln and began the extremely dangerous mission of seeking out and obtaining handwritten eyewitness affidavits to the Tunstall murder.

One day he was approached by a slender young cowboy with slightly protruding teeth who asked if he was the man from Washington looking for eyewitness statements to the Englishman's murder. When Angel warily admitted he was that man, the cowboy offered to give him one. A delighted Angel quickly accepted the offer and Billy the Kid signed the affidavit with his favorite nom de plume of William J. Bonney.

Alexander McSween, the Lincoln lawyer, friend of the Kid and Tunstall, was also helping Angel. As he wrote to the senior Tunstall in June 1878: "We have succeeded in getting to U.S. government to appoint and send out here a gentleman from New York to inquire about the murder of John. For the past week or ten days I have been busy taking testimony."

Robert Adolph Widenmann, another friend of Tunstall, was also working with Angel and the Kid to seek out and persuade the uneasy eyewitnesses to the murder to sign Angel's affidavits.

All that summer and early fall of 1878, McSween, Widenmann, and Billy the Kid helped Angel gather the statements—even from members of the gang accused of the murder.

Montague R. Leverson, a naturalized Englishman from Colorado, who had ranching interests in New Mexico and was an outspoken enemy of the Santa Fe Ring, wrote to President Hayes on June 28, 1878, warning him that plans were being made to kill Angel.

One wonders what Angel really meant when he cautiously wrote to Schurz that he had met "every opposition by the United States Civil officials and every obstacle was thrown in my way to prevent a full and complete investigation."

Leverson again wrote Hayes from his Colorado ranch, praising Angel's work and describing the Santa Fe Ring as a "misrule—a misrule to which that of [Boss] Tweed in New York was Justice and truth by comparison. . . . There is not one of the citizens who feels that if the Santa Fe Ring fails to buy up Mr. Angel—which is my belief that they will certainly fail to do so—they will murder him to prevent his report from reaching Washington."

The affidavits of Billy the Kid and others given to Angel give a stark description of the volatile county ready to explode and the grim scene on the lonely trail when the trustful Tunstall smilingly faced the thirteen killers riding toward him minutes before they blew out his brains, even killing his horse. One rancher told Angel:

"They [Murphy & Co.] intimidated crushed and oppressed people who were obliged to do business with them. They were a gigantic monopoly. They were reported to control the courts. The present troubles [The Lincoln County Wars] are the result of their tyranny and determination to put down competition in business."

Angel returned East, gave President Hayes an oral report, filed and numbered his more than three hundred pages of affidavits, then wrote an explosive final report for Schurz and Hayes, detailing the crime and official corruption in New Mexico. As a result Governor Samuel Beach Axtell was removed from office, a national scandal at the time, and Civil War hero Lew Wallace was appointed in his place.

Pat Garrett, sheriff of Lincoln County, who killed Billy the Kid.

While the political maneuvering was going on in Washington, Billy the Kid and his followers had ridden into Lincoln to join forces with McSween. A band of wanted men, killers, and rustlers, employed by the Murphy faction with the blessing of the Santa Fe Ring, began a siege of the McSween house.

For an unbelievable nine days and nights both sides traded shots until Colonel Nathan Augustus Dudley, a veteran of the Civil War and Indian attacks, appeared in Lincoln leading thirty troopers of the Ninth Cavalry armed with a Gatling gun. Dudley warned McSween he would level his house if his men were fired upon, and then ringed the McSween dwelling with his troopers. McSween protested but Dudley, hard drinking and belligerent and friendly to the powerful Santa Fe Ring, refused to listen. In the end Billy gathered his men about him, forced Mrs. McSween and her children to leave, then led the small group into a run from the house which had been put to the torch.

McSween was killed but Billy and some of his men made the river and escaped. He was now "on the dodge" from the law.

In Washington President Hayes said goodbye to Wallace after Angel had advised the newly appointed governor to seek out the Kid for advice and information.

On Monday night March 17—Saint Patrick's Day—in 1879 Wallace met Billy in one of the strangest scenes in Western history. In a lonely cabin near Lincoln, Wallace, friend of the martyred Lincoln, war hero, and astute politician, sat down with the young orphan and gunfighter to discuss the best way to bring peace to Lincoln County. Before the first meeting ended Wallace had persuaded Billy to become a witness before a federal grand jury and had received from the young outlaw a long statement naming names, revealing corruption and how rustling was taking place in the county.

Wallace returned to the Santa Fe Palace, not only to review Billy's statement but also to write one of the last chapters of his novel—*Ben Hur*.

Wallace, who had promised Billy amnesty, later proclaimed amnesty to all who would surrender.

For all his skill with a gun and cold-eyed courage, Billy was politically unsophisticated. He believed in the unbreakable frontier code that a man never goes back on his word. He trusted Wallace, first and always the politician, with disastrous results.

In his diary Wallace made clear he wasn't interested in New Mexico's tragic internal affairs; he was interested in obtaining some "mineral interests," possibly running for the Senate if the Territory became a state and was waiting for a minister's appointment by the State Department, a post Hayes had promised when Wallace helped him into the White House.

When that appointment came as Minister to Turkey, Wallace hastily left the dusty governor's "palace" in Santa Fe; the promises he had made to the young gunfighter had been forgotten.

When the Kid arrived in court, expecting all charges against him to be dropped as Wallace had promised, he

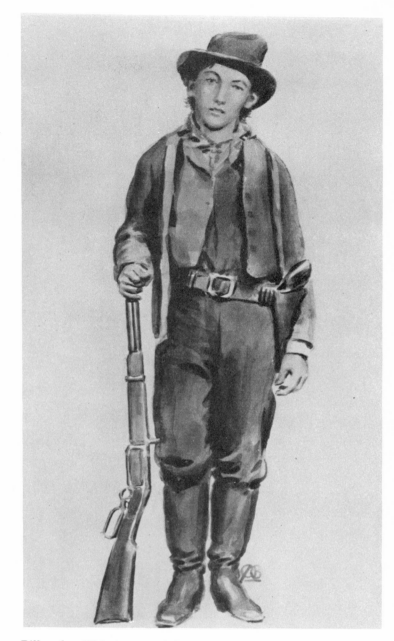

Billy the Kid, immortal legend of America's Wild West.

was stunned to discover District Attorney Catron eyeing him maliciously before he advanced to the bench and asked that Billy's case be transferred to his own county, in a change of venue. Catron knew that to hang Billy he had to try him outside Lincoln.

One can sense the bitterness, frustration, and rage in Billy's extant letters to Wallace pleading for the governor to remember his promises. When there was only silence Billy broke out of the makeshift jail in Lincoln and fled to the protection of his friends at Fort Sumner. He escaped capture in the Battle of White Oaks but finally at Stinking Springs the Kid's luck ran out. On December 19, 1880, Pat Garrett, who knew and liked the Kid, surrounded a small hut where Billy and his men were hiding out. The Kid's close friend Tom O'Folliard was killed, and he was forced to surrender.

On April 18, 1881, Billy again broke out of the Lincoln jail, this time killing the guards and returned to Fort Sumner. On a warm July night Garrett killed Billy at the

John Tunstall's store in Lincoln, New Mexico Territory, in the 1870s, as it was known to Billy the Kid. Later a peaked roof was added.

Fort where the Kid had almost fatalistically waited for their meeting. Billy had lived twenty-one years, seven months, and twenty-two days. Legend has him killing a man for every year of his life; the truth is three, possibly four.

He will always be the immortal legend of the Wild West.

Tom O'Folliard, Billy the Kid's closest friend, who was killed during the gunfight at Fort Sumner on December 19, 1880.

The knife and spurs that belonged to Billy the Kid. The spurs, brass with twenty rowels, were given to New Mexico's Governor Miguel A. Otero on December 30, 1880, while the Kid was in the Santa Fe jail. The bone-handled knife, 12¼″ long and made in Sheffield, England, was taken from the outlaw Chavez y Chavez, a member of the Silva gang, by Rafael Lucero, a mounted policeman of El Pino, New Mexico, when he captured the bandit. Chavez had won the knife from Billy in a horse race. Both the spurs and knife were donated to the library of the University of New Mexico by the Otero family. They are presently in the University's Thomas Bell Rare Book Room, Special Collections.

Kid Curry:
The Most Dangerous Man
in the Wild West

HE was no more than five foot seven inches tall with dark melancholy eyes, a thick black moustache, and black hair carefully parted to one side. At times he dressed like a banker on a holiday in double-buttoned conservative suit, winged collar, and tie. He came from a distinguished Kentucky family that had produced the eighth vice-president of the United States. His mother and father were hard-working farmers and everyone predicted that of all their sons, he was the most likable, had the most charisma, and, as they said in those days, "is the one to make his mark in life."

He intimately knew the rough trails, lonesome valleys, and rowdy cow towns of the Wild West but he liked the cities and enjoyed window shopping. He boasted that when he visited Denver he always bought his underwear in the "finest men's shops" and had them monogrammed. In a time when hard drinking was associated with range life, he preferred apricot brandy. His favorite weapon was a single-action Colt .44; on one occasion eyewitnesses claimed his draw was so fast they were sure he had shot through the pocket of his jacket but his gun was holstered on his hip.

TRAGEDY NEAR LANDUSKY

John Curry Shot by Jas. M. Winters and More Trouble Expected.

On Sunday evening Sheriff McLaughlin received the following telegram from Malta:

"James Winters shot John Curry. Winters is at John Brown's ranch and wishes to give himself up. Going after him you will need a posse.
R. W. GARLAND."

It has been rumored for some time past that trouble was brewing in the vicinity indicated, and it appears to have

An article from the *Fort Benton River Press*, February 3, 1896, giving the details of the killing of Johnny Curry, Kid Curry's younger brother, by Jim Winters, a neighboring rancher.

The death of Jim Winters, the rancher who was ambushed and killed by Kid Curry in revenge for Winters' killing his younger brother.

Winters' Wounds Were Fatal.

Sid Brockway, of Woody Island creek, came into Harlem last night from Landusky bringing the news that Jas Winters had died the evening before from the wounds received at the hands of an unknown assassin. He lived 14 hours after being shot. The wounds were both inflicted with 30 calibre soft nose bullets and were close to the navel an inch apart. The backbone was shattered by one of the bullets in passing out.

The story brought from Landusky is to the effect that there were three men cached in the brush at Winters' spring and that two of them did the shooting. Afterwards they mounted and rode up the creek, but were only seen for a short distance and were not pursued. The people of Harlem and most of those at Landusky are firmly convinced that the murder was the work of Harve Curry and his partners in the Wagner train robbery. Their theory is that after crossing the Missouri, immediately after the hold-up, they camped on one of the creeks flowing into the Musselshell from the east and took stock of their booty. Finding it to be a large sum they decided

The ranch house on the old Thornhill-Logan ranch south of Landusky in the Little Rockies country of Montana.

Rare photograph of miners' picnic, Landusky, Montana Territory, in Kid Curry's time.

He was soft spoken, courteous, fanatically loyal to friends, but never forgot an injury, insult, or threat. He had little respect for human life including his own. On the record he killed fifteen men. He was far from the legendary gunfighter who walked down the dusty lonely street of a cow town to face his opponent in a gun-for-gun duel. Once he waited all night like a frozen shadow to kill a man from ambush.

He attracted all types of women: frontier prostitutes, dance hall girls, and lonely housewives. A child recalled half a century later how he had stopped his horse, smiled down at her, and called out a greeting although a posse was gathering not far behind.

He was physically tough as pig iron and a tiger when cornered. An aging lawman said he still felt a chill when he remembered those sad dark eyes and the soft-spoken promise to kill him. A policeman broke his club over his head only to find himself hurled across a shattered barroom. Coatless, with a badly sprained ankle, he outwitted hundreds of possemen in subzero weather until half frozen and barely able to hobble he surrendered at gunpoint. But even then he refused to raise his hands.

"I have never raised my hands to any man," he said quietly, "and I don't intend to do so now. However I will hold them out in front of me and if that is not good enough you will have to kill me to take me."

He was the most dangerous man in the Wild West; his name was Harvey Logan but he was known to the frontier as Kid Curry.

For many years the early history of the Kid has been shrouded by myth and legend. However, with the publication of this writer's *The Authentic Wild West: The Gunfighters*, which contained the first detailed documented biography of Logan, a member of his family, who requested anonymity, revealed details of the gunfighter-outlaw's background.

Kid Curry came from an established Kentucky family that had links to the Lees of Virginia and produced Richard Merton Johnson, eighth vice-president of the United States. Johnson, a celebrated Kentucky lawyer, had been a congressman and senator for many years and a friend of Andrew Jackson. He served under Van Buren from 1838 to 1841.

On several occasions the Kid used his father's middle name of Neville as an alias.

There were six children, not four as tradition has claimed; five boys and a girl. The oldest, James, died in California. The girl, Eliza, married and raised a family. Her brothers were Henry, called Hank; Harvey, later to become Kid Curry; John and Louis, nicknamed Lonny (not Loney or Lonnie as many writers have spelled it). The boys had dark hair and black eyes, a heritage from their Cherokee grandmother.

In the 1870s, after the death of their parents, the family

Rare photograph of the Missouri River ferry south of Zortman, in Kid Curry's time. The boatman is Ruel Horner, early freighter and stagecoach driver out of Zortman and Landusky in the Little Rockies country.

split up, with James going to the West Coast, Eliza remaining in the South, while Hank, Harvey, Johnny, and Lonny left Rowan County, Kentucky, for Dodson, Missouri, to live with an aunt, Mrs. Elizabeth Lee.

Aunt Betty, as the Logan brothers affectionately called her, was the mother of two children, Elizabeth, or Lizzie, and Robert E. Lee, named after the illustrious Confederate general. Her husband, Hiram, had been permanently injured, either through an accident or from war wounds. He could be seen every day rocking silently on the porch while the Logan brothers and their cousin, Bob Lee, worked the farm.

The main house, the scene of a wild shootout in later years, was a two-story frame dwelling situated on the peak of a small hill between Dodson Road and Troost Avenue, about sixteen miles from Kansas City.

Neighbors recalled Harvey as quiet and reserved, Lonny as handsome, outgoing, and mischievous, Johnny as impulsive, a bully, and possessing an explosive temper. Hank, the oldest, "kept the boys in hand."

In their early teens the Logans and Bob Lee left Dodson "to go West and become cowboys." Hank and Harvey joined the Circle C outfit in Montana's beautiful Little Rockies country in the summer of 1884. John Ritch, historical writer for the Great Falls *Tribune* and a staff member of the Montana Historical Society, agreed with the memoirs of other Montana pioneer ranchmen that the

Logans worked hard for the first few years, punching cows in the summer and fall and spending the winters chopping firewood, which they sold for $8 a cord. Hank and Harvey, now called the Kid, were determined to some day own their own ranch.

There is no documentation on how the Logans gained the name of Curry. Legend has them stopping off in Wyoming on their way to Montana and meeting Flat Nose George Currie (also spelled Curry), then gaining a reputation as a rustler. The impressionable teen-age farm boys arrived after Wyoming's celebrated Johnson County War when cattle barons were the common enemy and rustlers were emerging as folklore heroes of a fading frontier. Again accepting legend, the Logans, in admiration for Currie or Curry, casually used his name in their travels and became known in Montana's history as the "Curry boys" or the "Curry gang," and Harvey Logan as "Harv Curry" and finally "Kid Curry."

After working some time as hands on the Circle C and selling firewood, Hank and Harvey pooled their savings with Jim Thornhill, another Circle C rider, to buy a ranch several miles south of a crossroads cow town and mining settlement, which one day would be named Landusky, after Powell (Pike) Landusky, one of the most colorful figures on the Montana frontier.

Landusky, a tall powerful man, left Missouri in 1872 to settle near the Last Chance mine. He soon won a reputa-

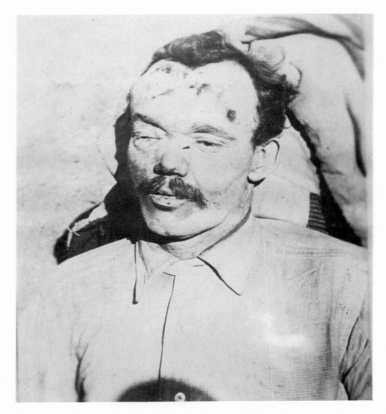

Flat Nose George Currie, or Curry. This photograph was taken shortly after Wyoming's celebrated rustler and train robber had been killed by a posse on April 17, 1900, while rustling cattle at Thompson, Utah.

tion as a fierce brawler; as Ritch wrote, even the toughest of miners went miles out of their way to avoid the Last Chance.

In 1935 Ritch remembered Landusky:

"I do not think Pike Landusky ever killed a white man. He just beat them with his fists so they didn't fight anymore. The true story of Pike Landusky would rival the best thriller Beadle ever published in his dime novel group."

In 1880 Landusky killed the wife of White Calf, a Blackfoot, while on a drunken spree. The warrior hunted him down and shot him in the face. The blast tore away part of Landusky's lower jaw. For days he lived on whiskey while his friends drove him overland in a wagon to the nearest physician. As the legend goes, the pain was so severe Pike tore away part of his dangling jawbone. When the wounds finally healed his face was a grotesque mask. As one pioneer recalled: "It was hard to tell how good looking he might have been."

In the 1880s Pike and Jake Harris, another colorful Montana frontiersman called Jew Jake, opened a combination saloon and general store in the settlement that had been used for years by ranchers and sheepmen driving their herds to the range between the Missouri and the Little Rockies and Bear Paw Mountains. Harris, whose leg had been amputated after a gunfight with the sheriff of Great Falls, walked with crutches but when he was "on the bar shift" he used only one crutch and kept a sawed-off No. 8 shotgun close at hand.

The settlement slowly developed until there were four

saloons, a hotel, a forty- by sixty-foot peeled log dance hall, a livery stable, and about twenty cabins. In 1894 the miners and stockmen of Chouteau County officially named the settlement Landusky in honor of Pike. It soon became a stopping-off place for fugitives "on the dodge," gunmen, rustlers, army deserters, along with respectable miners and ranchers. Harris expanded his stock and employed a gunman named Hogan to keep the peace in the rowdy saloon.

The Logans, Thornhill, and the other wild young cowhands soon adopted Landusky as their own. It became commonplace for them to ride in, whooping and yelling, shooting off their six-shooters and riddling the town's false fronts. When news arrived that the Logans were approaching, the townspeople cautiously stayed indoors, "letting the boys work off steam."

As one gambler described their visits:

"She [Landusky] sure was hot. I say hot. I could have gone out there in the street anywhere and swung a pint cup around and caught a quart of bullets in it."

The Logan-Thornhill ranch prospered. Judge Dudley, who claimed "to have known the Logan boys," told a Fort Benton newspaper in the 1890s that they had 15,000 head of stock, a large horse herd, and had erected some outbuildings in the short time they were working the ranch. Although Thornhill, the Logans, and their neighbor, Landusky, had been friendly, Hank had warned his brothers to avoid the fearsome Landusky "when he was liquored up."

After his wife died Landusky grew worse; only his partner, the one-legged Harris, could control him when he was on a spree, pounding the bar in the rough smoky saloon and challenging the world to a free-for-all with all rules barred.

At the Logan-Thornhill ranch Harvey was the hardest

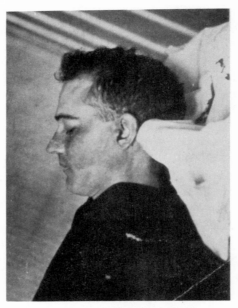

Lonny Logan, handsome and easy-going younger brother of Kid Curry who was killed by a posse outside his aunt's farmhouse in Dodson, Missouri, early on the morning of February 28, 1900.

Robert E. (Bob) Lee, Kid Curry's cousin who as a teen-ager accompanied the Logan brothers to the West "to become cowboys." Lee later became a partner with Lonny Logan in the Curry Bros. Club Saloon in Harlem, Montana Territory, and took part in the Wilcox, Wyoming, train robbery. He was captured by Pinkerton detectives in Cripple Creek, Colorado, and sentenced to a long term in prison. W. G. Walker, who took this picture of Lee when he was working as a gambler in Cheyenne, is noted for his rodeo and ranch life photographs.

worker of the clan; he, Hank, and Thornhill did most of the ranching chores; the two younger brothers had become problems. Johnny had started to wear a gun, practicing a fast draw and boasting that he would soon be better than any gunslinger on the frontier. Handsome, jovial Lonny had developed into a frontier beau who spent most of his time attending the weekly dances in Landusky's log dance hall and romancing the town's widows and the ranchers' daughters. Hank and Harvey warned both of them that guns and women were an explosive mixture but Johnny kept practicing at "marks" while Lonny continued to take the blushing ranchers' daughters and the eager widows for Sunday rides.

In the late 1880s Landusky married the "widow woman Mrs. Dessery, who had four lusty daughters." Two soon married while two remained at home. One, Elfie, or Elsie, as she was called, "became enamoured of Lonny." When Pike heard the rumors he rode to the Logan ranch and ordered Hank to warn his brother to leave his daughter alone or suffer the consequences. Hank urged Lonny to forget Elfie but Lonny only laughed off his fears.

The decade turned and it was 1890. The Logan ranch was prospering, members of the family had come from the South for a visit, and their sister married a man in Landusky but a shadow fell over the brothers—Hank developed tuberculosis and Johnny lost his right arm in a gunfight.

Both events had a devastating effect on Harvey Logan.

For over two years Johnny had swaggered about the county, bullying, taunting, and challenging cowboys and miners to a fight. Finally in July 1892 he selected a German miner as his favorite target. At Rocky Point "the

German," as the *Fort Benton River Press* described him, gave Johnny a savage beating. The battered young bully rode to the ranch, got his Winchester, and returned to Rocky Point.

Both met on the road. The German first killed Logan's horse. His next slug creased Johnny's right arm. Logan's bullet tore through the other man's hat. The German's return fire ripped open Johnny's right elbow shattering the bones. He waited a moment, then after he saw the boy was badly wounded, turned and rode off.

Logan staggered down the road, leaving behind a trail of blood. He fainted once; when he regained consciousness he walked and crawled until he reached a ranch house. He was taken in a wagon across the Little Rockies to the subagency where his arm was bandaged, then driven to Harlem and finally to Saint Clare's Hospital at Fort Benton. A week later, on July 20, 1892, surgeons amputated Johnny's arm between the elbow and shoulder.

When Johnny recovered, Hank brought his brother back to the ranch. The would-be gunfighter was now an embittered cripple, who carried a Winchester and a challenge whenever he rode into Landusky. Miners and ranchers avoided him as a killer.

Kid Curry dressed as a banker and his girl friend, Annie Rogers, in a photograph taken in Nashville in the fall of 1901. Annie, an attractive redhead, was arrested as Curry's accomplice shortly after this photograph was taken. She was later acquitted when the Kid swore she was not aware of his identity and he had told her his money came from gambling.

Finally when Hank's racking coughing spells began to bring up blood Harvey insisted he consult a doctor. At Fort Benton a surgeon told him he had advanced tuberculosis and his only hope for survival was to leave the Little Rockies country with its harsh winters for Arizona's dry hot climate. Hank kept delaying his trip until Harvey forced him to go with him to Arizona.

They had been at the hospital only a short time when Hank suffered a massive hemorrhage and died. Harvey's telegram to his brothers announcing Hank's death was carried to the ranch by a rider from Landusky who had received it from the driver of the Harlem-Landusky stage who in turn had picked it up from the telegraph office at Harlem, the nearest railhead.

Harvey buried Hank in Arizona and returned to the ranch; Thornhill, Johnny, and Lonny now accepted him as the boss.

Elfie Landusky, or Elsie, had developed into a buxom attractive girl, and once again Lonny began driving her about in a carriage and taking her to the weekly Landusky dances. Gossip about Elfie and Lonny reached Pike and once again he rode over to the Logan ranch, this time to warn and threaten Harvey. The one-armed Johnny wanted to challenge Pike to a gunfight but Harvey quietly told him and Lonny that one day he would settle things in his own fashion. He wanted nothing to interfere with the development of the ranch.

As Ritch wrote: "The countryside looked on and wondered how it would end. . . . Everyone felt that some day there would be a showdown and somebody would be hurt."

The feud finally exploded when Landusky charged Harvey and Lonny with changing cattle brands. The outraged brothers were taken into custody by the sheriff of Chouteau County who left them in Pike's custody while he looked for Thornhill.

Landusky chained both Logans to a log, then began "working on a quart." In between drinks he taunted both

The log kept by Lowell Spence, the Pinkerton detective who trailed Kid Curry for years. It was Spence who formally identified the outlaw in the Knoxville jail following his capture. Half a century later Spence told the writer of this book he still felt a chill when he recalled coming face to face with Kid Curry in his cell.

men, then as his drunken rage increased, he began beating one, then another. As the battered Harvey told him when they were finally released by the sheriff:

"I'll give you the damnest workin' over a man ever got and lived to tell about."

The sheriff took Harvey and Lonny to Fort Benton where friends at the Circle C ranch put up bail with the Logan herd as collateral. The charges were quickly dismissed and both Logans returned to the Little Rockies country. Ranchers, miners, and sheepmen held their breath and waited. Legend has an uneasy Landusky sending an emissary to Harvey asking to call off their feud but Logan sent the messenger back with a terse warning; the feud would end only when he had Pike on his knees begging for mercy.

In the fall of 1894 someone suggested a community Christmas party. After riders spread invitations across the lonely area, guests began to drift in from the badlands sixty miles away, from grassy valleys in the foothills, alkali flats, posts far down the river, from isolated ranches, and cabins deep in the gullies of the Little Rockies. On Christmas Eve a hundred guests assembled in Landusky, the largest gathering recorded in the Territory.

For two days and nights the guests danced, drank, ate, and attended a dance held at the new Logan barn. Guns were checked at the door.

On December 27 a light snow fell. About 10:30 A.M. Pike Landusky, wearing a heavy overcoat, walked into

Harvey Logan, Kid Curry of the Wild West, taken shortly after his capture by a posse outside of Knoxville in December 1901.

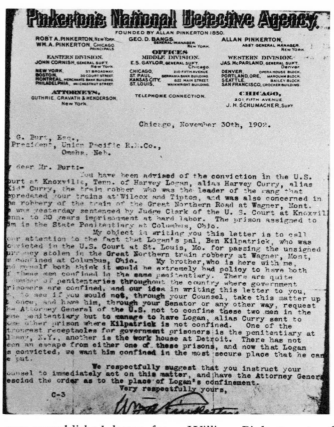

A rare unpublished letter from William Pinkerton to the president of the Union Pacific, urging him to use all his influence with the Attorney General not to put Curry and Ben Kilpatrick, the Tall Texan of the Wild Bunch, together in a federal penitentiary.

his saloon and ordered a drink. Behind the bar was Hogan, the hired gunman, and Jew Jake, his sawed-off shotgun close at hand. Several customers were drinking and discussing the Christmas party.

Suddenly the door opened. Thornhill, followed by Harvey and Lonny, walked in. Harvey unbuckled his gun belt and handed it to Thornhill, who stood with his back to the bar, gun in hand. Then Harvey slapped Pike on the shoulder. As he turned, Logan hit him in the face to send him sprawling. Thornhill and Lonny, also with a gun in his hand, warned Hogan, Harris, and the saloon's customers that this was a private fight and to stay out of it.

Pike, then about fifty years of age but still powerful, fought desperately. Eyewitnesses remembered it was a brutal frontier brawl with both men standing toe to toe exchanging blows. Once while rolling about on the floor Pike got on top of Harvey and tried to gouge his eyes out but the younger Logan finally got his arm free and hit Landusky a stunning blow to the side of his head.

Pike was finished. He weakly waved his hand and mumbled, "I'm all in, kid."

Harvey, his lungs working like bellows, slowly stood up. Pike fumbled in the pocket of his heavy coat for a handkerchief to wipe his bloody face but as he pulled out

Kid Curry's .45-caliber Colt revolver, which he dropped in the Knoxville saloon brawl. Eyewitnesses said he drew so fast they were sure he had fired from his jacket pocket instead of from his hip.

the handkerchief a gun appeared. Thornhill threw Harvey's six-shooter to him. The Kid fired twice and Landusky fell back dead, two bullets in his forehead.

In the best of Hollywood fashion Harvey, Thornhill, and Lonny backed out the door to jump into a wagon driven by Johnny. Patrons poured out into the street with Jake Harris hobbling after them and Hogan, that vaunted gunfighter, at his heels. Residents attracted by the shots began running to the saloon as the wagon bounced along the frozen road and out of town.

At the ranch Thornhill, Lonny, and Johnny argued with Harvey to surrender to the sheriff with a plea he had killed Landusky in self-defense but their brother refused to listen. There was only one thing to do, he said, pull out until things calmed down.

Harvey rode off to vanish in Wyoming's Hole-in-the-Wall where he joined Flat Nose George Currie's gang of rustlers and horse thieves. It was a case of environment shaping the man. In a few years the soft-spoken orphan from Missouri, who once had dreamed of becoming a cowboy and rancher, appeared on the outlaw trail as Kid Curry, rustler, train robber, outlaw, and the deadliest man in the Wild West.

There is little doubt that if Logan had surrendered to the sheriff he would not have been convicted of murder. Though Landusky had his friends and admirers, the majority of the residents of Chouteau County feared him. As Teddy Blue, cowboy-author of the well-known *We Pointed Them North*, wrote:

"Pike Landusky was a hard man and a fighter . . . a maniac when he got in one of his rages."

Harvey Logan was well liked by the ranchers who viewed him as a loyal friend and good neighbor. Had he remained he possibly would have gone on trial with Lonny and Thornhill who were later acquitted in Fort Benton by a judge who dismissed the state's case.

Johnny became more violent without Harvey's restraining influence. In March 1895 he went on trial in Fort Benton for assault with a deadly weapon but the jury disagreed and he was discharged with continued bail. He was retried in May, found guilty, and fined $50.

A short time later the wife of a nearby rancher left her home to live with him. When the cuckolded husband sold his outfit to James M. Winters and Abram Gill, his wife demanded that she also be paid for her share, but the new owners refused. Then one day Johnny, rifle in hand, rode to the ranch and warned Winters that if he didn't get off the ranch within ten days he would kill him. Winters laughed off the threats.

In the meantime a bench warrant had been issued in Fort Benton for Johnny's arrest in another assault case, and a deputy sheriff set out on the long journey for the ranch to arrest Logan.

The ten-day deadline passed. On a bright February morning in 1896 Johnny rode up to the ranch house and called out to Winters. When the rancher appeared Johnny fired and missed. Winters ran back into the house and emerged with a double-barreled shotgun. As the one-armed gunfighter tried to aim, Winters fired. The blast flung the boy off his horse; he was dead before he hit the ground.

Winters, who knew Lonny and Jim Thornhill would come looking for him with guns, immediately started out for Malta to surrender for the killing. About eight miles from the town his horse gave out and he sought refuge at the John Brown ranch. A rider rode to Malta where a telegram was sent to Sheriff McLaughlin in Fort Benton advising him that Winters had killed Johnny and wanted to surrender.

There was one significant last line:

"Going after him you will need a posse."

R. W. Garland, who sent the telegram from Malta, undoubtedly knew that Thornhill, Lonny, and their friends would try to kill Winters.

McLaughlin's undersheriff, Charles Howell, who knew the Logans, volunteered to bring back Winters. He gathered a small posse, rode to the Brown Ranch, and escorted Winters back to Fort Benton. The *Fort Benton River Press* reported there had been no confrontation "as none of the Curry element had put in an appearance."

After a brief trial Winters was acquitted on his self-defense plea. One witness testified that Winters had gone out to meet Johnny without carrying a gun. A shot was fired, then Winters rushed in to get his shotgun to return

Johnny's fire. The same witness told the jury he had been present when the one-armed gunfighter told Winters he had ten days in which to get off the ranch.

After he buried his brother, Lonny sold his share of the ranch to Jim Thornhill and moved to Harlem where he opened a saloon with his cousin, Bob Lee. Handsome, friendly Lonny was well liked and the Curry Bros. Club Saloon prospered. When Kid Curry heard the news of Johnny's death he sent word to Lonny that some day he would avenge their brother's death.

From stealing horses and rustling cattle Kid Curry and Flat Nose George Currie turned to bank and train robbery. In April 1897 the Kid killed Sheriff William Deane who foolishly rode up to the K-C Ranch on the Powder River where Curry had his headquarters to demand that the Kid surrender. On June 28 of the same year Curry led his men into Belle Fourche, South Dakota, to rob the Butte County bank. He ordered his gang to scatter but was himself cornered in Fergus County, Montana. The Deadwood jail couldn't hold him; he escaped after a few days.

When Butch Cassidy joined the Kid the gang expanded to become the Wild Bunch, one of the last and largest bands of outlaws in the fading days of the Wild West. The likable Cassidy became the publicized personality but Kid Curry was the brains, the planner, and a ferocious menace that made lawmen cautious about going after him.

A former wagon boss for the Circle C recalled he had counted eighty-six saddles in the yard of the Winters-Gill ranch where a posse stayed overnight when chasing the Kid and his men after a train robbery. The gang was camped on Thornhill Butte, their campfires visible for miles, but the posse never closed in on them.

On June 2, 1899, Kid Curry, Flat Nose George, and Elza Lay, a Wild Bunch rider, held up the Union Pacific's Overland Flyer near Wilcox, Wyoming; Lonny Logan and Bob Lee temporarily left their saloon in Montana to act as horse holders. A special Union Pacific train carrying a sheriff's posse and ten railroad detectives picked up the gang's trail outside Casper, but walked into an ambush at Casper Creek. Sheriff Josiah Hazen of Converse County was shot in the stomach as he bent over to examine hoofprints; an intense rifle and handgun fire pinned down the other possemen. Hazen died the following morning. Kid Curry is believed to have fired the shot that killed Hazen.

The generally reliable *History of Natrona County, Wyoming, 1888–1922*, written by Alfred J. Mokler, has a posse of "United States Marshals, ten deputies, ten picked men from the Buffalo Militia, a dozen railroad detectives, half a dozen bloodhounds and at least a hundred men," joining in the manhunt, but Kid Curry led his men to Hole-in-the-Wall where they picked up fresh horses and provisions. Later they met Butch Cassidy and continued on to Arizona, then crossed the border to Alma, New Mexico, where the members of the Wild Bunch were always welcomed as cowhands on the WS ranch.

They had passed through some of the wildest and most picturesque country in the West—canyons, deserts, and rivers—in the season's hottest period. It was one of the longest rides the Wild Bunch had ever made. They arrived so quickly in New Mexico some lawmen refused to believe Kid Curry and his men had held up the train. Ironically the WS had been suffering from rustling; when the Kid and his riders appeared the cattle stealing abruptly ended.

Working as cowhands on the WS, the gang drove a herd across a desert to a railhead three hundred away without losing a head. Other outlaws who worked on the ranch included Tom "Blackjack" Ketchum and his brother, Sam; Blackjack would soon die on the gallows and Sam from gunshot wounds following a gun battle with a posse.

Lonny was next of the brothers to die by the gun. Detectives had traced some of the bills taken in the Wilcox train robbery to him. When he was warned lawmen were on their way to Harlem, Lonny and Bob Lee quickly sold their saloon and left town. Bob Lee pushed on to the Colorado mining towns, finally stopping at Cripple Creek where he became a gambler. Lonny, who had always preferred playing the fiddle for the Harlem dances or courting the widows and daughters of ranchers rather than robbing trains, fled to Dodson, Missouri, where he joined Aunt Betty and his cousin Lizzie in the weatherbeaten farmhouse.

Mrs. Lee, "an estimable little old lady who had no knowledge of the sort of life her nephew led," as the *Kansas City Post* later reported, gave Lonny a prodigal's return. For six weeks he hid out in the house on the top of the small hill. Finally, either through necessity, carelessness, or overconfidence, he cashed one of the stolen bank notes. Routine banking procedures in Kansas City discovered the bill and traced it to Dodson. Pinkerton operatives joined by local police surrounded the Lee farmhouse about 6:00 A.M. on February 28, 1900.

Lonny, who it is believed wanted to draw fire away from the house, ran out. Although he was wearing a heavy overcoat and the snow was deep, he tried to reach a strip of woods. When the first warning shots whistled about him, he turned and began firing. After a brief savage shootout he suddenly jumped up from behind a small mound to advance on the posse, his six-shooter blazing.

In moments he was riddled and fell dead in the snow.

A few weeks later Bob Lee was captured in Cripple Creek; a jury found him guilty of train robbery and he was sentenced to twenty years in the Wyoming Penitentiary.

Kid Curry was now the last of the four brothers who had come to the Montana frontier to fulfill their romantic dreams of becoming cowboys. The climax to his career in outlawry took place on the morning of July 3, 1901, when the Wild Bunch riders held up the Great Northern near Wagner, Montana. They blew apart the express box with charges of Hercules black powder and escaped with an amount variously described as $75,000, $65,000, and

Sketch in the *Knoxville Sentinel* based on eye-witness accounts of the saloon brawl in which Kid Curry beat up two young thugs attempting to rob him, shot his way past two patrolmen, and escaped only to be captured later by a posse.

Sketch based on an eyewitness account of the suicide of Kid Curry after he had been trapped by a posse in a Colorado canyon following a train robbery.

$41,000. The latter is believed to be correct.

After the robbery the Wild Bunch scattered for the last time. Cassidy urged Logan to accompany him, the Sundance Kid, and Etta Place to New York, and then on to South America, but Kid Curry refused. He had one more mission to accomplish in Montana before he left—that was to kill Jim Winters.

He arrived at the Winters-Gill ranch in the early hours of July 25. Tracks later showed that he had a companion. They patiently waited all night. When the first streaks of dawn appeared in the east one man, undoubtedly Kid Curry, placed his rifle over the top bar of a pigpen and looked down the barrel. The sun slowly rose, finally the back door of the ranch house opened, and Winters stepped out, a tin plate and toothbrush in his hand. As he bent over to brush his teeth, Kid Curry slowly and very carefully squeezed the trigger. Two shots shattered the morning stillness; Winters fell over, with two .30-caliber soft-nosed bullets an inch apart in his stomach.

Winters' partner, Abram Gill, had left the night before for Fort Benton but there were six visitors, "pilgrims," as a frontier newspaper described them, staying at the ranch. Whether they were friends or strangers just staying overnight has never been made clear. When two ran out on the back porch they were driven back into the house by rifle fire. One later testified he saw a man he could not identify leap onto his horse after a crouching run.

While Winters was made as comfortable as possible, two of the visitors rode for Landusky. A posse returned with them and began a futile search for the bushwackers as Winters was taken in a wagon to the nearest physician in Harlem, sixty-six miles away. It was a harrowing journey for the dying rancher whose spine had been shattered. He died several hours after reaching Harlem.

The killing of Winters, denounced by the Fort Benton newspaper as the "most cold-blooded and cowardly crime to have been committed in Montana," was investigated by two deputies who brought back some empty rifle shells and disclosed there had been other attempts to ambush Winters and Gill. Lawmen quickly identified Kid Curry as Winters' assassin, pointing out he had crossed the Missouri after the Wagner train robbery, camped on one of the creeks flowing into the Musselshell from the east, then returned to the Little Rockies, perhaps not only to kill Winters but also to dig up a cache of bills from a previous train robbery.

However, there were no eyewitnesses to the shooting and a coroner's jury sitting in Fort Benton on July 27, 1901, handed up a verdict that Winters had been killed by persons unknown. The murder of the cattleman and the Wagner train robbery raised the rewards for Kid Curry, dead or alive, to $10,500, and for the first time a deputy sheriff was stationed at Landusky to "exercise a salutary influence on the criminal element which has lately come to the surface in northern Montana."

In the fall of 1901 Kid Curry began a leisurely tour of the South with Annie Rogers, a young attractive redheaded prostitute from San Antonio. Curiously the Kid didn't fear cameras and they had their portrait taken in Nashville. Logan, by now the most wanted man in the country, looked sadly into the camera while Annie, slightly taller, lovingly draped her arm around his shoulder. They could have been a banker and his wife on a holiday.

Annie, cashing one of the forged bills, was arrested in Nashville but the Kid escaped to Knoxville. As he later said, he liked the city with its glittering Christmas windows and decided to stay for a few weeks. He selected Ike Jones' combination pool hall at Central and Commerce streets as his headquarters. As a mark of his affluence, the Kid drank nothing but apricot brandy and smoked only the best cigars. The bartender judged him to be a drummer "passing through."

The Kid's dark streak of violence, hidden behind his soft voice and mild manner, suddenly exploded when two young thugs tried to rob him while he was playing pool. He had flung one across the table and was strangling another when two local policemen burst into the saloon. When they couldn't break the Kid's grip on the young thug's throat, one broke his club over Curry's head. The Kid dropped the gasping robber and turned to the patrolmen. When they rushed toward him he shot one in a draw so fast the saloon's patrons assumed he had fired a gun hidden in his jacket pocket, kicked open a rear door, and jumped into a deep railroad cut.

He badly sprained his ankle but in a hobbling gait managed to reach some woods and disappeared. Battered, bleeding, and coatless in the subzero weather, the Kid dodged the posses for three days until he was finally captured by three merchants from Jefferson City.

When one ordered him to put up his hands he replied:

"I have never raised my hands for any man. But I will hold them out in front of me. If you're not satisfied with that you will have to kill me to take me."

The civilian posse accepted his proposal and Kid Curry was brought to the Knoxville jail.

He became an overnight celebrity with crowds numbering in the thousands, waiting in line to pass before his cell to say hello or reach in and shake his hand. After countless postponements and delays he was finally tried, convicted on all counts, and sentenced to a long term in the federal penitentiary.

A few days before he was to be transferred Logan, using the wire from his cell broom, lassoed a jailer, took his gun, and escaped on the sheriff's best horse. Somehow he managed to travel across a wild mountainous section known as Jeffrey's Hell, months later he appeared in a Denver hotel carrying a valise that a bellboy said was filled with bills. When the police arrived the Kid had disappeared.

Some legends have Kid Curry fleeing back to the Little Rockies or joining Butch Cassidy and the Sundance Kid in South America. Neither are true. On June 7, 1904, leading a small band, he held up the Denver & Rio Grande Railroad at Parachute, Colorado. In a subsequent gun battle with a posse, one man was hit in a gully near Rifle. Possemen heard his companions call out and ask if he was hurt.

"I'm hard hit and going to cash in quick . . . you go on," was the reply.

At dawn the posse rushed the gully to find a dead man, six-shooter in hand, and a bullet in his head. His companions had made their escape during the night. The corpse was identified as Tap Duncan, who had worked as a cowboy on nearby ranches.

A sheriff, hoping to collect a reward, sent a series of photographs of the dead man to the Pinkerton's National Detective Agency in Chicago where William Pinkerton told his staff he was sure the corpse could be that of Kid Curry. Lowell Spence, a Pinkerton operative who had hunted the Kid for years, was assigned to exhume and photograph the body and fully establish that the dead man found in the gully was Kid Curry.

As Spence told this writer many years ago, he had the body exhumed on July 16, 1904. The corpse was badly decomposed but Spence recorded as many scars and bullet wounds as possible. He brought the sheriff's criminal photographs and his own physical descriptions to Knoxville and showed them to the sheriff, the jailers who had spent two years guarding Kid Curry, the United States Attorney who had prosecuted him, the judge, defense counsel, and members of the jury that had convicted Curry. All agreed the man buried as Tap Duncan was Kid Curry.

"I knew that man and hunted him for years," Spence said. "There was never any question in my mind that the dead man was the Kid. I am sure he took his own life in the gully because he could not face spending the rest of his life behind bars. I also think it is significant that after the Parachute train robbery we never again heard of Kid Curry."

Legends never die and in the Little Rockies country the few remaining old men who knew Kid Curry when he and his brothers first rode in looking for work as cowboys will always insist that after his escape from Knoxville the Kid lived out his life as a rancher in Chile, a stockman in Washington, a horse dealer in Wyoming who made frequent trips back to the Little Rockies to visit old friends who would be drawn and quartered before they revealed his identity.

However, one of the principal actors in the Kid Curry legend *did* actually reappear. Elfie Landusky as a spry old lady of seventy-eight, accompanied by a sister, paid a visit to the Little Rockies in November 1958. A party was given for them and she recalled the old days on the frontier when a handsome, laughing young cowboy named Lonny would come to take her to the Landusky dances or for a ride in a rented carriage.

The Restless Ghost of Butch Cassidy

A FEW days after Jesse James had been killed by Bob Ford in Saint Joseph, Missouri, a local newspaper declared that Jesse had not been killed, that there was a stranger in the coffin of Sidenfaden's Undertaking Parlor and Jesse was gathering a new band to soon prove to the world he was alive and well. This ridiculous statement was made despite the identification of the body of the legendary bandit leader by men who had ridden with him in the guerrillas, his wife, Zerelda, his mother, and law enforcement officials who had hunted him for years.

Down through the years other Jesse Jameses appeared, the last one in 1948 accompanied by a blare of national headlines. This time he said his name was J. Frank Dalton, age one hundred and one. Homer Croy, the Western writer, asked the bearded old man what happened to his left hand? The old man, who was living on whiskey and doughnuts, was startled until Croy explained that Jesse, as a boy, had shot off the tip of the third finger of his left hand but J. Frank Dalton had all his fingers!

Despite his foolish claim Dalton appeared at a number of shows and fairs. Al Jennings, the most overrated bandit in the history of the Wild West—his career lasted 109 days and his total loot was $60—met the old fellow in Oakland, California. As the Associated Press of July 3, 1948, reported, Jennings, his eyes brimming with tears, cried out: "It's him! It's Jesse!" There is no historical evidence that Jennings and the real Jesse James had ever met.

Now Butch Cassidy has been resurrected. His sister, Lula Parker Betenson—she was an infant when he left home—insists her brother was not killed in Bolivia but returned home in 1925 driving a Ford.

Matt McGuire's Trading Post on Wyoming's Wind River Reservation in the early 1930s, where historian Blanche Schroer, then bookkeeper of the firm, first met William Phillips, the Butch Cassidy impostor. As Mrs. Schroer recalled, it was a "comic opera" scene of Phillips skipping about the reservation informing anyone who would listen that he was the outlaw but not to disclose his identity because he could be "strung up." Here, eighty some years ago, the real Butch Cassidy bought supplies from J. K. Moore who built the post, the first at Fort Washakie.

Saint John's saloon, The Mint, on the main street of Lander, Wyoming, where the real Butch Cassidy played cards.

Among absurd statements Mrs. Betenson makes in her book *Butch Cassidy, My Brother* is that Charles Siringo and Frank Dimaio (she misspelled both names) were sent to South America to find and capture Cassidy. Nothing could be further from the truth. Shortly after the end of World War II this writer located Dimaio in a small hotel in Wilmington, Delaware, and was given the first of a series of interviews the gallant old detective ever granted. He had a veteran policeman's mind, and his recollections of how he located Cassidy, the Sundance Kid, and Etta Place in Argentina were clear, precise, and supported by his original handwritten notes, maps, and posters he had printed in Spanish and had distributed up and down the South American coast to shipping offices, banks, police, army posts, and to small but closely knit American colonies.

Dimaio described in detail how he had located the trio in a homesteading ranch at Cholilo, Province of Chubut, District 16 de Octubre, their bank account in the River Platte Bank in Buenos Aires, and how he was prevented by the rainy season from entering the jungle with a company of soldiers to storm the ranch.

Percy Seibert, an official of the Concordia Tin Mines in Bolivia, also gave this writer exclusively all the information, maps, and photographs he had on the outlaws who

had worked for years under him at the mine and described how they died.

Seibert had never been interviewed before, nor did he talk to any other writer. Victor J. Hampton, who built the smelting ore plant at San Vincente, Bolivia, where the outlaws were killed, revealed to the writer details of how the outlaws died and supplied photographs of the Indian cemetery where they were buried and the walled barrio where they fought their last gun battle with a segment of the Bolivian army.

At no time were Siringo and Dimaio teamed up and sent to South America to hunt for Cassidy and the Sundance Kid. In fact Dimaio and Siringo never met. Dimaio's work as a detective for the Pinkerton's was confined to the investigation of major jewel thefts, confidence rackets, and the Mafia. He played a major part in the celebrated New Orleans Police Chief Hennessy murder by the Mafia on October 15, 1890.

Dimaio was assigned to the hunt for Cassidy, the Sundance Kid, and Etta Place only because he was in South America chasing an international jewel thief.

Siringo's work as the famous "cowboy-detective" was confined to the West, hunting down the riders of the Wild Bunch and later to the violent strikes in the minefields.

In recent years old cowboys who claimed to have rid-

The cabin on Trout Creek, seven miles from Fort Washakie, Wyoming, where guide Will Boyd gathered saddle horses and a supply wagon and set out with impostor William Phillips for "Cassidy's Cabin" in the mountains. When he neared the place Boyd "hung back" and let Phillips take the lead, but Phillips-Cassidy became confused and couldn't find the cabin.

den with the Wild Bunch or delivered messages and supplies to the gang have come forward with weird stories of having seen Cassidy in many parts of the country, getting on trains, drinking in saloons, walking down streets, visiting the weather-beaten old towns. If they claimed they were outlaws they were the most unwanted in the West; there are no telegrams, posters, or even mention of their names in the mass of correspondence between Western lawmen that I have examined down through the years.

Mrs. Betenson also charges in her book that in this author's *Desperate Men*, first published in 1949, Cassidy, the Sundance Kid, and Etta Place are named as participants in the Colorado train robbery with Harvey (Kid Curry) Logan in which Logan committed suicide. Nowhere is this ridiculous statement made.

As Dimaio revealed, Cassidy, the Sundance Kid, and Etta had arrived in New York City in February 1901 to stay at the boardinghouse of Mrs. Julia Taylor, 235 East 12th Street. During a shopping tour up Fifth Avenue the pair bought Etta a hundred dollar watch at Tiffany's. Later the Kid and Etta posed for photographs in the studio of DeYoung, a well-known Manhattan photographer; the Kid was dressed formally holding a top hat and Etta Place was dressed in a gown. This writer first published these photographs in *Desperate Men*, along with photographs

of Kid Curry and an attractive redhead, Annie Rogers, and Fanny Porter who ran the San Antonio bordello where the gang hid out.

Mrs. Betenson has Cassidy, the prodigal, telling her and their family that Percy Seibert identified two other Americans as himself and the Sundance Kid only to give the outlaw pair a chance to change their lives.

It makes a moving story with one important hitch: Seibert never identified the bodies of any outlaws, that task was done by Roberts, general manager of the Compania Aramayo, whose payroll Cassidy and the Kid had robbed on a lonely trail. Roberts, Seibert's friend, told both him and Victor Hampton the story at different times.

Seibert was asked shortly before he died how he would describe the stories of the return of Butch Cassidy. His reply was a terse "rubbish." This writer agrees.

Another version offered by the Cassidy-returned-home group has the outlaw living in the Northwest under the name of William Phillips, who became a businessman in Spokane, went bankrupt during the Depression, and died on a poor farm in 1937.

In April 1970, a man who claimed he was the "son" of the Sundance Kid wrote a lengthy letter to this writer from Dayton, Washington, expressing surprise at some of the never-before-published details in *The Wild Bunch*

Blanche Schroer, the Wyoming historian, who helped to shatter the myth that William Phillips, the Seattle businessman, could have been the outlaw Butch Cassidy.

(continuously in print since 1958). He also discussed the background of Etta Place and the last battle of Kid Curry, who committed suicide in a Colorado canyon when he was trapped with a gang following a train robbery.

He claimed he met Cassidy in Jackson, Wyoming, on July 4, 1935, and the outlaw told him, "Your father is still alive and is still looking for you."

Interest in the Cassidy/Phillips myth began to emerge following the 1972 death of a man in a hotel fire in Missoula, Montana. A year previously this same man had told

reporters he was the son of the Sundance Kid and had attended Cassidy's funeral in 1937 and that Cassidy's assumed name was William Phillips.

The first name of the man who died in the fire was "Robert"; the man who wrote to this writer signed a different first name and middle name.

It is amusing to speculate that two "sons" of the outlaw had themselves been hoodwinked by that pathetic fraud, William Phillips.

Cassidy was born in 1866. If he returned to the United States in 1925, as his sister asserts, he would have been fifty-nine. Phillips' followers have him appearing in Spokane in about 1910 when the outlaw would have been forty-four.

The factual material available on the life of Phillips certainly proves he was an amusing impostor. His widow wrote to Charles Kelly, author of *The Outlaw Trail*, the first full-length book on Cassidy, giving some details on the background of her husband, who she said was born in the East, not in Utah as was the real Cassidy. Phillips, she wrote, "did mural decorations in New York City for two or three years," and, as she stated flatly to Kelly, was *not* the outlaw.

Phillips' Michigan marriage license describes him as a "mechanical engineer" who lived in Des Moines; one Spokane city directory lists him as the second vice-president of a typewriter company. Later he became the head of a successful company manufacturing business machines. He was a prototype of Sinclair Lewis' Babbitt, a successful businessman of the 1920s who faithfully attended the meetings of the Elks and Masons. Another friend, who was "convinced" Phillips was Cassidy because he had said so, claimed he once displayed interior decoration work he supposedly had done in the state capitol building in Saint Paul, Minnesota.

Cassidy's education on the frontier was meager, undoubtedly consisting of what he was taught in the small

A rare photograph of William Boyd, the guide for William Phillips, the Butch Cassidy impostor, and Matt McGuire, Indian trader, to whom Phillips revealed in a comic opera scenario that he was Butch Cassidy. The photograph was taken on a hunting trip in the Saint Lawrence Basin, Wind River Reservation. *Left to right:* Fred Schroer, Sequoyah Fox, Indian Agency employee Will Boyd, Matt McGuire, and George N. Tunison, Omaha attorney for the Shoshone in their claim against the Arapaho.

local schoolhouse or in Sunday Bible class. As he later demonstrated, his only talents were confined to rustling cattle, stealing horses, and robbing banks and trains.

How then could an aging ex-outlaw, whose only business experience consisted of counting stolen bills or forging the names of bank officials to unsigned bank notes taken in train robberies, have gained the business acumen to establish and organize a successful company dealing with office equipment?

There is no mention in the memoirs of any members of his family, fellow cowboys, or the lawmen who hunted him that Cassidy possessed a talent for either sketching or drawing. One wonders how he suddenly became such an accomplished draftsman and artist that he was invited to decorate the capitol building of Minnesota?

Mrs. Betenson has made one remark the writer agrees with: Phillips was not her brother, Butch Cassidy.

The Cassidy-Phillips theory was also supported by the appearance of *The Search for Butch Cassidy* by Larry Pointer, a disjointed attempt to reconcile the errors in a manuscript Phillips left, supposedly his autobiography, although it was written in the third person. Pointer proudly revealed he had "proven" Phillips was Cassidy through the comparison by a handwriting expert of one letter from Phillips with a handwritten letter said to have been sent by the outlaw from South America to a friend in Utah. One wonders what proof there is to establish beyond any reasonable doubt that Cassidy actually wrote the letter? For example, is there an envelope with the Argentine postmark and date?

There is also a ring inscribed by Phillips to a woman who was reported to have been Cassidy's friend during his days as an outlaw. How does that establish Phillips was the outlaw? Pointer's frantic and at times amusing attempts to put together a case to prove that William Phillips was Butch Cassidy crumbles very quickly under the intent probing of a skillful historical investigator such as Blanche Schroer, a Wyoming writer and historian whose research proved that Sacajawea, a young Shoshone girl who accompanied Lewis and Clark on their historic journey across the West, was not buried on the Wind River Shoshone Reservation as had been claimed for many years.

Mrs. Schroer's father, Dr. A. Moore, first came to Fort Washakie to take over the Wind River Reservation hospital, and his daughter soon followed to become bookkeeper-clerk at McGuire's Trading Post at Fort Washakie, Wyoming. As Mrs. Schroer informed this writer:

"One hot afternoon in 1934, William Phillips came into the post and whispered to me and Mike Ryan, the butcher, that he was Butch Cassidy. He begged us not to reveal his secret or he would be strung up. For the next two days Phillips skipped about the reservation confiding *sotto voce* to many people that he was Butch Cassidy but was trying hard to keep it quiet. The performance was, in retrospect, very funny. Gilbert and Sullivan never dreamed up an operetta as wild as the Phillips scenario."

As Mrs. Schroer pointed out, Phillips curiously never visited the two people who had been very close to the real

Butch Cassidy—Alice Stagner Burnaugh and John Henry.

Mrs. Schroer recalls: "Alice Burnaugh with her husband, who was deceased at the time of Phillips' travels to Fremont County, had been in constant touch with Cassidy during the Owl Creek days. In fact Cassidy had spent the better part of two winters at their ranch on the Muddy. It was Butch, the budding outlaw, who had made the rough ride to Washakie for the doctor when Alice's first child was born. From the Burnaugh Ranch, Sheriff Stough once picked up Butch to question him on a horse rustling charge."

Frank Diamio, the detective who hunted Butch Cassidy, the Sundance Kid, and Etta Place in South America. This photograph was taken when Diamio was wearing what he called "my Mafia uniform." Diamio was an early expert on the Mafia and had played an important role in the murder investigation of New Orleans Police Chief Hennessy who was killed by Mafia gunmen before the turn of the century.

John Henry, another close friend of the real Butch Cassidy, was asked after Phillips' visit to the reservation if he had seen the newly risen outlaw and Henry told Mrs. Schroer:

"No, and if Butch Cassidy had ever returned to Lander or near it, he surely would have come to my place. He was the closest friend I ever had, so close that he stood up for me when I was married in Vernal, Utah. I saved his life over there after I warned him I had overheard two men who were waiting by the hitching rack telling how they planned to shoot him when he came for his horse. I went to the house, told Butch to saddle up a little race mare I owned and ride out of town in a hurry and I would go out and get his horse!"

Mrs. Schroer has carefully researched the movements

of Phillips and interviewed many pioneering ranchmen and Wyoming residents who intimately knew Cassidy and had seen Phillips. At one time Phillips visited a rancher in an attempt to get information on Cassidy but was stunned when the rancher recognized him as the same William Phillips "who ran a poker game at Lost Cabin during shearing time, many years before."

During the late summer of 1934 Will Boyd, a member of a Wyoming pioneering family and frequent customer at McGuire's Trading Post where Mrs. Schroer worked, accompanied Phillips to a cabin used by Cassidy during his outlaw years.

As they neared the spot, Boyd "fell back on purpose" leaving Phillips-Cassidy to find the cabin. As they got closer to the old trail, Boyd said Phillips "got confused and didn't know which direction to take."

Mrs. Schroer concluded her investigation with this comment:

"My solid conclusion is that the Phillips-Cassidy thing is in a class with the cliché statement 'Jesse James really was not shot by Bob Ford in Saint Joseph, Missouri, but changed his identity to become head of a financial empire.'"

This writer agrees most heartily.

LOS RETRATOS, SEÑAS PERSONALES Y LA HISTORIA CRIMINAL DE CADA UNO DE LOS INDIVIDUOS SOSPECHOSOS, SE DAN Á CONTINUACIÓN.

NOMBRE......Harry Longbaugh, (a) "Kid" Longbaugh, (a) Harry Alonzo, (a) Frank Jones, (a) Frank Body, (a) el "Sundance Kid."
NACIONALIDAD......sueco-americano.........PROFESION.........Vaquero; tratante
OCUPACIÓN CRIMINAL......Salteador de caminos, ladrón de bancos, de ganado y de caballos.
EDAD......35 años.........ESTATURA......5 pies 10 pulgadas
PESO......de 165 á 175 libras.........CONSTITUCION......Buena
OJOS......Azules ó pardos.........COLOR......Trigueño claro
BIGOTE Ó BARBA......[si tiene] castaño natural con matiz rojizo.
FACCIONES......tipo griego.........NARIZ......Más bien larga
COLOR DEL PELO......castaño, puede habérselo teñido; se peina pompadour.

ES ESTEVADO Y TIENE LOS PIES MUY SEPARADOS.

OBSERVACIONES......Harry Longbaugh estuvo 18 meses cumpliendo sentencia en la cárcel de Sundance, Condado de Cook, Wyoming, cuando era muchacho, por robo de caballos. En Diciembre de 1892, Harry Longbaugh, Bill Madden y Henry Bass asaltaron un tren del Ferrocarril "Great Northern" en Malta, Montana. Bass y Madden fueron juzgados por este crimen y sentenciados á 10 y 14 años de presidio, respectivamente; Longbaugh se escapó y desde entonces es un prófugo. En 28 de Junio de 1897 y bajo el nombre de Frank Jones, Longbaugh en compañía de Harvy Logan (a) Curry, Tom Day y Walter Putney, tomó parte en el robo de un banco en Belle Fourche, South Dakota. Todos cayeron en manos de la policia, pero Longbaugh y Harvy Logan lograron escaparse de la cárcel de Deadwood, en 31 de Octubre del mismo año. Desde entonces Longbaugh no ha vuelto á estar preso.

HARRY LONGBAUGH.
Retrato tomado el 21 de Noviembre de 1900.

NOMBRE......Sra. de Harry Longbaugh
ALIAS......Sra. de Harry A. Place; Sra. Ethel Place
NACIONALIDAD......Americana
OCUPACIÓN......desconocida
OCUPACIÓN CRIMINAL......
EDAD......de 27 á 28 años [en 1906].........ESTATURA......5 pies 5 ó 5 pulgadas
PESO......de 110 á 115 libras.........CONSTITUCION......Regular
COLOR......Trigueña.........COLOR DEL PELO......Castaño oscuro
OBSERVACIONES......Usa peinado alto formado por un moño enroscado desde la frente.

AL IR Á PRENDER Á CUALQUIERA DE LOS INDIVIDUOS DE ESTA BANDA DE LADRONES, SE RECOMIENDA Á LOS POLICIAS QUE LO INTENTEN QUE ESTEN BIEN REFORZADOS, PERFECTAMENTE ARMADOS, QUE NO SE ARRIESGUEN, PUES DICHOS CRIMINALES RESISTEN TEMERARIAMENTE ANTES DE RENDIRSE, Y NO TITUBEAN EN MATAR SI ES NECESARIO PARA SALVARSE. SON BUENOS TIRADORES, EXPERTOS GINETES, ACOSTUMBRAN Á VIVIR EN LAS LLANURAS Y SON HÁBILES EN LA CRÍA DE GANADO.

LA ESPOSA DE HARRY LONGBAUGH.

Harvey Logan (a) Harvey Curry, (a) "Kid" Curry, (a) Tom Jones, (a) Bob Jones, se escapó el 27 de Junio de 1903 de la cárcel del Condado de Knox, Knoxville, Tenn., E. U. de A., donde estaba esperando á ser trasladado al presidio de Columbus, Ohio, para cumplir la sentencia de 20 años que se le impuso por circular billetes de bancos alterados, robados del carro del "Great Northern Express" en el ferrocarril "Great Northern," el 3 de Julio de 1901, por asaltadores de caminos de los que Logan era el jefe, y los cuales asaltaron dicho tren, contuvieron con armas de fuego á los empleados del tren, saltaron con dinamita la caja de hierro y sacaron de la misma $45,000 en billetes de banco sin firmar, que se llevaron.

SEÑAS PERSONALES.

NOMBRE......Harvey Logan
ALIAS......Harvey Curry, "Kid" Curry, Bob Jones, Tom Jones, Bob Nevilles, Robt. Nelson, R. T. Whelan.
RESIDENCIA......Se huyó de la cárcel del Condado, Knoxville, Tenn., el sábado 27 de Junio de 1903.
LUGAR DONDE NACIO......Dobson, Mo.....COLOR......blanco
OCUPACIÓN......Vaquero, tratante
OCUPACIÓN CRIMINAL......Asaltador de bancos y trenes, ladrón de caballos y ganado asaltador de caminos y asesino.
EDAD......38 años [en 1903].
OJOS OSCUROS......Estatura, 5 pies 7½ pulgadas
PESO......de 145 á 150 libras.........CONSTITUCIÓN......Regular
TEZ......trigueña, atezada.........NARIZ......Prominente, larga, grande y recta
COLOR DEL PELO......Negro
BARBA......afeitada cuando se escapó, pero puede dejarse crecer una barba espesa y bigote de color algo mas claro que el pelo.

ADVERTENCIAS. Tiene una herida de bala en el brazo derecho, entre la muñeca y el codo; habla despacio; es un poco estevado y de carácter reservado. Padece bronquitis aguda, jadea mucho; su estado físico no es del mejor; tiene dos cicatrices en la espalda que parecen proceder de una descarga con perdigones; tiene el hombro izquierdo mucho más bajo que el derecho, á causa de la herida; tiene los brazos más largos que la generalidad de las personas de su estatura; tiene los dedos bastante largos. HARVEY LOGAN también asesinó á Pike Landusky, en Landusky, Montana, el 25 de Diciembre de 1894, y tomó parte en gran número de asaltos y robos, entre ellos el robo del tren del Ferrocarril Unión del Pacífico, en Wilcox, Wyoming, el 2 de Junio de 1899, después de lo cual la fuerza civil alcanzó á Logan y su banda cerca de Casper, Wyoming, y al tratar de prender á los ladrones, el alguacil mayor, Joseph Hazen, del Condado de Converse, Wyoming fué asesinado.

HARVEY LOGAN.
Retrato tomado en 1...

NOMBRE......George Parker
ALIAS......"Butch" Cassidy (a) George Cassidy; (a) Ingerfield
NACIONALIDAD......Americano
OCUPACIÓN......Vaquero, tratante
OCUPACIÓN CRIMINAL......Ladrón de bancos y asaltador de caminos, ladrón de ganado y caballos.
EDAD......36 años [en 1901]
ESTATURA......5 pies 9 pulgadas
PESO......165
CONSTITUCIÓN......Regular
TEZ......Clara
COLOR DEL PELO......Blondo
OJOS......Azules
BIGOTE......Leonado, si lo usa
OBSERVACIONES. Tiene dos cicatrices en la nuca; cicatriz pequeña debajo del ojo izquierdo, pequeño lunar en la pantorrilla. "Butch" Cassidy es conocido como un criminal principalmente en Wyoming, Utah, Idaho, Colorado y Nevada, y ha cumplido sentencia en Laramie por robo, pero fué perdonado el 19 de Enero de 1896.

GEORGE PARKER.
Primer retrato tomado el ... de Julio de 18...

GEORGE PARKER.
Último retrato tomado el 21 de Noviembre de 1900.

Rare wanted poster in Spanish for the Sundance Kid, Etta Place, and Butch Cassidy, written by Frank Diamio and distributed by him along the South American coast.

They Told the Story

THE excitement, drama, humor and glamour of the West was excellent material for writers. The public clamored for accounts, stories and shows about the fabulous West, and they got it. Desperadoes, marshals, Indian chiefs, generals, scouts, stage-drivers, cowboys and even horses were portrayed as heroes capable of fantastic achievements. Also desperadoes, Indian chiefs, rustlers and cowboys were portrayed as vicious villains, capable of the cruelest of crimes.

Probably widest circulated of this immensely popular and quite inaccurate school of writers was Ned Buntline (Col. E. C. Judson), whose name is virtually synonymous with Western dime thrillers. He is reputed to have written over a thousand novels, but that is undoubtedly an exaggeration. It is true, however, that thousands of such stories about the West were published and they helped to create the popular image of the West that persists even until now.

But there were serious writers also whose reports, essays, stories and books did present a faithful view of the Western scene. Most notable among these were Mark Twain and Bret Harte, whose writings about the West achieved fame and great circulation not only all over the country, but almost all over the world. Mark Twain's *Roughing It* is full of excellent descriptions of prospecting, mining camp life, ranch life, the Pony Express and other important elements of the West. His "Celebrated Jumping Frog of Calaveras County and Other Sketches," published in 1867, is a classic of western humor.

Mark Twain (Virginia City years). *Photo by Charles Watkins.*

"Ned Buntline," Colonel E. Z. C. Judson.

Bret Harte. *Photo by Sarony.*

Bret Harte wrote stories about the gold camps for the *Overland Monthly* which were published in 1870 as *The Luck of Roaring Camp and Other Sketches*. That and his famous ballad about the "Heathen Chinee" called "Plain Language for Truthful Jones" are also among the still widely-read great classics of the West. The writings of Theodore Roosevelt, previously mentioned, also achieved wide publication and had considerable influence.

Wild West shows and exhibitions like Buffalo Bill's were enormously popular in the East and the West and vied with regular theatrical fare for the public's attention. Although famous actors, actresses and various stock companies toured the West in successful plays, the Wild West melodramas and shows were almost always sure-fire attractions.

And, as previously mentioned, the photographers and artists such as Catlin, Bodmer, Schreyvogel, Moran and Remington, and many others supplied illustrative material for lectures as well as for magazines and books.

All these portrayed the West. The amount of truth in what they told varied and some of it assayed very low, but they helped to build the colorful legend of the Great American West.

California Theatre showbill. Note that Bret Harte was in the cast.

Mark Twain, in his later years.

William F. "Buffalo Bill," Cody, in his younger years.

Annie Oakley, famous markswoman, star of Buffalo Bill's show.

Lillie Langtry, the "Jersey Lily," the actress most popular with western audiences in the late 1870's and 80's.

A Wild West show poster.

An 1876 show poster.

Pawnee Bill (G. W. Lillie).

Stanley J. Morrow, photographer.

Frank Leslie, publisher of *Leslie's Weekly. Photo by I. W. Taber.*

John K. Hillers, photographer, in the field, 1871.

Tim O'Sullivan, photographer.

Twilight of the Great Chiefs

DURING the long struggle of the red man against the white man in the West, there were always some peaceful tribes, herders and farmers who accepted what fate and the Great White Father gave them. But the warrior tribes kept fighting bitterly, and it took many years of tragedy and disaster to make the Indian chiefs accept the inevitable.

The first notable acceptance of the white men's way was that of Washakie of the Shoshones of Montana. He had been a fierce fighter, leading his tribe nobly against the neighboring tribes. But he made friends with the white men and when, as early as the 1840's he saw the hordes of emigrants coming over the Oregon Trail, he persuaded his tribe, and later others, to submit to the white men's rule. "We can make a bow and arrows," he said, "but the white man's mind is strong and light!"

Quanah Parker, chief of the Kwahadi Comanches, led a powerful alliance of Comanches, Kiowas and Cheyennes in the bloody battle of the Adobe Walls in the Panhandle Country in 1874. Quanah was the half-breed son of Peter-Nakomi and Cynthia Ann Parker of Baker Fort, Navasota County, Texas. As chief of the Kwahadi, he resolved to get all the Indians of the plains together to fight off the invading white men.

A great council was called and the united braves decided to attack, one by one, the various white men's camps in the Panhandle.

The trading post at Adobe Walls was the first target.

Washakie. Photo taken about 1882. *Photo by Baker and Johnston.*

Big Tree, a Kiowa sub-chief, 1871.

White Horse, famous Kiowa warrior.

Long Wolf's son, 1872.

Now the white man's "strong and light mind" was working too fast. Quanah Parker's defeat was the first note of eventual submission for the tribes. Chief Joseph of the Nez Percés had an even more dramatic encounter with the new arms, the new god of the white man.

Quanah Parker.

Asa-tu-at, a Comanche chief.

Kiowa braves, 1876. *Photo by W. P. Bliss.*

There were just 30 buffalo-hunters there, but they were alerted in time to the impending charge of Quanah Parker's Indians. They barricaded themselves behind their stockade and were ready for a siege. And they had powerful new long-range weapons which the Indians did not expect and could not match. Charge followed charge and the fight lasted three days. Quanah was wounded, many of his men were killed or wounded, and the Indians knew that reinforcements would come for the white men.

Quanah knew there was no point in fighting any more. The red men could not beat the white men, and the only thing left to do was to join them. "I can learn the ways of the white men," he said. And he did. He became a successful businessman and won full citizenship for himself and the members of his tribe.

Chief Joseph and the Nez Percés

In 1876 a commission set up by Washington decided that the Nez Percés had to leave their beloved Wallowa Valley in Oregon and return to a reservation. In May of the following year Major General O. O. Howard, commanding the Military Department, was ordered by Washington to carry out the order.

Several councils were held at Fort Lapawi, Idaho. Chief Joseph, accompanied by a younger brother, Ollicut, White Bird and Looking Glass, attended the council.

Hoping to keep peace, Joseph agreed reluctantly to go on the reservation. While he was gathering his people and their pony herds, a band of young warriors murdered some settlers and raped their women. Also, a party of whites fleeing to Mount Idaho was massacred.

The young bucks rode into the camp of White Bird, waving their bloody scalps and calling upon Too-hul-hul-suit, the powerful head of the warriors' organization called the Dreamers, to demand war. His fierce oratory soon had the tribesmen united in a desire for battle. When Joseph

General O. O. Howard, 1881. *Photo by Rieman & Co.*

Chief Joseph, leader of the Nez Percés. *Photo by C. J. Curtis.*

Chief Joseph, in his younger days.

arrived he found his people calling for him to lead them. Reluctantly he obeyed.

The whole countryside was in a panic. Settlers were fleeing their ranches and hurrying to the larger settlements. Messengers were sent from Mount Idaho to Fort Lapawi with the news of the massacres. Howard, one-armed hero of the Civil War, sent part of his skeleton First Cavalry under Captains Perry and Trimble and Lieutenant Teller of the Twenty-First Infantry to protect the settlers.

Perry made a forced march covering 80 miles in 30 hours over terrible terrain. On the 17th of June he was joined by a handful of civilian volunteers.

Once the gauntlet was dropped, Chief Joseph plunged into organizing his small tribe into a mobile fighting unit. He joined White Bird's band on the Salmon River and pitched his camp with his back to the river and his front toward White Bird Canyon.

At dawn when the first soldiers appeared confident that the Nez Percés would not fight, Joseph ordered his women, children and spare horses across the river. Then he prepared an ambush at the mouth of the canyon.

Lieutenant Teller, leading a point of eight soldiers, moved cautiously into the canyon. The fours came up behind at 50 yards. The canyon was quiet until suddenly a body of hard-riding redskins charged out of the ravine toward the cavalrymen. A devastating cross-fire knocked the blue-coated soldiers out of their saddles. When Captain Perry arrived he ordered his force up a small hill. The soldiers traded shot for shot, although they were almost surrounded by Joseph on one side and White Bird on the other.

Looking Glass, 1871. *Photo by W. H. Jackson.*

The cavalrymen managed to retreat in good order though they had to abandon a small force which was wiped out to the man. A rear guard was slaughtered by the Nez Percés, and Teller and his whole command of 36 men were killed. It was only Captain Perry's cool leadership that saved the entire force from being destroyed. Joseph had demonstrated that he was a brilliant strategist.

General Howard quickly organized the largest force he could manage—300 soldiers—and marched to the Salmon River. When Joseph's lookouts caught the advancing troops in their glasses they galloped into camp and gave him the news. By late afternoon, Joseph had established his lines across the river in the mountains. If the soldiers wanted to fight, it was going to be on the battlefield of his choice.

Howard sent a troop under Major Whipple to Cottonwood Creek, where White Bird's camp was located, then moved in on Joseph. The Nez Percés' chief vanished, leaving the general entangled in the mountain vastness while the Indians struck Whipple's force and then almost destroyed a large civilian force coming to Whipple's defense.

When Howard finally made his way out of the mountains and hurried to help the besieged Major Whipple, Joseph, who had excellent scouts, retreated, to be joined by Looking Glass. His force now numbered about 250 warriors and 400 women and children.

Chief Joseph's movements were superb. Accompanied by the tribe's women, children, ponies, and livestock, he had swung his army in and out of the mountains cutting

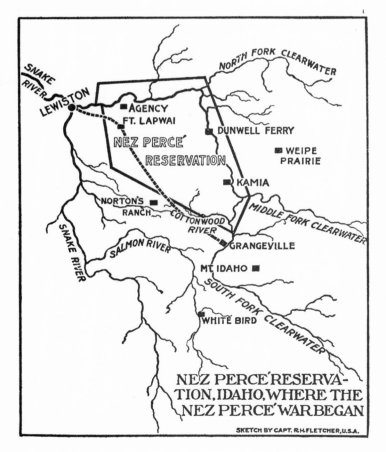

NEZ PERCÉ RESERVATION, IDAHO, WHERE THE NEZ PERCÉ WAR BEGAN

SKETCH BY CAPT. R. H. FLETCHER, U.S.A.

down Howard's force while he led the general on a chase like a bouncing jackrabbit luring on a tenderfoot.

Chief Joseph next moved to the Clearwater, a rushing mountain stream, with steep banks rising to level plateaus cut by ravines. When Howard appeared, Joseph attacked, and the fighting continued with charges and counter-attacks for several days.

When Joseph saw Howard trying to turn his right flank he sent word he wanted to parley. Howard halted his advance while he listened to the ramblings of the sub-chief Joseph had sent in order to gain time while he prepared to flee away; he had finally decided to leave his beloved Idaho, cross the mountains to Montana and then join Sitting Bull in British Columbia.

With his women, children, stock and pony herds he struck north, then eastward along the famous Lo-lo Trail, which wound through ragged ravines and deep forests. It began raining and the muddy, slippery trail became almost impassable.

Howard, aware of Joseph's objective, was in pursuit. Some distance behind came the weary infantrymen and the cavalry troops. The singing wire, however, was Howard's ally and Joseph's enemy. Orders were flashing over the wire to commands in Montana. The Seventh Infantry under Gibbon made a forced march from Helena to Fort Missoula. In the meantime a detachment had left the fort to try to stop Joseph at Lo-lo Pass in the Coeur d'Alenes. But Joseph and the warriors fought so fiercely that the civilian volunteers vanished, leaving the troops no alternative but to move back to Missoula.

After a 75-day journey in which he kept two and three days ahead of Howard, Joseph made camp in a meadow on the south side of Big Hole River, without knowing that Gibbon was moving in on him from Fort Missoula.

On August 8, Gibbon attacked. For once Joseph's scouts had failed him. The attack was a complete surprise. However, Joseph, White Bird and Looking Glass rallied their men who put up such a fierce counter-attack that Gibbon soon realized he was fighting for his own life.

The fighting went on all day. The Indians drove Gibbon's force back across the river and even attacked his strongly fortified position. When they couldn't dislodge him Joseph set fire to the tall dried grass; only a freakish wind saved the soldiers from cremation. That night Joseph and his people vanished behind the screen of smoke.

Gibbon had sent messages to Howard, urging him to put on a forced march to save his command and so on the day after the battle Howard led an advance party of 50 weary men into Gibbon's camp. After one look at the number of wounded, Howard ordered Gibbon to return to Missoula while he continued with a number of volunteers from Gibbon's force.

On August 7, 1879, Howard led "150 rifles," as he called them, on Joseph's trail. This tenacity was rewarded when he found Joseph's camp in Big Hole. He attacked at dawn and another fierce fight took place. The Indians captured Howard's howitzer but were forced to leave 85

General David Perry.

dead on the field, many small children and women, and Joseph's best field commander, Looking Glass.

Once again Joseph led his people on a long, weary pilgrimage, a tortuous journey of many hundreds of miles, back and forth over much of the West—Idaho, across the Yellowstone, Wyoming, Montana. And Howard was always behind him, relentless in pursuit.

The famous Seventh was detailed to assist Howard, but Joseph outwitted them and escaped. Finally General Miles joined Howard. At Cow Island on the Missouri, Joseph attacked a large freight depot, then repulsed another force of the Seventh which had come down the river by steamboat from Fort Benton. Joseph finally halted on Snake Creek on the north slope of the Bear Paw Mountains. He could have easily escaped into Canada, but he would not desert his wounded and his women and children.

On October 3, Miles, armed with howitzers and Gatling guns, attacked the camp. After a bloody fight in which the soldiers suffered heavy losses, Miles decided to starve out the Indians. Only White Bird and a small force of warriors escaped to join Sitting Bull.

The artillery began a methodical shelling of the camp with devastating results. Meanwhile, Howard came up to join Miles and his troopers. The thermometer dropped and troopers and Indians alike suffered from the numbing cold. But although the shells were bursting among his people and the Gatling guns cutting them down, Joseph's marks-

Chief Joseph's surrender to General Miles. *Painted by J. N. Marchand.*

men made the troopers pay; one company lost 35 per cent of its numbers.

But the Nez Percés could not keep up the uneven fight; it was now rifles against howitzers and Gatling guns. On October 3 Joseph sent word he was surrendering. When the dead were counted, Miles had lost 20 per cent of his entire command; Joseph only 17 killed. With him were 87 warriors, 40 of whom were wounded, 184 squaws and 147 children.

The great Nez Percé rode into camp escorted by a delegation of five warriors. His scalp lock was tied with otter fur. The rest of his hair hung in thick plaits on each side of his head. He wore buckskin leggings and a gray woolen shawl through which could be seen the marks of four or five bullet-holes received in the last fight. His head and wrist were also scratched by bullets. He gave his rifle to Miles, then smiled as he shook hands with Howard.

All in all, Joseph's journey was remarkable. With a force never numbering more than 300, at different times he had engaged more than 2,000 soldiers. Of these his warriors had killed 176 and had wounded 140. He himself had lost 151 killed and 89 wounded. He had fought 11 engagements, five of which were forced, bloody pitched battles. He won three, drew one and lost one. He had marched more than 2,000 miles across the roughest terrain in the West.

Howard rightly called him one of the great chiefs of Indian history.

Nez Percé warriors.

The Surrender of Sitting Bull and the Sioux

On the morning of July 10, 1881, leading 187 men, women and children, Sitting Bull left Grandmother Land, as the Sioux called Canada, to return to the United States. Their journey to Fort Buford, North Dakota, was a sad one as the creaking carts rolled across the plains and past the skull and bones of the buffalo herds that littered the grass. Ten days later they entered Buford and the settlers along the borders of Montana and the Dakotas breathed more freely.

On July 29, Sitting Bull and his people were placed aboard the steamer *General* and the boat headed into the muddy Missouri for the three-day trip to Fort Yates and Standing Rock Agency. After a short stay at the agency, the Sioux were again moved, this time to Fort Randall as "prisoners of war."

There, Sitting Bull held court for visiting Sioux from all over the West who came to seek his advice; he told each one to lay down his rifle and move behind the plow. The white man was just too strong and now, with the buffalo gone, it was suicide to continue the wars. According to his biographer, Stanley Vestal, the old Sioux chief also received "fan mail" from all points of the globe.

On May 10, 1883, Sitting Bull was returned to Standing Rock Agency, where he lived out the rest of his years.

A view of the Sioux camp at Fort Randall. This and the other pictures of the Sioux camp shown on this and the following page and a half are from a series a number of which are believed to have been taken by Bailey, Dix and Meade.

Sitting Bull and his favorite wife, his eighth. At this time she was thirty years old and had borne six children.

One Bull, nephew of Sitting Bull.

Steps, a Nez Percé Indian, who joined the Sioux. His right hand and his feet had been frozen in a blizzard.

Winter quarters.

Eat Dog and family.

Battalion drill of the 25th Infantry, garrisoning Fort Randall and guarding the Sioux.

One Bull and Black Prairie Chicken examining a hide, while an officer's wife and child observe.

Standing Rock and the other Indian agencies, forts and military posts in the North—from Wisconsin and Minnesota to Oregon and Washington—played an important part in Indian affairs for many years.

Fort Snelling was the most notable of these, a bulwark throughout all the Indian wars, the base from which early Dragoons and later cavalrymen and infantrymen went out to engage the Sioux, the Mandans, Pawnees, Flatheads and numerous others. The early fur-trappers also knew its stout stone walls, which never failed to impress the nomadic Plains tribes.

Snelling was built on a triangle between the Minnesota and Mississippi Rivers. Across the Minnesota, at what is now Mendota, was the headquarters of the famous American Fur Company. The site was established in 1820 on the orders of President Monroe. First named Fort Saint Anthony, it was later changed to Snelling.

Like most western forts and military installations, Snelling was located on a bluff, the site of an ancient Indian village. A magnificent panoramic view of the surrounding area could be seen from the palisades, while the steep bank of the bluff made attack almost impossible. The fort's famous long wooden stairway, which led from the Snelling Ferry to the post, was noted by many early Indian agents, missionaries and scouts in their letters and memoirs.

Another important fort built on the site of an old Indian village was Fort Abraham Lincoln, one of the most colorful and important posts on the western frontier.

Engineers originally sent out from Fort Rice, Dakota Territory, in 1872 to establish a military fortification which would protect the surveyors, engineers, and workmen building the Northern Pacific, wisely selected the site of an old Mandan village on the bank of the Missouri and near the mouth of the Heart River.

Like Snelling, the Mandan site on the bluff commanded

Sitting Bull with two wives, his twins and youngest child.

the ancient barren plain below it, while a steep bank protected one side. Stout cottonwood trees were dragged up from the river's bank for the palisade, and blockhouses and lumber was hauled in wagons from nearby Bismarck for construction of the officers' quarters and other structures.

The fort was first named McKeen after Colonel Henry Boyd McKeen of the First Pennsylvania Volunteers, but on November 19, 1872, the installation was renamed Fort Abraham Lincoln in honor of the martyred president.

The finished fort was one of the most impressive on the frontier. It was situated in a triangle area with blockhouses at each corner, palisade walls connecting them on two sides, and the steep bank protecting the third side. There were officers' quarters, barracks, a hospital, laundry and stables.

Through the gates of Fort Lincoln rode some of the most colorful figures in western History. Heading the list is General Custer and his Seventh Cavalry. When they rode into Lincoln in 1873, the installation became a nine-company cavalry and infantry post.

For the troopers of the famed Seventh, life at the fort, between expeditions and skirmishes with the Plains tribes, was dull and monotonous. In the summer they were plagued by hordes of mosquitoes that descended on men and horses like great buzzing blankets. In the winter, bone-numbing cold seeped through their thick buffalo robes.

Their only relief was an occasional visit to the "Point," a small settlement of saloons and gambling halls on the bank across the Heart. There was no bridge, and only a small ferry connected the point and the fort. In the winter the troopers walked across the ice. In the spring the thaw made it impossible to cross the torrent.

The fort's most momentous night was the stifling one in July, 1876, when the steamer *Far West*, loaded with wounded from Reno's command at the Little Big Horn, brought the news of the annihilation of Custer's command. The captain had made the 700-mile run in 54 epic hours, to inform 26 wives at the fort that they had become widows.

Inseparable with Fort Abraham Lincoln in the shaping of the Western frontier is the Standing Rock Agency, South Dakota. The great war captains of the Sioux, the

Seated, left to right: Sitting Bull, Swift Bear, Spotted Tail. *Standing,* Julius Meyer, an Indian interpreter, and Red Cloud. *Photo by Frank Currier.*

medicine men, warriors and the families moved in and out of this famed agency during the Indian Wars from 1866 to Wounded Knee in 1890.

Here, Sitting Bull was buried under the slender granite shaft in the corner of the Roman Catholic Cemetery. Most men have forgotten how soldiers kept walking, one at a time, into the carpenter's shop where the Old Bull's coffin was kept, and then seized the opportunity to "drive a nail in the chief's coffin." His big body was finally crammed into the crude box, and a husky soldier "sat on the lid to close it." The hole was dug and the chief's last remains were interred in quicklime, like those of a common felon.

Standing Rock, so closely related to the history of the Sioux, was named after the stone (Inyan Woslata) sacred to the Arikaras. The stone first placed on Proposal Hill was supposed to be the figure of a small shawled woman holding a child. Dakota legend tells how a young woman became jealous of her husband's second wife and refused to leave when the camp moved on. She was left standing before the fire with her child on her back. Later, when she

This is probably the only known photograph of the original Standing Rock sacred to the Sioux. *All the photos on this page and the next four pages are by General John T. Pitman, except as otherwise stated.*

A blockhouse at a corner of Fort McKeen, later Fort Abraham Lincoln. *Photo by General Pitman.*

Sioux chiefs and braves with soldiers at the Standing Rock Agency.

Sioux warriors, 1880's.

Sioux squaws, Standing Rock Agency, 1880's.

did not appear at the new camp, her husband sent his relatives to find out what happened. His in-laws returned to the old camp to find the woman and the child transformed into stone.

From that time on, the rock was carried with the tribe and occupied a position of honor in the center of each camp. The rock is one of two revered by the Sioux. The second (Inyan Bosdata-Erect Rock) is on the Cheyenne River.

Closely connected with Fort Lincoln and Standing Rock Agency was Bismarck, the small bustling town whose rooftops could be seen from the blockhouses of Fort Lincoln by the troopers of the Seventh, counting the days until their next pass.

Fort Abraham Lincoln.

A group in front of "Custer's house" at Fort Abraham Lincoln, 1889. *Left to right, seated:* Mrs. L. Powell, General Crook, Major Powell's wife; *Standing:* Governor Fasler, Major Powell, Major Warner, Major Randall. *Photo by D. F. Barry.*

Parade grounds at Fort Abraham Lincoln.

A group at Fort Abraham Lincoln, 1889.

The famous Rosebud Indian Agency of the Dakota Territory as it appeared in
1889. *Photo by J. A. Anderson.*

Fort Snelling, 1862. *Photo by J. E. Whitney.*

A view of Fort Snelling, 1880's. *Photo by General Pitman.*

A view of the long stairway up to Fort Snelling, 1880's. *Photo by General Pitman.*

Crow prisoners at the Crow Agency, Montana, 1887.

The Crow Reservation, Montana, 1890.

Geronimo

By 1882 the strength of the Plains tribes had been broken. There would be only a few last flare-ups before the fire died out. But in Arizona Territory the sullen, embittered Apaches were restless and ready to take to the warpath.

In the spring of 1882 the situation had so deteriorated that General Crook ("Three Stars" to the Plains tribes, "Gray Fox" to the Apaches) was reassigned to the Territory. Crook returned at once to Prescott and set out to get a first-hand account of what had happened. He learned that there had been some skirmishes with the Apaches, that the Apaches had heard talk that they were to be driven out of their reservation, that the Indian agent at San Carlos was crooked and involved in a swindle with Army contractors.

Crook arranged a meeting with the Apache leaders. Alchise, the leader of the 26 warriors, told Crook in detail of the grievances against the Indian agent at San Carlos, who had refused them food and had in fact ordered them to give up their farms and move to the malaria-breeding San Carlos Agency. Alchise plaintively asked the same question that had echoed across the plains for years: why does the white man break his promises?

The Indians had been making progress, were nearly self-supporting. But there was a close ring of crooked contractors in Tucson, determined that the Apaches would not be self-supporting, for if they did what would become of their lucrative business? To disturb the Indians' progress all they had to do was telegraph Washington that

Geronimo, 1884. *Photo by A. F. Randall.*

The San Carlos Agency, 1880.

the Indians were "restless" and jittery. The Indian Bureau would demand that the War Department send troops at once. Then, the contractors knew, there were always the rebels on the reservations who would incite the bucks and create the trouble that had been reported.

Also, coal had been discovered on the reservation and crooked Indian agents were trying to acquire that part of the land for speculation. They hoped to interest the Southern Pacific Railroad Company. There were rumors—unconfirmed—that silver also had been discovered, and every possible means was used to trick the Apache.

Crook investigated Alchise's charges and found that the rations issued by a man named Tiffany had shrunk to a shocking degree. A shoulder of beef was supposed to feed 20 persons; a cup of flour was issued every seventh day. The Indians told Crook they were forced to eat every part of the animal, from intestines to hoofs.

Before the arrival of Crook, Alchise, determined to get proof, had sent scouts to trail the wagons from the agency. The redskins found the wagons loaded with rations intended for tribesmen going to Globe or other towns where the supplies were sold.

One of the Apaches who spoke Spanish and English was delegated by the tribe to protest to the Indian agent. The warrior-spokesman found himself sentenced to six months' imprisonment without a trial and his cattle were confiscated. After his release he tried in vain to find out what his crime had been.

Captain Emmet Crawford, although firm with the warriors when he caught them drinking tizwin, was the one Army officer treated with respect by the Apaches at the post, but they regarded the agents with contempt. At San Carlos Crook talked to some of the chiefs who had returned and found that a number had been forced to leave their cool lands near the Cibicu for the searing flats of San Carlos. Before they left they had seen their fields of corn deliberately trampled. Crook reorganized the military affairs at San Carlos and put Captain Crawford, one of the finest officers in the Territory, in charge. Crawford ordered a spring planting and the Agency was prepared for the arrival of the Chiricahua Apaches.

The Chiricahuas had been on the warpath for years after they had fled into the Sierra Madre Mountains. Crook was now prepared to force them to come in and hold a council.

In March 1883 the Chiricahuas under Chief Cato broke out of their mountain strongholds and left a trail of fire and blood along the frontier. One of the band, Panayotishn, better known to frontier history as "Peaches," deserted Cato and came to San Carlos, offering to betray the Chiricahuas' hiding place. Crook organized a force of 193 Indian scouts and a company of the Sixth Cavalry and personally led it into the mountains. Among the scouts under the frontiersman Al Seiber was ugly Mickey Free, who had been captured as a boy and raised by the Apaches and Alchise.

Geronimo and his staff meet with General Crook and his staff, 1886. Geronimo is seen left center; General Crook is second from the right. *Photo by Camillus Fly.*

The attack was successful. Peaches led them to the stronghold camp and it was captured after a brief battle. Most of the warriors were absent raiding the Mexicans, and when they returned with their squaws they were put under arrest and sent back to San Carlos.

In July 1883, by the terms of a conference entered into between the Secretary of War, the Secretary of the Interior and Crook, it was agreed that the entire policing of the Apaches should be turned over to the War Department. Five hundred and twelve Chiricahuas were then sent to a spot on the White River, where they started to farm. In one year after Crook's reassignment Captain Crawford reported that the Indians were producing large barley crops and had cut with knives 400 tons of hay and 300 cords of wood, "for which they have been paid a liberal price."

However, Crook was infuriated about one matter—the selling of whiskey to the Indians. "It is a dead matter," he wrote bitterly to the Secretary of the Indian Rights Association in Philadelphia. "Indians who so desire can obtain from unprincipled whites and others all the vile whiskey for which they can pay cash. . . ."

On January 20, 1885, Crook requested to be relieved of the responsibility of policing the Indians and asked that such duties revert to the Department of the Interior. Major General John Pope, commenting that "General Crook's management of these Indians had been marked by unusual and surprising successes," told the Army's adjutant general that instead of relieving Crook he would recommend that "the entire control of the Indians be turned over to him."

Two months later, Secretary of War William C. Endicott, following Pope's recommendation, suggested to the Department of the Interior that the "entire control of the Indians in the Territory be placed under the charge of General Crook."

But before the Washington brass could make up its mind the Chiricahuas broke out after a dispute over the blasting of an irrigation ditch. The Army under Captain Crawford had told them to go ahead; the Indian agent had refused to give them permission.

If there was such discord between the white men, the Apaches said in council, why stay? Under Geronimo and

Captain Emmet Crawford.

Nachez and Geronimo, 1885.

Apaches on guard. *Photo by Camillus Fly*.

[269]

Nachez 124 took to their mountain strongholds. However, Cato and the others stayed behind.

In the months which followed, Geronimo, a wily old scoundrel who loved to get drunk on tizwin, led his bucks on many raids. Thirty-nine white men in New Mexico and 34 in Arizona were burned or tortured to death, together with a number of friendly White Mountain Apaches.

It was the battle of the lava beds all over again, and it was almost impossible to run down the Apaches.

In January, 1886, Crook's most valuable officer, Captain Crawford, was killed near Sonora, Mexico, in a skirmish with Mexican troops. It was after his death that Geronimo sent in word he wanted to talk in the Cañon de los Embudos, in the northeast corner of Sonora on the Arizona line. Crook, Alchise, the mayor of Tucson and Camillus Fly, the Arizona photographer, attended the meeting.

Geronimo's talk was long and rambling. Crook took him to task for lying and told him, "Think it over tonight and let me know in the morning."

The next day, March 27, Geronimo came down with word that he was "thinking better" and would surrender his people. After a speech about how the sun was at last looking down at him and the earth was listening, he shook hands and gave in. The other war chief, Mangus, was still at large with 13 Chiricahuas.

The Apaches were due to move out the next morning,

"Peaches," General Crook's guide.

Noncommissioned officers of the First U. S. Infantry, Turkey Springs, New Mexico, in the 1885-86 Apache campaign.

Geronimo's wife and child.
Photo by A. F. Randall.

Geronimo and his warriors after their surrender in the Sierra Madre Mountains, New Mexico. Geronimo is at the right of the horse. Chief Nana is mounted.

the 28th. But at dawn Crook was awakened with the news that a Mexican trader had sold the Indians a load of mescal and the Indians were drunk.

Geronimo and Nachez escaped with a number of their braves and the fight had to be fought all over again. But before the search for the Apache remnants could be renewed friction with Washington caused Crook to resign and General Nelson Miles took charge.

With the aid of cavalry Miles pursued the Apaches relentlessly and finally Geronimo and Nachez agreed to a peace. The war with the Apaches was over. Eventually, the Apaches were settled and found a permanent home in the Indian Territory, Oklahoma.

Chief Nana. *Photo by A. F. Randall.*

Geronimo just before leaving Arizona for Fort Sill, Oklahoma.

The Ghost Dancers and the Massacre at Wounded Knee

As the last decade of the nineteenth century approached there was little doubt that the Wild West was now tamed. The buffalo were gone, the great war chiefs dead, the old ways were ended. The Plains tribes confined on the reservations were beaten, spiritless, sick at heart. But there was one final eruption before the Indian Wars could be considered at an end.

About 1888 a Paiute Indian named Wovoka claimed he had a vision in which he was named the Messiah, and the defeated red men believed that he was the Christ of the Second Coming.

This time, because the Messiah had been crucified by the white men, He was returning to earth as an Indian. With him would be legions of dead Indians and vast herds of buffalo that would once again darken the great western plains. A new earth would appear in which there would be no white men. To the starving, beaten Sioux this tale of a new religion promised the restoration of all they had lost.

Wovoka promised that those who danced his sacred dance would be spared. It was a simple dance of holding hands and moving toward the left. The dancers had a special shirt which the Messiah claimed could stop the bullets of the white men.

The new movement was peaceful. "Do not harm anyone. Do right always. Do not tell lies. Do not fight. When your friends die you must not cry."

In all the agencies there was a tremendous religious revival. Dances were held daily. The more experienced Indian agents just shrugged and said that the cold weather would stop the dancing and it would be best to let them blow off their head of steam.

But in 1889 the Democrats swept the Republicans out of office. Indian agents were dismissed and green hands took their place. At Pine Ridge Dr. T. V. Gillicuddy had kept Red Cloud and his savage Ogalalas in hand for years without calling on the troops. But now the new agent, Royer, got panicky and called for troops.

General John R. Brooke, who wasn't familiar with Indians, arrived at Pine Ridge November 19, 1890, and the Ghost Dancers fled to the Badlands. The only damage the Indians did was to burn their own houses and haystacks, but the reporters who accompanied the so-called "Ghost Dance Expedition" sent back hair-raising stories of a new Indian outbreak.

At Standing Rock Agency the Army saw an opportunity to step into Indian affairs. An order was sent for the arrest of the Sioux. Early on the morning of December 15, 1890, Lieutenant Bullhead led his members of Indian police force into Sitting Bull's log cabin and dragged him from his bed.

Before they could start the policemen were surrounded

This photograph of Wovoka, taken in 1928, was given to the Bureau of Ethnology by Tim McCoy, the old-time movie star. It is one of the few in existence.

Red Tomahawk, who killed Sitting Bull.

by a crowd of angry Sioux. Catch-the-Bear, leader of Sitting Bull's bodyguard, who hated Bullhead, shot his old enemy. As Bullhead fell he fired into Sitting Bull's body. At the same moment Red Tomahawk shot the chief in the head, killing him instantly.

Then a fierce battle of Sioux against Sioux broke out. Within minutes 12 were dead and three others gravely wounded. Only the arrival of troops saved the policemen.

The killing of Sitting Bull swept across the plains like an evil wind. Sioux families left their homes, seeking shelter in the camps of their relatives along the Cheyenne River Reservation. One small band reached the camp of Big Foot.

On Christmas Day the Cheyennes' government scouts clashed with Kicking Bear's Sioux on Battle Creek north of the Badlands. When an order came for Big Foot's arrest he started toward the bleak badlands with 356 men, women and small children. Three days later they surrendered to troops and were taken to Wounded Knee Creek, 20 miles northeast of the Pine Ridge Agency. Altogether there were eight troops of Seventh Cavalry armed with four Hotchkiss guns in addition to a company of scouts, the entire command totaling 470 fighting men.

The soldiers surrounded the camp, and the next morning the Indians were ordered to come out. The four Hotchkiss guns mounted on a small rise had the camp in their sights. The Indians were plainly frightened; it was only a few weeks after the killing of Sitting Bull at Fort Yates. There had been rumors that they were going to be sent down to the swamps of Florida in chains and their horses butchered.

In searching the Indians for weapons—the most foolhardy thing for a white man to do was to lay his hands on a half-savage Plains Indian—"a scuffle occurred between one warrior who had a rifle in his hand and two soldiers. The rifle was discharged."

What took place was one of the most dreadful massacres in our plains history. Within minutes, more than 200 Indian warriors, their wives and children were dead along with 60 troopers. The remnants of the band ran frantically down a dry ravine pursued by soldiers with their blood lust up; it was now "Remember the Little Big Horn. . . ."

The few straggling survivors staggered into Pine Ridge

Mass burial of Indians who died at Wounded Knee.

Agency and lit the fuse. Two Strike and his Brulé warriors swarmed in to attack the agency while a handful of outraged Sioux drove off the soldiers at the Wounded Knee camp. On the 30th a Sioux band attacked the Ninth "Buffalo Soldiers" and later forced Forsyth's Seventh to call for reinforcements. Now it was the Sioux remembering Wounded Knee, and so savagely did they bring the fight to Forsyth that it was only the arrival of the Ninth which saved the whole command.

For 32 days the pitched battles lasted; then suddenly they broke off and the Ghost Dance War was finished.

In Mason Valley, Nevada, in a small wickiup, Wovoka, the false prophet, covered his head with a blanket after he had told a visitor that the Sioux had "twisted things" so badly that everybody had better "drop the whole business."

Now it seemed that all hope was gone for the red man. Even the Messiah, with all his great dreams, had failed; there was only one thing to do. . . .

The wrinkled old warrior, his blanket wrapped toga-fashion about his shoulders, walked about the Cheyenne camp and harangued his people: "Hoo-oo! My children, my children. In days behind many times I called you to travel the hunting trail or to follow the war trail. Now those trails are choked with sand; they are covered with grass, the young men cannot find them. My children, today I call upon you to travel a new trail, the only trail now open—the White Man's Road. . . ."

Viewing the hostile Indian camp, Pine Ridge, January, 1891. *Left to right:* Buffalo Bill, General Miles, Captain F. Baldwin, Captain M. P. Marco. *Photo by Grabill.*

Lieutenant Pratt's Indian School

THE government's Indian education policy began in 1819, but little progress was made for more than half a century in teaching the Indians the white man's way. The efforts to educate them came from outside; the teachers were white men and therefore the Indians were suspicious of them, resisted and opposed them. But a young Army lieutenant turned the tide. He was Lieutenant Richard H. Pratt of the 10th Cavalry and beyond any doubts, he is one of the true heroes of the West, much more important than the manufactured heroes —the Jameses, Billy the Kid and the assorted gunfighters who have been presented as authentic "greats" of our last frontier.

Pratt, like many great men, was not a legend in his own lifetime. Even today he is known only to the scholars and the specialists. Shy, unassuming, a gentle man, he wanted nothing for himself, only for the children of the red men against whom he had fought for so many years.

He fought in the Civil War with the Ninth Indiana Infantry, then with the Indiana Cavalry in which he achieved the rank of captain, a grade he still held when he left the service after Appomattox. In 1867 when the War Department was reorganizing the Regular Army to fight the Plains tribes, he re-enlisted as a lieutenant and was sent to join the famous 10th, or the "Buffalo Soldiers."

Pratt made his first contact with the red men in the Cheyenne, Kiowa and Comanche war, 1868-69, and again in 1875 when he was a commander of the Indian scouts.

In 1875 Sheridan ordered Pratt to make an investigation of crimes committed by the Kiowa and Comanche prisoners at Fort Sill. The interrogation of the prisoners and their families gave Pratt a deep insight into the savage mind. In 1875 as a result of his findings, 75 of the chiefs and warriors were ordered to Leavenworth, then to St. Augustine. It was a dangerous journey. Pratt was well aware that his wild charges, despite their arm and leg chains, would kill him and his small guard at the first opportunity. At Nashville Lean Bear, a chief, killed himself after stabbing a corporal to death and slashing another. Another time Graybeard, a Cheyenne chief, leaped from the car window and was killed by the guards.

So depressed were the Indians that many had to be removed by litter on arrival at St. Augustine. The young officer, although firm in his dealing with the prisoners, could not help feeling a great compassion for the once-free rovers of the plains who were now chained like animals. It was Pratt who unchained them and let them roam the yard under surveillance.

Gradually the redskins began to ask Pratt to teach them the "way of the white men . . . we first want our wives and our children . . . then we will go anywhere you say and learn to support ourselves as the white men do . . . we want to learn how to make corn and work the ground. . . ."

In 1875 Pratt wrote a letter to Washington outlining his plan to educate the Indians. "The duty of the govern-

Tom Torlino, a Navajo (*left*) as he arrived at Carlisle and Tom Torlino (*right*) three years later. *This and all other Carlisle photos are studio photos taken by Choate in the 1880's, unless otherwise stated.*

ment to these Indians seems to me to be the teaching of something that will be of permanent use to them. Teaching them to work is one thing, but St. Augustine offers practically nothing to them in this line. They have besought me repeatedly to try to get Washington to give them the opportunity to work. They say they want to learn to build a house, to make boots and shoes, to do blacksmith work, to farm, etc. . . ."

Pratt, with his wife, then enlisted the help of Florida curio dealers, who gave him sea beans for necklaces. Soon the Indians were making souvenirs, arrows, bows, moccasins. Local ladies' societies, who once were afraid to even look at the proud, hawk-faced men who stared at them with such impassiveness, organized classes to teach them to read and write. When they learned English, Pratt organized religious services. Pratt begged, borrowed and bought out of his small salary equipment for the crude classrooms.

A few months after their imprisonment, Pratt gave them guns and told them to guard themselves. For more than two years there was not one violation recorded.

By this time the idea of an Indian school was branded in Pratt's heart. He sent scores of letters, pleading to be allowed to form such a school. He paid his own way to Washington to plead his cause. For years he was tolerated as an Indian-loving pest. By this time the people of St. Augustine had employed all the red men; they were oper-

Ernest, son of White Thunder, who died at the school, 1880.

American Horse, Jr., on a visit to Carlisle in the early 1880's to see his son, Robert.

Spotted Tail and Iron Wing.

Yellow Bear and daughter, Minnie.

ating sawmills, blacksmith shops. In fact, they became so skilled that local workers petitioned Washington to get them out of Florida; they were making it hard for white men to get a job!

In 1878 General Hancock was sent to Fort Marion to see what "Pratt's Indian business is all about." Hancock was astounded at what he saw and wrote a glowing report endorsing Pratt's suggestion that 22 of the young men be allowed to remain in the East for further study and development.

Pratt now had his foot in the door. He was not too proud to beg, and beg he did. He soon had a following of wealthy, influential men who were willing to subsidize his experiment. Next Pratt had to find a building. He reluctantly agreed to house his charges at the Hampton Negro Institute. Now the government was weakening and ordered him to corral 50 more wild youngsters from Chief Joseph's recently defeated Nez Percés, imprisoned at Leavenworth.

That same year the Army ordered him, through an amendment to the Army Appropriation Bill in 1878, to a permanent post "with reference to the Indian education."

Pratt was not satisfied with Hampton. He felt the problems of both races were not the same, so he went to Secretary of the Interior Carl Schurz and presented a plan to educate the Indians as Indians at the old Army barracks in Carlisle, Pennsylvania. Schurz was cool to the plan until Pratt—probably with his heart in his mouth—pointed out that it was only the great freedom of democracy that had enabled Schurz himself to gain such an important post in his adopted country.

Schurz saw the light and approved Pratt's plan. But there was a great deal of red tape to overcome. A special bill had to be drawn and passed by Congress; the Military Committees of both houses had to be soothed and pampered to agree to this rather radical experiment. Pratt was tireless. He lobbied strenuously day and night, but the bill was too late to be introduced. Then Pratt went to the Secretary of War, who was impressed by his enthusiasm and more importantly by the results he had achieved. He got Sherman to declare the barracks unfit for the Army. General Hancock, whose department took in Carlisle, went along with Sherman, and the barracks and old buildings were tentatively assigned to the Department of the Interior for the school.

"What do you plan to do?" Schurz asked.

"Feed the Indians to America. America will do the assimilating and annihilate the Indian problem," was the reply.

The Last Indian Raid

While the Battle of Wounded Knee marked the end of Indian tribal resistance to the white man's way, there were occasional minor local outbreaks. The last raid occurred in 1911 in Humboldt County, Nevada. It was led by Shoshone Mike who, with a band of his tribesmen, attacked a group of stockmen near Getchell's mine, killing several people. The outraged citizens of the area, led by the local sheriff, organized a posse to hunt down the Indian raiders. When the posse found Shoshone Mike and his raiders, a bitter gunfight took place. His ammunition exhausted, Shoshone Mike led his people, now armed with bows and arrows, in a suicidal charge. There were only three Shoshone survivors, a young squaw, a boy and a girl. They are shown here with Sheriff Ferell.

The war bonnet shown is the one Shoshone Mike was wearing when he was killed.

Pratt now began roaming the West looking for children to come to Carlisle. He sat in countless councils, argued, pleaded, cajoled and listened with patience to the long-winded oratory of the Indian speakers. In Rose Bud and Pine Ridge he corraled 72 boys and girls, many the sons and daughters of principal chiefs. Spotted Tail sent five of his own clan, which Pratt considered a major victory.

On October 6, 1879, the first contingent of copper-skinned children arrived at Carlisle. Crowds packed the depot and stared in silence as the stern-faced boys in blankets and wearing claw necklaces and feathers marched up the street. On November 1, 1879, the school formally opened with an enrollment of 147 pupils, 27 more than the Army had authorized. Pratt just did not have the heart to say no.

Two months later he happily reported to Congressman Pound in Washington that the children "were responding to discipline" and showed "eagerness to learn." So rapid had been the advancement of the school, he said, that they were including agriculture and mechanics.

That year, when the glowing letters began to arrive at the agencies, the western chiefs began bombarding Pratt with demands that he take more of their children. They also sent delegations to Washington begging that the school be enlarged. So strong was the movement that Congress passed a bill ordering several abandoned posts to be turned into Indian schools patterned after Carlisle. Re-tiring Army officers also volunteered to act as superintendents. However, the course was not followed immediately for budgetary reasons and Carlisle remained the sole Indian school until the Haskell Institute in Lawrence, Kansas, was opened.

Pratt not only wore himself out physically, but by the winter of 1880 was wrecked financially. It took an eight-year uphill fight before Pratt was able to force Congress to foot some of the bills. In the interim it was Pratt's energetic campaign with his wealthy benefactors and the Society of Friends which kept the school going. More than $125,000 was donated in three years.

Using Indian boy labor, Pratt turned the old stables into shops. Soon classes in tinsmithing, cabinet-making, shoe repairing, tailoring and many other crafts were being taught. When the school began to burst at the seams the Indians, under Pratt's supervision, built another building. Here the girls were taught dressmaking, nursing, laundry work and child care. Nothing was overlooked by the zealous officer; the girls even made their own dresses.

By now he had implanted in their minds that "God helps those who help themselves." Within five years the school was one of the most efficient in the country. Hundreds of savage "blanket Indians" were transformed into efficient workmen and their sisters into nurses, dressmakers, and teachers. And now all these could lead their brothers and sisters to the white man's way.

The Carlisle Indian School Track Team, about 1908. No. 1 is Jim Thorpe; No. 2 is Louis Tewanima, Hopi runner from Arizona who scored for the United States in the 1908 and 1912 Olympics; No. 4 is Glenn L. "Pop" Warner; No. 3 is unidentified.

The Last Frontier—The Cherokee Strip

ON the morning of April 19, 1889, a detachment of U. S. Army troops led thousands of settlers across the Cherokee Outlet, commonly called "The Strip," to the edge of the Oklahoma border, 62 miles to the south. There they would wait until high noon, April 22, when at the sound of a signal gun they would ride on horseback, in wagons, buggies—or even run—to plant their stakes and claim 160 acres each of America's last frontier.

There were more than 10,000 men, women and children in that strange column that morning; there were sodbusters who were weary of seeing their corn wither under the blazing Kansas sun; there were settlers from Nebraska with only a few dollars more than the $15 filing fee that was required; there were tinhorn gamblers from Dodge City, Santa Fe and Creede, Colorado, all riding sleek racehorses; there were soft-looking tenderfeet self-consciously wearing side-arms and a brand-new Winchester but who readily confessed they had never fired a shot in anger; there were the "boomers," whose raids into Oklahoma had drawn national attention to the unspoiled lands, creating the boom that gave the raiders their name and the land rush its greatest push.

There were farmers with many children who owned little more than a rickety prairie schooner, with a trail-worn cow bringing up the rear, a few treasured dollars and hearts full of golden dreams.

There were also hard-eyed men "on the dodge," as they called it in those days, wanted in a hundred towns and cities across the West, wondering how soon they could hold up the gambling tent.

Farmer, doctor, adventurer, tenderfoot and gunman—they all had one goal: to make the Run on the 22nd and stake their claim in the land that even the President had called "The Promised Land."

They had moved out that morning from Arkansas City, Kansas, the outlet to the Strip. It lay directly north from the land to be opened. It had the only railroad which went into that otherwise empty land. It had bridges over the Arkansas River which must be crossed by those coming from east and north. It was the last place to buy supplies; it had the last post office.

Almost overnight Arkansas City had been turned into a roaring boom town. The Central Hotel was crowded twice over; men slept three and four in a bed, on the floor, in the corridors, in the lobby chairs, in the cellar, for weeks at a time. In the last three weeks before the

Moving up to the starting line, April 22, 1889.

The long caravan of prairie schooners on the way to Oklahoma, April, 1889. *This and all other Land Rush pictures are by W. S. Prettyman unless otherwise specified.*

The opening of the Cherokee Strip in 1893 as the line of 10,000 men, women and children surged forward.

In Oklahoma City the day of the 1889 run. This settler arrived too late to plant a stake.

Oklahoma City two months after the run, June 18, 1889. *Photo by D. A. Miller.*

Army would guide the settlers across the Strip to the Border of Oklahoma, men wrapped in blankets, their Winchesters within easy reach, slept in the streets.

Stretched along the banks of the river were hundreds of boomers and settlers from all over Kansas and Missouri. Some had been camped on the river banks for more than a year.

The land they all were so eager to occupy had been set aside by the terms of the treaty of 1866 between the United States and the Indians of the Five Civilized Tribes —Cherokee, Choctaw, Chickasaw, Creek and Seminole— that part of the Indian Territory that was not assigned to any tribe. This tract had been called Oklahoma and was officially designated as the "Unassigned Lands."

The rush for the free lands officially began on March 27, 1889, when President Benjamin Harrison issued his proclamation opening Oklahoma for settlement. To give every settler an equal chance, the proclamation provided that "any person who should enter upon and occupy any of such lands before the hour of 12 noon on April 22 shall thereby forfeit his right to claim land," and soldiers from Fort Sill and Fort Reno constantly patrolled the area to keep out lawbreakers.

On the 19th, all settlers were permitted to cross the Kansas border and enter the Cherokee Outlet—popularly known as The Strip—to make the journey to the border of Oklahoma, where the Run was to begin. It was a two- or three-day ride, across a beautiful but empty land.

From the first, there had been that hunger for land in America, that desire to put down roots. The original set-

tlers from Europe had been drawn by the vast continental expanse across the ocean—land enough for anybody, and to spare. Later, as the coastal lands became more and more heavily populated, a man could always find room by moving westward. Plains that for centuries had known only Indians now sprouted farms. Farms that a few years before had marked the outward limits of civilization suddenly found themselves way stations on the road to a still farther West.

The advance picked up great momentum after Appomattox, spurred by the Homestead Act of 1862. More families moved along the rutted trails, more wagons. Log cabins appeared, then villages, then cities. All the land a man could ever want . . . free. . . .

Then, unexpectedly—to some men it seemed to happen overnight—the frontier had vanished.

The great herds of buffalo that once had roamed the prairies were now gone. In their places were cattle and sheep. The Plains tribes had been subdued, and the Indian Wars were virtually a thing of the past. The West of the explorers and the pioneers was already a legend; the men who had helped to tame it had begun their memoirs.

That was when men started to look covetously at the last remaining unsettled farm land: the Unassigned Lands of the Five Civilized Tribes, which had been promised to the Indians for as long as the waters should run . . . in other words, forever.

By sad, bitter experience the people of the Five Civilized Tribes knew perhaps better than any other Indian nation exactly what the white man's promise was worth.

Map of the Land Rush area.

Once these related tribes, so named because they had adopted many of the white man's ways, had hunted and camped across almost the whole of the American South: the Seminole in Florida, the Cherokee in northern Georgia and the western Carolinas, the Creek in Alabama and southwest Georgia, the Choctaw in central and southern Mississippi and Louisiana, the Chickasaw in Arkansas.

Little by little, as the white man pushed out from the sea-coast, these Indians had been pushed back—by smooth talk, by force of arms, by gifts of hard drink, by trickery and even, surprisingly, by occasional legal sales of land. Each backward step was usually accompanied by a new treaty; virtually every treaty was ultimately broken.

The white man made his first move to cross the borders of the Oklahoma Indian Lands in 1879. That year a man named C. C. Carpenter gathered some 20 families along the southern border of Kansas and announced they were going to enter the Unassigned Lands and claim farms. They were quickly discouraged from trying by the presence of federal troops. But an interested observer was Captain David Payne, a Union cavalry veteran, and a member of the Kansas legislature. After Carpenter's failure, Payne took over leadership of the boomers. He made eight unsuccessful attempts to establish Oklahoma settlements.

After Payne died in 1884, William L. Couch took over leadership of the boomers and established a camp near the present city of Stillwater. But troops under Colonel Ed-

In Guthrie, April 27, 1889. *Photographer unknown.*

ward Hatch evicted Couch and his boomer trespassers.

The invasions of Carpenter, Payne and Couch had failed, but they did bring the attention of the public to the Unassigned Lands. Then, while Washington argued the question of opening the lands to settlement, the harassed leaders of the Five Civilized Tribes themselves resolved the issue.

In January, 1889, a delegation of chiefs traveled to Washington with an offer to sell their lands. An agreement was soon reached with the Secretary of the Interior. The Creeks sold 1,392,704 acres of their land for $1.25 an acre, and additional acreage in the Cheyenne and Arapaho Reservations for $1.05 an acre. The United States paid $280,000 in cash, while the sum of $2,000,000 was held in trust with five per cent interest paid to the tribes. The Seminoles got $1,912,942 for 1,669,080 acres in the Cheyenne-Arapaho reservation and 500,000 acres in the Unassigned Lands.

On March 2, 1889, a homestead measure was rushed through Congress. The Unassigned Lands were opened by Presidential proclamation, with 1,887,796 acres ready for settlement. East to West the area extended about 30 miles, north and south about 50 miles.

The white man once again had begun his relentless march. The canvas-topped wagons rolled across the virgin land.

April 19. The dusty streets of Arkansas City were emptied now of the lines of wagons that had toiled through during the past months; now the wagons were deep in the Cherokee Outlet, heading for the Oklahoma border, where the Run would begin in three days. People were still arriving by rail; Arkansas City was the dividing point; here trains making the Run were to be made up.

In Arkansas City beds and lodging were no longer available. The Gladstone House, as stylish as any Kansas City hotel, was filled to capacity. Settlers slept in back yards, behind sheds, wherever they could find room. Hundreds rolled themselves up in their blankets on the sidewalks in a three-block area about the Santa Fe station—and waited for the train.

During the morning 15 Santa Fe trains of ten cars each left Arkansas City for the Oklahoma border. Six came northward from Purcell. In Arkansas City thousands crowded the area about the station, fighting for seats or

Street scene in Guthrie. *Photographer unknown.*

standing room on the cars. The trains were filled before they could grind to a stop. Men hung from the windows or clung to the raised section of the roofs. When they reached the Oklahoma border the trains stood in one long line, waiting for noon of the 22nd. It was a long wait, but the people in the cars and even those on the roofs refused to give up their places. They munched their sandwiches, smoked their pipes, passed jugs of water and waited.

April 20. Captain Hays of Troop F, Fifth Cavalry, was up long before dawn, readying his patrols and defenses against sooners, those desperate men who hid out in the gullies and brush, hoping to beat the gun, get to the "Promised Land" sooner and file choice tracts of land.

Captain Hays and his troopers fanned out in a straight line to sweep their section of the Unassigned Lands clean of sooners. It was twilight by the time they returned to camp, reasonably sure that no man, no matter how cunningly hidden, could have escaped their sharp eyes.

Yet some men did, such as Frank Hilton Greer, a brilliant young Kansas newspaperman. Just 21, Frank had an idea he wanted to publish the first newspaper in Okla-

homa. He named it the *State Capital*, had it printed in Wichita and mailed the issues to Guthrie—a town not yet in existence—addressed to himself. With what remained of his savings he bought a printing press and instructed his friends to take it apart and ship it to him in Guthrie so he could start printing immediately after the Run.

He had $39 left after buying the press. He gave his wife $10 and set out for Arkansas City on the Santa Fe with two friends. Within an hour after their arrival in Arkansas City, Greer knew that their chances of getting a choice town lot were indeed slim. It seemed there were ten men for every acre in Oklahoma. If they wanted land they had to become sooners.

On their way in, Frank had seen piles of telegraph poles on flatcars lined up in the railroad yards of Arkansas City. He recalled that someone had said you had to be a telegraph pole to get past the soldiers. At eleven o'clock that night the three young men crept up to a flatcar loaded that afternoon with poles. Each man slipped through a large crack arranged conveniently by a friendly trainman to whom Frank had slipped a dollar. One of his friends, a

Crossing on a railroad bridge.

Boomers on the Kansas state line ready for the Strip Run of 1893.

huge man, had some difficulty; it took a lot of grunting and shoving to wriggle into their hideout.

They also discovered they weren't alone. When Greer slid down into the space under the piled poles a deep voice floated up from under his feet: "Step on me, sonny —but not on my face." There were at least two others hidden among the poles.

They shivered through the night. Just about dawn the train jerked to a start. As the men held their breath it inched its way along the sidings and onto the main line.

The train sped across the Cherokee Outlet and slowed as it came to the Oklahoma line. They caught glimpses of troopers on both sides of the tracks, but the train did not stop.

At last they were in Oklahoma. The train chugged rapidly across the wilderness. Two miles outside Guthrie a trainman came back to the flatcar and told them to get off. Greer peered at the landscape racing past.

"We'll be killed jumping now!" he said. "Slow her down."

A hand reached in. Greer wearily took another dollar and gave it to the hand. It vanished. Minutes later the train began to slow down. At ten miles an hour they scrambled from under the poles and leaped, one by one. Greer and his two friends ran to the woods and camped in a small, beautiful ravine with a pool of clear water, using their coats for makeshift tents.

April 21. At twilight a strange quiet descended all along the Oklahoma line. Men were breaking up their camps, caring for their stock, greasing their wagon wheels; the women, helped by the children, packed the last of the food, the few clothes and the household goods. Tomorrow at noon the Run would begin. There was no singing, no shouting, no firing of six-shooters. In this wood-scarce prairie there were few camp fires.

In the cavalry's main camp at Taylor's Spring northeast of Guthrie, General McDuff, after reviewing reports from his men in the field, estimated to reporters there were more than 10,000 persons before nightfall, and thousands more were waiting at other jump-off points.

The trains backed up at the line, ready to chug across the Unassigned Lands, were crowded to suffocation. Men hung from every platform and lay like cordwood on the roofs. There was one press car, and the authorities back in Arkansas City had already disclosed that many top-hatted gentlemen had tried to force their way into the car with forged credentials. It took the *Tribune* man all morning to fight his way to his car.

All trains were required to run not more than 15 miles an hour—which was regarded as about equal to the speed of other means of transportation—so all would have a fair chance. Although some passengers would drop off and stake a claim near the railroad, the majority preferred town lots in Guthrie and Oklahoma City.

Tension mounted during the morning. Captain Hays, who had set his watch by railroad time, had his troopers spread out in a thin blue file across the prairie, a few hundred yards inside the line. The agreed signal was to be the bugle call reveille.

Long before dawn, sooners had slipped in from the south and from the Pottawatomie Indian country in the east, and from the wild lands in the west—sections not patrolled by the few troops.

At five minutes of twelve, on the northern line, thousands of eyes were glued on the right hand of Captain Hays as it slowly rose. At Purcell the settlers shaded their eyes from the sunlight dancing on the sandy Canadian to study Lieutenant Fraser on his white horse.

To those watching Captain Hays the signal brought the sound of thunder. The blue-clad arm fell, the high bugle notes had just sounded when the long line of farm wagons, horses, spring wagons and carriages leaped forward. The rumbling of the wheels shook the earth. There were shouts, curses, shrieks and prayers. The sound of guns mingled with the crack of whips.

Within two minutes the line was all strung out, horsemen in the lead, buggies and wagons coming up in the rear. A carriage hit a rock and overturned. Men fell out, cut their horses free and rode off.

Captain Hays, suddenly weary, gathered his men together and rode off to camp. Their big job was done.

Seconds after twelve o'clock, sooners popped out of their hiding places and staked their claims. Back in his ravine by the bubbling waterfall, Frank Greer timed his walk to reach Guthrie and stake a choice lot where he would begin publishing his Oklahoma *State Capital*. Shortly after he arrived baggage and mail were dumped off to one side of the Santa Fe tracks and Greer found his precious bundles. Tents were going up when he sold the first copies of the newspaper he had printed in Kansas.

Back in Arkansas City, train after train pulled out of the Sante Fe station. As the *Tribune* correspondent wrote,

"All along the land after we had passed the Oklahoma line, we could see wagons and riders racing like mad across the prairie. Some wagons were abandoned and more than one horse was riderless."

Not all men who won their land rode to it. Some ran on foot. The *Harper's* correspondent saw one man carrying on his back a tent, blanket, dishes and an axe, with food enough for two days, run down the Santa Fe tracks for six miles. He made it in 60 minutes. Then he staked his claim, crawled under a large tree and lay for some time unable to speak.

That first afternoon thousands of persons milled around in Guthrie. The only water came from the muddy Cottonwood. Enterprising settlers, after registering their lands, peddled water in buckets. Most of it was undrinkable. Red dust was everywhere. The streets were ankle-deep. A thick film hung over everything and stuck to the sweaty, bearded faces.

In Guthrie and Oklahoma City trains kept dumping lumber and boxes alongside the Santa Fe tracks. The railroad representative put up a sign, "Pick up your stuff." It is to the settlers' credit that not one theft was reported. Food was scarce. Dusty ham sandwiches sold for a quarter, pork and a teaspoonful of beans for $2. One bitter Missourian estimated that if he wanted to eat normally it would cost him $7.50 a day—exactly what he spent in a week back home. He stayed one day.

Within 24 hours Oklahoma City, Guthrie, Norman and Kingfisher were established—with a singular lack of violence. The thousands of settlers who crowded these new-born cities were unknown to one another and had come from different parts of the country. Yet while the first tents were being raised they gathered together to demonstrate the American capacity for self-government. Barely 24 hours after the first wagons had leaped across the Oklahoma line, calls were issued for mass meetings to

Moving into line for the 1893 run into the Cherokee Strip.

Standing in line to register in El Reno.

Just before the first number was drawn at El Reno. The boxes in the foreground
held all the regulations for the lottery.

organize governments and establish law and order. Temporary regimes were set up which, with few changes, managed local affairs for a year, until legal government was provided by Congress. Ironically, one of the few men killed in Oklahoma City was Couch, the leader of the boomers, who had done so much to draw national attention to the need for settling the Unassigned Lands, and who became the elected mayor. He was shot to death in a dispute over a claim.

It had been a magnificent frontier melodrama. The Run of 1889 was the beginning. There would be several more. In 1893 the Cherokee Outlet itself was opened for settlement and more than 100,000 men, women and children would repeat, on a larger scale, what had taken place on that bright, crisp day of April 22, 1889.

There was a final run in 1911 when the last section of free land was opened for homesteading. But it was really during the 1889-93 land rushes that the last frontier was reached.

The dust had settled not only over Oklahoma, but essentially over all the West.

What had happened in the half-century since the first wagon trains of emigrants moved west over the Oregon Trail was, and is, unparalleled in history. In just about fifty years, a vast wilderness of some 2,000,000 square miles was made into a vast and flourishing empire. A virgin land, populated only by hostile tribes of savages, had been tamed by singularly independent men and women who were never satisfied until they had seen what lay beyond the rim of the next hill.

They had conquered this unknown land and its natural hazards with their hands and their hearts. They had broken trails where there had been seemingly impassable wilderness. They had delivered their mail by horse, pony, and stagecoach, at the cost of many lives. They had crisscrossed this land with railroad tracks and telegraph wires although lesser men said it could not be done. Their vigor and vitality had built towns and cities between dawn and sunset. They had dug fortunes from the earth that were greater than Solomon ever dreamed. Yet all of this had not been accomplished without some injustices, not without wounding the land they loved.

In their ruthless advance they had ended a way of life. They had not only wiped out the red man's culture by violence, broken promises, whiskey and bribery, but they had carelessly exterminated his buffalo. They had destroyed forests without thinking of the future. They had, without protest, allowed cattle barons to usurp enormous privileges and had granted almost tyrannical power and great land-holdings to railroad kings. In their rush to build an empire their indifference often bred corruption and lawlessness.

But they won the land. They had dug their mines, drilled their wells, plowed their fields, sown their seeds, thrust down their roots.

The troubles and tragedies of their early days were really only growing pains. Now the West had come of age; its people were ready to reap a rich harvest from a challenging land that had already demanded a full measure of sacrifice and iron courage.

First train leaving the line north of Orlando, bound for Perry, September 16, 1893.
The trains were ordered to travel at 15 miles per hour, the estimated speed of horses and wagons.

Epilogue
The Great Western Belt Buckle Fraud

IN recent years the Butch Cassidy story has produced twists more bizarre than the claim of William Phillips that he was the outlaw. The latest addition to the legend had its beginning at the end of World War II when the hobby of collecting Americana became big business. In the 1950s, 1960s, and 1970s buyers swarmed into auction galleries, flea markets, and antique shops buying everything from Depression-era comic books to arrowheads. Choice items were connected to America's Wild West. Photographs, guns, wanted posters, branding irons, spurs, saddles—prices mounted as they became rare.

In the late 1960s and early 1970s brass Western belt buckles, supposedly issued by Wells Fargo, Adams Express Company, Colorado State Penitentiary, and many other companies and institutions popularly connected with the days of the Wild West, began to flood the United States at gun and antique shows and soon became part of respectable collections.

The buckles were stamped as made by Tiffany's, the famous New York jewelry concern and Emerson Gaylord, a Civil War leather accouterment manufacturer. The buckles had a heavy wire loop held in place by a flat

TIFFANY & GAYLORD
EXPRESS & EXHIBITION
BELT PLATES

by
PERCY
SEIBERT

The title page of the fraudulent book supposedly written by the late Percy Seibert, the American engineer who employed Butch Cassidy and the Sundance Kid at the Concordia Tin Mines in Bolivia after the turn of the century. Seibert was the principal source of information as to how the outlaw pair died. Seibert never wrote this book, which has a phony copyright of 1950. Most of the text was stolen from a pamphlet on military design written by J. Duncan Campbell and Edgar M. Howell and published by the Smithsonian Institution in 1963; the majority of photographs and prints were plagiarized from books written by this author. This spurious book, undoubtfully issued to boost the authenticity of the fake Western belt buckles, appeared shortly after Seibert's death in 1971. Obviously his name had been selected from the obituary columns.

Frank Fish, a legitimate collector of Americana, was dead when this foreword supposedly was written. He had never met nor did he know Percy Seibert. Fish was found dead at his home in Amador City, California, April 6, 1965. His museum had been looted. The photograph of Seibert used here was plagiarized from a volume on the West written by the author of this book.

1000 Sets Cadet Equipments

Consisting of Small Leather Cartridge Box with nickled Cartridge Box Plate, adjustable Waist Belt with small Eagle plate; Leather Bayonet Scabbard for 16 inch bayonet. Small Cap Pouch when desired for use with Muzzle-loading Arms.

All made of black harness leather; suitable for Military Schools. All in fine order. Price, 88 cents set.

U. S. Regulation Waist Belt and Plate.

100 Sets U. S. Regulation Equipments.
FOR CALIBRE 45 BREECH-LOADING RIFLE.

Consisting of McKeever Cartridge Box; Web loop for 20 cal. 45 cartridges; Steel Bayonet Scabbard with swivel frog, either plain or stamped U. S. Adjustable Waist Belt with either the U. S. Regulation Belt Plate or the Eagle Belt Plate, as generally used by the G. A. R. and Military Academies. Black harness leather, bridle quality. Price, $2.50 set.
200 Sets in cleaned and repaired order, $1.75 per set.

100 Sets Sportsmen's Equipments,

Consisting of Russet Leather Waist Belt, nickled buckle and U .S. wool-lined Cartridge Pouch; makes very neat and light set for sportsmen. Cartridge Pouch will hold 30 cal. 45 cartridges. NEW. Price per set, 75c.

300 Wool-lined Cartridge Pouches.

With Russet Leather, adjustable shoulder slings; in good order, 75 cents set.

Waist Belts and Plates.

1000 U. S. PRIVATES' WAIST BELTS AND PLATES,
Fair order, each 25 cents.
Infantry Eagle Belts and Plates, good condition, 50 cents each.
10,000 U. S. Artillery Waist Belts, with Eagle plates and Sword frog, all made of best black harness leather; wax finished on flesh side. English style.
NEW.
Have a large quantity of these belts and will put the price at 40 cents each.

This is another page of Bannerman's catalog. Note the "Waist Belts and Plates."

RELICS.
COLLECTION OF 50 DIFFERENT KINDS OF ARMS.
AS USED BY THE U. S. GOVT. LAST 75 YEARS.

List on application. All in fine order, having been refinished. Price, $300.00

A Collection of 15 Different Kinds of Revolvers and Pistols,
Used by U. S Government, last 40 Years.

List on application. All in fine Order, having been refinished. Price, $75.00

A Collection of Bombshells, as Used in Civil War.

List on application. Free from Powder. Total weight, 1,500 lbs. Price for lot, $100

6 Swords, as used by the U. S. Cavalry, 1840, straight blades, in good refinished order. Price, each, 2.50
1000 Flints for flint lock muskets and pistols. Each, .05
25 Dragon Horse Pistols with extension stocks; primer locks; in fine order, swiveled ramrod. Cal. 58. Each, 2.50
Lot of 50 Assorted Rifles, Muskets and Carbines, part of the lot surrendered by the Indian Chief, Sitting Bull, to the U.S. Government, after the Custer Massacre; some of the rifles are the Leman Indian Sporting Rifle with heavy barrels and fine sights; stocks and woodwork are worn thin; some stocks are repaired with buckskin; some are still loaded. Charges will be withdrawn before shipment. Prices: Carbines, $3; muskets, $4; sporting rifles, $5; some Henry Repeating Rifles in lot. Price, $7.00

Signature of Patrick Henry, to a Land Grant,

With the Seal of the Commonwealth of Virginia, A. D. 1783. Price, $100.00

Reindeer Skin Fur Coats
WITH HOODS.

Made for use of the Greeley Relief Expedition; no style, but lots of comfort in cold weather; reindeer skins have thickest fur known; flesh side is nicely alum or Indian tanned. Price, $10.00
100 Pair Greeley Rubber Sandals purchased from U. S. Navy on the return of the Greeley Relief Expedition from Arctic regions; sizes very large—10s, 12s and 14s, new, with heel strap and buckles; useful in cold weather. Price, .75

10 Sleeping Bags of Elk or Reindeer Skin,
Six feet long, with flaps and buttons, new, from Greeley relief expedition, Price, $15.00

5000 Lbs. Pemmican Prepared Meat.

Put up by Kemp, Day & Co. of New York, for the Greeley relief Exhibition; will keep for 20 years. Packed in 1½ and 7 lb cans. Price, 10 cents per lb.

RELICS.
COLLECTION OF 50 DIFFERENT KINDS OF ARMS.
AS USED BY THE U. S. GOVT. LAST 75 YEARS.

List on application. All in fine order, having been refinished. Price, $300.00

A Collection of 15 Different Kinds of Revolvers and Pistols,
Used by U. S Government, last 40 Years.

List on application. All in fine Order, having been refinished. Price, $75.00

A Collection of Bombshells, as Used in Civil War.

List on application. Free from Powder. Total weight, 1,500 lbs. Price for lot, $100

Waist Belts and Plates.

1000 U. S. PRIVATES' WAIST BELTS AND PLATES,
Fair order, each 25 cents.
Infantry Eagle Belts and Plates, good condition, 50 cents each.

10,000 Wells Fargo Steamship Belt Plates by Louis Tiffany New York. All complete with black hide belts and holsters for 38 cal. Colt Revolver. Price, $1.00

Reindeer Skin Fur Coats
WITH HOODS.

Made for use of the Greeley Relief Expedition; no style, but lots of comfort in cold weather; reindeer skins have thickest fur known; flesh side is nicely alum or Indian tanned. Price, $10.00
100 Pair Greeley Rubber Sandals purchased from U. S. Navy on the return of the Greeley Relief Expedition from Arctic regions; sizes very large—10s, 12s and 14s, new, with heel strap and buckles; useful in cold weather. Price, .75

10 Sleeping Bags of Elk or Reindeer Skin,
Six feet long, with flaps and buttons, new, from Greeley relief expedition, Price, $15.00

5000 Lbs. Pemmican Prepared Meat.

Put up by Kemp, Day & Co. of New York, for the Greeley relief Exhibition; will keep for 20 years. Packed in 1½ and 7 lb cans. Price, 10 cents per lb.

This is the doctored poster issued by the scam artists. Note how they combined both catalog pages and inserted their recently manufactured "10,000 Wells Fargo" belt buckles.

This is an example of how the operators of the "Western Belt Buckle Sting" made up a fake poster to authenticate their fraudulent products, which swept across the country in the last twenty years selling from $25 to $500. The first page comes from a rare nineteenth-century catalog issued by Francis Bannerman, a celebrated dealer in Civil War and Western frontier artifacts. Collectors can only groan at the prices of the now very rare items listed.

piece brazed to the plate. No American belt buckle made from 1865 to 1900 was ever manufactured in this fashion. Some of the words stamped on the plates were meaningless.

J. Duncan Campbell, a former United States Army Colonel, a noted authority on military insignia, consultant to the Smithsonian Institution and director of the William Penn Memorial Museum in Harrisburg, Pennsylvania, began to investigate the authenticity of the belt buckles, then selling at prices from $25 to $400. During his thirty years as a collector, researcher, and writer on the subject, Colonel Campbell had examined over 10,000 belt plates but had never seen one issued by Wells Fargo, Western Union, Adams Express Company, and Union Pacific.

THE GAYLORD COLORADO STATE PENITENTIARY BELT
PLATE

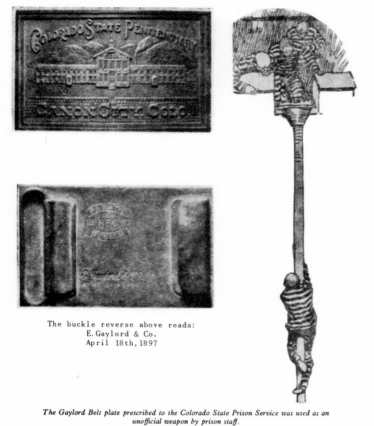

The buckle reverse above reads:
E. Gaylord & Co.
April 18th, 1897

The Gaylord Belt plate prescribed to the Colorado State Prison Service was used as an unofficial weapon by prison staff.

come from old prints or from the imagination of the manufacturer.

Tiffany's had not issued the buckles; Emerson Gaylord, after the Civil War had brought him prosperity, bought an ironworks that produced steel pins and mailboxes and continued his production of mailbags. The company went out of business in 1889 and at no time did Emerson Gaylord return to his old trade nor did any successor use his name. The Gaylord Company never made belt buckles.

Suddenly a strange book appeared in the early 1970s with the title *Tiffany & Gaylord Express & Exhibition Belt Plates.* It was shocking to discover the alleged author was Percy Seibert, who, the book boasted, was the man who "actually employed Butch Cassidy and the Sundance Kid at the Concordia Tin Mine in Bolivia and became a close friend to the two most wanted men in America."

THE TIFFANY STUDIO'S ADAMS EXPRESS CO. BELT
PLATE

Alvin Adams founder of the famous Adams Express Co. Adams was Wells Fargo's biggest opposition in those early banking and express days.

A page from the spurious *Tiffany & Gaylord Express & Exhibition Belt Plates.* It purports to show a belt buckle issued by the Emerson Gaylord Company, a Civil War manufacturer, at the request of the State of Colorado, which wanted a brass belt buckle "used by superior officers in the prison service." Colorado authorities had never approached any manufacturer with this request; in fact the Gaylord Company had been out of service for seven years when this buckle was supposedly issued. No such plate was ever made in 1897, nor was any patent issued.

To add a frontier flavor to the phony Colorado belt buckle, the mysterious publisher of the book used the drawing on the right of a prisoner supposedly escaping from the Colorado State Penitentiary. The drawing had been plagiarized from a book written on the West by this author; the sketch was of Oliver Perry, the New York train robber, escaping from Dannemora, New York State Penitentiary for the Criminally Insane.

Campbell soon determined that the sale of the millions of supposedly Western frontier belt buckles was one of the biggest confidence games to have been pulled on the American public in years. The buckles, he discovered, had been manufactured in England. The plates were not even reproductions; designs such as Annie Oakley and her dog, riverboats, stagecoaches, steamboats, and trains had either

The phony Adams Express Company belt buckle, which sold in the tens of thousands across the United States in the 1960s and 1970s. At no time did Adams ever issue a belt buckle. According to the fraudulent book, "over one million" of these buckles were distributed by Adams to its employees, yet not one was ever seen until 1967! Adams, the major public carrier in the Civil War and on the frontier, was the principal target of the outlaw gangs of the Wild West from the James-Youngers to the Wild Bunch. The company had about 1,000 employees; thus each one would have been given 1,000 belt buckles!

THE E. GAYLORD MASSACHUSETTS
WELLS FARGO & CO. EXPRESS PLATE

The 1877 Parade design plate by Gaylord was the most widely used of all Wells Fargo plates during the 1870's.

This plate displayed a primitive iron horse of the Union Pacific Railroad, and a great deal of artistic licence was given to Gaylord in the creation of this very popular belt plate.

The train does not appear to be pulling a Wells Fargo Express car, which must have been overlooked by Gaylord in the die sinking of this plate.

Gaylord, unlike Tiffany was not a perfectionist, but on all of the Gaylord products sharp detail and quality was of first importance.

THE AMERICAN EXPRESS COMPANY,
WELLS, BUTTERFIELD & COMPANY —
TIFFANY BELT PLATE

Another phony Western belt buckle supposedly issued by the American Express Company. In the 1850s American Express controlled northern New England with lines into Canada, the Middle West, and the Northwest. The design for the fake buckles was taken from an 1858 lithograph used in *Old Way-bills* by Alvin Harlow, a history of the express companies published in 1934.

One of the most popular of the fake Western belt buckles was the Wells Fargo & Co. Express Plate, supposedly issued by the famous public carrier in the 1870s and manufactured by Gaylord. No such buckle was ever manufactured by Emerson Gaylord's Company.

Seibert, at the time, was dead. He had never written a line in his lifetime on belt buckles nor had he any interest in them.

When Colonel Campbell got in touch with this writer we discovered that the text of the book had been stolen from Campbell's work on military insignia, written with Edgar M. Howell and published by the Smithsonian Institution in 1962. This immediately proved that the book's copyright of 1950 was fraudulent.

The photographs in this weird book had been plagiarized from this writer's many books on the West, including Percy Seibert's picture, taken on orders of the writer on March 11, 1961.

The book had been copyrighted in the name of a reputable New York City manufacturer of military insignia. The Fifth Avenue address was wrong; the company before moving to New Jersey had actually been based on Twenty-third Street. The spurious authors undoubtedly had plucked out of air a more impressive Fifth Avenue address.

When this writer contacted the firm a bewildered spokesman informed him the company knew nothing of the book, had never manufactured belt buckles, and had never heard of Percy Seibert.

It is evident that the book was published simply to authenticate the buckles and help to increase the sagging sales. Ads for the articles were appearing in magazines and in major newspapers across the country. A close examination of the text of the book revealed words, phrases, and spelling to be associated with England. Colonel Campbell believes, as this writer does, that the book may have been published there or the manuscript sent from England and printed in this country.

Colonel Campbell also pointed out another bizarre and grim angle to the story. The author of the book's foreword was Frank Fish who claimed a "close friendship" with Percy Seibert. Campbell identified Fish as a legitimate collector who operated a museum close to Campbell's home in Amador, California. Friends say that he had one or two valuable belt buckles in his collection of Americana. On the morning of April 6, 1965, Fish was found dead in his home; his museum had been looted before or after his death.

Friends insist Fish never knew Seibert; in all the years this writer was acquainted with Seibert, he had never mentioned the name of Fish or discussed Western belt buckles.

The plagiarism in the book clearly proves it could not have been written before the death of Fish or published after 1970. It is evident that the operators of this fraud simply selected the names of Fish and Seibert from the

This very unusual belt plate was minted by the **Tiffany Company** for employees of Wells Fargo on the West Coast.

Only a limited amount were minted and the collector is very fortunate indeed to possess one of these fine plates today.

Correct front plaque markings are as follows: —

Red Bluffs—Yankee Jims—Angels Camp—Diamond Springs—Colama—Charley's Rancho—Fiddle Town—El-Dorado—George Town—Grass Valley—Poverty Hill—Rattle Snake Bar—Empire Ranch —Nevada Calico—Sacramento City—Amador City—Oakland—Timbuctoo—Smartville—Sucker Flat—Negro Hill—Mud Springs—Spanish Town—Pence's Ranch—Cotton Wood—Marysville and Lynchberg.

The Author feels that this plate was manufactured purely as an exhibition piece for sale in the Parrott Building in San-Francisco. There is not enough documentary evidence to show that this plate was actually issued to Wells Fargo employees.

THE CENTRAL & UNION PACIFIC RAILROAD COMPANY PLATE

This Tiffany plate was issued to guards and railroad employees during the 1870's.

The early version of the Central and Union Pacific Railroad Company plate was based on the Wells Fargo series.

This fine looking plate depicts the loading of Texas Long Horn Cattle into an awaiting freight car bound for the Chicago stock yard.

Percy Seibert, the American engineer and official of the Concordia Tin Mines, Bolivia, was one of the few men trusted by Butch Cassidy and the Sundance Kid. After his death, the belt buckle fakers used his name as the author of a fraudulent book to help the sale of their phony product.

The Western belt buckle fakers outdid themselves on this phony product. Belt plates marked Central & Union Pacific Rail Road Co. are an impossibility. The Union Pacific and the Central Pacific printed a joint timetable to cover the geographical area they served as a convenience to passengers whose travels required both roads. The belt buckle scam artists, using a joint timetable as their point of reference, dreamed up both a belt buckle and a railroad!

obituary columns, as men who could not legally retaliate from the grave.

The fraud continued. Some time later as the boom for the buckles started to sag, a letter supposedly written by Seibert was sent to a magazine devoted to the study of antiques. In it the writer stated he had meticulously researched the subject of the belt buckles in London mu-seums and found them to be authentic. The box number signed to the letter was proven to be nonexistent.

Millions of American consumers and innocent businessmen have been defrauded, the names of Seibert and Fish have been defamed, and somewhere in England a scam artist has grown rich on the legends of Butch Cassidy and America's Wild West.

Bibliography

GENERAL REFERENCE WORKS

Aberly, Lloyd, *Pursuit of the Horizon: A Life of George Catlin.*

Baker, Ray Stannard, "The Great Southwest," *Century Magazine*, May–November, 1902.

Beadle, John H., *The Undeveloped West*, or *Five Years in the Territories*, Philadelphia, 1873.

Botkin, Benjamin Albert, *A Treasury of American Folklore*, Crown, N. Y., N. Y., 1944.

Davis, Clyde Brion, *The Arkansas*, N. Y. and Toronto, Ont., 1940.

Day, P. C., "The Winds of the U. S. and Their Economic Uses," *Yearbook of the U. S. Department of Agriculture*, Government Printing Office, 1911.

Dick, Everett, *The Story of the Frontier*, N. Y., N Y., 1941.

Galloway, Tod B., "Private Letters of a Government Official in the Southwest," *Journal of American History*, 1909.

Gard, Wayne, *Frontier Justice*, University of Oklahoma Press, Norman, Okla.

Griswold, Don and Jean, *Colorado: A Century of Cities.*

Havighurst, Walter, *Upper Mississippi: A Wilderness Saga*, N. Y., N. Y., 1937.

Jones, Charles J., *Buffalo Jones' Forty Years of Adventure* compiled by Henry Inman, Topeka, Kans., 1899.

Journal of the Expedition under the Command of Col. Henry Dodge to the Rocky Mountains during the Summer of 1835, report of the Secretary of War, February 27, 1836.

King, *Memoirs of Clarence*, N. Y., N. Y., 1914.

McClintock, Walter, *The Old North Trail*, London, 1910.

Otero, Miguel Antonio, *My Life on the Frontier*, N. Y., 1935.

Smith, Henry Nash, *Virgin Land: The American West as Symbol and Myth*, Cambridge, Mass., 1950.

Taft, Mrs. Walter, "Across the Plains in the Early Sixties," *The Trail*, July, 1910.

Thwaites, Reuben Gold, ed., Edwin James' *Account of an Expedition to the Rocky Mountains Performed in the Years 1819-1820 under the Command of Maj. S. H. Long*, Cleveland, Ohio, 1904.

Turner, Frederick J., *The Frontier in American History*, N. Y., N. Y., 1920.

MANUSCRIPTS

The West (two bound books of clippings covering every subject from reports of stagecoach robberies to frontier political feuds), owned by the author.

Collection of personal and business letters (c. 1850–1860) from a frontier lawyer, owned by the author.

NEWSPAPERS

Bad Lands Cowboy, The (Little Missouri, Medora P. O., D. T.), February 7, 1884–April 9, 1885.

Bismarck *Tribune*, The (Bismarck, D. T.), July 11, 1873–December 27, 1876.

Black Hills Pioneer (Deadwood, D. T.), June 8, 1876, January 6, 1877–February 14, 1878.

Cheyenne County Rustler (Wano, Kans.), July 10, 1885–October 30, 1885.

Deadwood *Pioneer-Times* (Deadwood, D. T.), 1876–1877.

Dodge City *Times* (Dodge City, Kans.) October 14, 1876–October 6, 1877.

Hays City *Railway Advance* (Hays City, Kans.), June 23, 1868.

Kansas Cowboy (Dodge City, Kans.), June 28, 1884–December 27, 1884.

Mining Journal, The (Black Hawk, Colo.), November 30, 1863–January 2, 1864.

Missouri Intelligencer (Franklin, Mo.), March 1824–December 1826.

Montana Post (Virginia City, Mont.), August 27, 1864–April 15, 1865; November 3, 1866.

Nebraska News (Nebraska City, Neb.), January 17, 1857–May 8, 1858.

Omaha City *Times* (Omaha, Neb.), June 11, 1857–July, 1858.

Sioux City *Tribune* (Sioux City, Iowa), March 24, 1876–June 15, 1877.

THE SPANISH INFLUENCE

Abbott, John S., *History of Cortès*, N. Y., N. Y.

Acton, Arthur Scott, *Secret Visita against Viceroy Mendoza*, Los Angeles, Calif., 1932.

Bandelier, A. F., *The Gilded Man*, N. Y., N. Y., 1893.

Bandelier, Fanny, *The Journey of Alvar Nunez Cabeza de Vaca*, N. Y., N. Y., 1905.

Bawne, Edward Gaylor, ed., *Narratives of the Career of Hernando de Soto as Told by a Knight of Elvas*, N. Y., 1922.

Blackmar, Frank W., *Spanish Institutions of the Southwest*, Baltimore, Md., 1891.

Bolton, Herbert E., *Spanish Explorations in the Southwest*, N. Y., N. Y., 1916.

Butler, Mrs. C. E., pub. *The Coronado Magazine*, Coronado Quarto Centennial, N. M., 1940.

Catlin, George, *North American Indians*, Philadelphia, Pa., 1891.

Davenport, Herbert, and Wells, Joseph K., "The First European in Texas," *Southwestern Historical Quarterly*, Vol. XXII.

Dellenbaugh, Frederick S., *The True Route of Coronado's March*, American Geographical Society, Washington, D. C., 1897.

Donoghue, D., *Coronado and Quivira*, Chicago, Ill., 1936.

Dunn, William E., "The Apache Mission on the San Saba River," *Southwestern Historical Quarterly*, Texas State Historical Association, Austin, Tex., Vol. XVII, 1914.

Hackett, C. W., *Revolt of the Pueblo Indians*, Albuquerque, N. M., 1940.

Hammond, George, and Rey, ed., *Narratives of Coronado's Expedition 1540–1542*, Albuquerque, N. M., 1940.

Keating, Maurice, transl., Bernard Diaz del Castillo's *True History of the Conquest of New Mexico*, London, 1800.

Morris, J. Bayard, ed., *Hernando Cortès' Letter to Charles V*, N. Y., N. Y., 1929.

Pfefferkorn, Ignaz, *Sonora: A Description of the Province*, 1949.

Ruberica, Juan de Cubas, "Coronado's Muster Roll," *American Historical Review*, Richmond, Va., 1939.

Thomas, A. B., *The Plains Indians and New Mexico, 1751–1758.*

Winship, George Parker, *Coronado's Expedition, 1540–1542*, Washington, D. C., 1892.

Winship, George Parker, transla., Pedro de Casteñada's *Coronado's Journey to New Mexico and the Great Plains*, N. Y., N. Y., 1894.

Wissler, Clark, "The Influence of the Horse in the Development of Plains Culture," *American Anthropologist.*

NATIVE WILD LIFE

Dodge, Richard I., *The Hunting Ground of the Great West*, London, 1877.

Merriman, C. Hart, "The Prairie Dog of the Great Plains," *U. S. Department of Agriculture Yearbook*, Government Printing Office, 1902.

Nelson, E. W., "The Rabbits of the United States," U. S. Department of Agriculture, Bureau of Biological Survey, Government Printing Office, Washington, D. C., 1909.

Palmer, T. S., "The Jackrabbit of the United States, U. S. Department of Agriculture, Bureau of Biological Survey, *Bulletin No. 8.*, Government Printing Office, Washington, D. C., 1897.

Santee, Ross, *Men and Horses*, N. Y., N. Y., 1926.

Stone, Witmer, and Cram, William E., *American Animals*, N. Y., N. Y., 1913.

LEWIS AND CLARK

Bakeless, John E., *Partners in Discovery*, N. Y., N. Y., 1947.

Brooks, Noah, *First Across the Continent*, N. Y., N. Y., 1922.

Burroughs, Raymond D., *Explorations Unlimited*, Detroit, Mich., 1953.

De Voto, Bernard, ed., *Journals of Lewis and Clark*, Boston, Mass., 1953.

Flandraus, Grace C., *Lewis and Clark Expedition*, St. Paul, Minn., 1927.

Fletcher, Robert Henry, *American Adventure*, American Pioneer Trails Association, N. Y., N. Y., 1954.

Gass, Patrick, *Journals of Lewis and Clark*, Philadelphia, Pa., 1812.

Guiness, Ralph B., "The Purpose of the Lewis and Clark Expedition," *Mississippi Valley Historical Review*, Cedar Rapids, Iowa, 1933.

Thwaites, Reuben, ed., *Lewis and Clark Journals*, N. Y., N. Y., 1904.

ZEBULON PIKE

Hafen, Leroy R., "Zebulon Pike," *Colorado Magazine*, Denver, Colo., 1931.

King, Nicholas, *An Account of Pike's Journey*, Washington, D. C., 1807.

Pike, Zebulon, *Journals*, Philadelphia, Pa.

Pritchard, Jesse L., "To Pike's Peak in Search of Gold in 1859," *The Trail*, September, October, 1911.

Quaile, Milo, ed., *Southwestern Expedition of Zebulon Pike*, Chicago, Ill., 1925.

THE FUR TRADE

Chittenden, Hiram Martin, *The American Fur Trade of the Far West*, N. Y., N. Y., 1902.

Gregg, Joseph R., *History of Oregon and the Santa Fe Trail*, Portland, Ore., 1935.

Inman, Henry, *The Old Santa Fe Trail*, Topeka, Kans., 1916.

Parsons, Eugene, "The Story of the Trapper," *The Trail*, July, 1911.

Vanderwalker, Victor, "Over the Santa Fe Trail in '64," *The Trail*, June, 1909.

Vandiveer, Clarence A., *The Fur Trade and Early Western Exploration*, Cleveland, Ohio, 1929.

EARLY TEXAS

Barker, Eugene C., *The Life of Stephen F. Austin, Founder of Texas, 1793–1836*, Nashville, Tenn., 1925.

Gillett, James Buchanan, *Six Years with the Texas Rangers, 1875–1881*, Austin, Tex., 1921.

Gray, A. C., ed., *Diary of Col. William F. Gray*, Houston, Tex., 1909.

James, Marquis, *The Raven*, Bobbs Merrill, N. Y., N. Y., 1929.

King, W. H., *The Texas Ranger Service and the History of the Rangers with Observation on Their Value as a Police Protection*, Dallas, Tex., 1898.

Reid, Samuel C., *The Scouting Expedition of McCulloch's Texas Rangers*, Philadelphia, Pa., 1848.

Webb, Walter Prescott, *The Texas Rangers*, Boston, Mass. and N. Y., N. Y., 1935.

THE OREGON TRAIL

Driggs, Howard, and Meeker, Ezra, *The Old Oregon Trail*, N. M., 1922.

Meeker, Ezra, *Old Oregon Trail*, Omaha, Neb., 1906.

Old Oregon Trail, The, compiled by the WPA., N. Y., N. Y., 1939.

Old Oregon Trail, The, hearing before Congress on roads, Washington, D. C., 1925.

Page, Elizabeth, *Wagons West*, N. Y., N. Y., 1930.

Parkman, Francis, Jr., *The Oregon Trail*, N. Y., N. Y., 1847.

Spaulding, Kenneth, ed., *On the Oregon Trail* by Robert Stuart, University of Oklahoma Press, Norman, Okla., 1953.

Wade, Mason, *The Oregon Trail*, from the notes of Francis Parkman, N. Y., N. Y., 1943.

JOHN CHARLES FRÉMONT

Bigelow, John, *Life of Frémont*, Cincinnati, Ohio, 1856.

Derby, G. H., *John Charles Frémont*, Buffalo, N. Y., 1849.

Frémont's Reports on Explorations to the Rocky Mountains, 1842, Washington, D. C., 1845.

Gudde, Erwin G. and Elizabeth K. (ed.), Charles Preuss' *Exploring with Frémont*, University of Oklahoma Press, Norman, Okla., 1958.

Harrington, Fred H., "Frémont and the North Americans," *American Historical Review*, Richmond, Va., 1939.

Nevins, Allan, *Frémont: The West's Greatest Adventurer*, N. Y., N. Y., 1928.

Nevins, Allan, *Frémont: Pathmarker of the West*, Appleton-Century, N. Y., N. Y., 1939.

Nevins, Allan, ed., John Charles Frémont's *Narratives of Exploration and Adventure*, N. Y., N. Y., 1956.

THE MORMONS

Driggs, Howard, *Mormon Trail*, Manchester, N. H., 1947.

"Hand Cart Brigade," *Huntsman's Echo*, Wood River, Neb., July 26, 1860.

THE GOLD RUSH

Allen, W. W., and Avery, R. B., *The California Gold Book*, N. Y., N. Y., 1893.

Delano, Alonzo, *Life on the Plains and Among the Diggings*, N. Y., N. Y., 1857.

Delano, Alonzo, *Pen Knife Sketches*, San Francisco, Calif., 1857.

Delavan, James, *Notes on California and the Placers*, N. Y., N. Y., 1850.

Hambleton, Chalkley J., *A Gold Hunter's Experiences*, Chicago, Ill., 1898.

Jackson, Joseph Henry, *Gold Rush Album*, N. Y., N. Y., 1949.

Johnson, W. C., *Experiences of a Forty-Niner*, N. Y., N. Y., 1892.

McIlvaine, William, Jr., *Sketches and Notes of Personal Adventures in California and Mexico*, N. Y., N. Y., 1850.

Pritchard, Jesse L., "To Pike's Peak in Search of Gold in 1859," *The Trail*, September, October, 1911.

Revere, J. W., *A Tour of Duty in California*, Chicago, Ill., 1849.

Stokes, George W., and Driggs, Howard R., *Deadwood Gold*, N. Y., N. Y., 1926.

Webster, Kimball, *The Gold Seekers of '49*, Manchester, N. H., 1917.

UNCLE SAM'S CAMELS

Bonsal, Stephen, *Edward Fitzgerald Beale*, N. Y., N. Y., 1912.

Hoffman, Velma Rudd, "Lt. Beale and the Camel Corps through Arizona," *Arizona Highways*, October, 1957.

Lesley, Lewis B., *Uncle Sam's Camels: The Journals of May Humphreys Stacey Supplemented by the Report of Edward Fitzgerald Beale (1857–1858)*, Harvard University Press, Cambridge, Mass., 1929.

"Report upon the Purchase, Importation and Use of Camels and Dromedaries to Be Employed for Military Purposes," *Senate Executive Document N 62*, 34th Congress, Government Printing Office, 1857.

THE PONY EXPRESS

Chapman, Arthur, *The Pony Express*, N. Y., N. Y. and London, 1932.

Driggs, Howard R., *The Pony Express Goes Through*, N. Y., N. Y., 1935.

Jones, Lloyd, "Pony Express," *Collier's*, September, 1910.

Pack, Mary, "The Romance of the Pony Express," *Union Pacific Magazine*, August, 1923.

Visscher, William Lightfoot, *A Thrilling and Truthful History of the Pony Express*, or *Blazing the Westward Way*, Chicago, Ill., 1908.

THE TELEGRAPH

Merriam, Lucius S., "The Telegraphs of the Bond-Aided Pacific Railroads," *Political Science Quarterly*, Vol. IX, No. 2.

Rush, David H., "Singing Wires in the Wilderness," *The Westerners' Brand Book*, Chicago, Ill., May, 1958.

STAGECOACHES

Beitleman, John L., "An Attack on the Stage Stations," *The Trail*, June, 1909.

Collins, William Oliver, drawings of the interiors and exteriors of early stage stations, Library, Colorado State Archives.

Davis, Theodore R., "A Stagecoach Ride to Colorado," *Harper's Monthly*, July, 867.

Greeley, Horace, *An Overland Journey*, N. Y., N. Y., 1860.

STEAMBOATS

Chittenden, Hiram Martin, *History of Early Steamboat Navigation on the Missouri River*, (2 vols.), N. Y., N. Y., 1903.

Hunter, Louis C., *Steamboats on the Western Rivers*, Cambridge, Mass., 1949.

Petersen, William J., *Steamboating on the Upper Mississippi*, Iowa, 1937.

RAILROADS

Buchanan, J. R., "The Great Railroad Migration in Northern Nebraska, *Proceedings* of the Nebraska Historical Society, Lincoln, Neb., Vol. XV, 1907.

"Creighton, Edward, Biographical Sketch of," *Nebraska History Magazine*, Vol. XVII.
Cruise, J. D., "Early Days of the Union Pacific," Kansas State Historical Society, Topeka, Kans., Vol., XI, 1910.
Davis, John P., *The Union Pacific*, Chicago, Ill., 1894.
Dodge, Grenville M., "Wonderful Story of the Building of the Pacific Roads," Trans-Continental Railways, Omaha, Neb., 1889.
Eastwood, Colin S., "Construction Work on the Old U. P.," *The Trail*, June, 1910.
Galbraith, R. M., "He Railroaded in Wyoming in Days When Peril and Romance Were Merely a Matter of the Day's Work," *Union Pacific Magazine*, September, 1922.
Harlow, Alvin F., *Old Waybills: The Romance of the Express Companies*, N. Y., N. Y., 1934.
Hibbard, Benjamin H., *A History of the Public Land Policies*, N. Y., N. Y., 1924.
Paxson, Frederic L., "The Pacific Railroads and the Disappearance of the Frontier in America," *Annual Report of the American Historical Association*, Vol. I, 1907.
Settle, Mary Lund, and Raymond W., *Empire on Wheels*, Stanford, Calif., 1949.
Trottman, N., *History of the Union Pacific*, N. Y., N. Y., 1923.
Waters, L. L., *Steel Trails to Santa Fe*, Lawrence, Kans., 1950.

THE INDIAN WARS

Aken, David, *Pioneers of the Black Hills*, or *Gordon's Stockade Party of 1874*, Milwaukee, Wis., 1920.
Arnold, Lt. Col. Frazier, "Ghost Dance and Wounded Knee," *Cavalry Journal*, Vol. XLIII, May-June, 1934.
Bourke, John G., *An Apache Campaign in the Sierra Madre*, N. Y., N. Y., 1886.
Bourke, John G., *Mackenzie's Last Fight with the Cheyennes*, Governors Island, N. Y., 1890.
Bourke, John G., *On the Border with Crook*, Scribner's, N. Y., N. Y., 1891.
Bourke, John G., "General Crook in the Indian Country," *Century Magazine*, March, 1891.
Brininstool, Earl A., *Fighting Red Cloud's Warriors*, Columbus, Ohio, 1926.
Carrington, Frances C., *My Army Life and the Fort Phil Kearny Massacre*, Philadelphia, Pa., 1910.
Congressional hearing on the Chivington massacre, 1865. Report of the Joint Special Committee, Washington, D. C., March 3, 1867.
Connolly, Alonzo P., *The Sioux War and the Minnesota Massacre*, Chicago, Ill., 1896.
Crook, George, *Resumé of Operations against Apache Indians, 1882–1886*, Omaha, Neb., 1886.
De Land, Charles Edmund, "The Sioux Wars," South Dakota Historical Society, Pierre, S. D., Vol. XV, 1930.
Dixon, Joseph K., *The Vanishing Race*, Garden City, N. Y., 1913.
Donaldson, A. B., "The Black Hills Expedition," South Dakota Historical Society, Vol. VII, 1914.
Dorsey, George A., "The Sun Dance," Field Museum, Chicago, Ill., Anthropological Series, Publication 103, Vol. IX, No. 2, 1905.
Dunn, Jacob P., *Massacres of the Mountains: A History of the Indian Wars of the Far West*, N. Y., N. Y., 1886.
Fee, Chester A., *Chief Joseph: The Biography of a Great Indian*, N. Y., N. Y., 1936.
Finerty, John F., *Warpath and Bivouac*, or *The Conquest of the Sioux*, Chicago, Ill., 1890.
Gibbon, Col. John, "Hunting Sitting Bull," *American Catholic Quarterly Review*, October, 1877.
Gibbon, Col. John, "Last Summer's Expedition against the Sioux," *American Catholic Quarterly Review*, pp. 271-304, April, 1877.
Hieb, David I., "Fort Laramie," National Park Service, *Handbook No. 20*, 1954.
Hodge, Frederick Webb, ed. *Handbook of American Indians North of Mexico*, Bureau of American Ethnology, Government Printing Office, Washington, D. C., 1912.
Hughes, Col. Robert Patterson, "The Campaign against the Sioux," *Journal of the Military Service Institution of the United States*, January, 1896.
Hyde, George E., *Red Cloud's Folk: A History of the Oglala Sioux Indians*, Norman, Okla., 1937.
Keim, D. Randolph, *Sheridan's Troopers*, Philadelphia, Pa., 1885.
Libby, Orin Grant, ed., *The Arikara Narrative of the Campaign against the Hostile Dakotas*, 1876, North Dakota Historical Society, Bismarck, N. D., Vol. VI, 1920.
Lockwood, Frank C., *The Apache Indians*, N. Y., N. Y., 1938.
Lounsberry, C. A., "Account of Life at Fort Abraham Lincoln," *The Record*, Fargo N. D., June, 1898.
Malin, J. C., "Indian Policy and Westward Expansion," Kansas Humanistic Studies, Lawrence, Kans., Vol. II, No. 3, 1921.
Marcy, Randolph B., *Thirty Years of Army Life on the Border*, N. Y., N. Y., 1866.
Miles, Nelson A., *Personal Recollections and Observations*, Chicago, Ill., 1896.
Mills, Anson, *My Story*, Washington, D. C., 1918.
Mooney, James, "The Ghost Dance Religion and the Sioux Outbreak of 1890," 14th Annual Report, Part II, Bureau of American Ethnology, 1895.
Mumey, Nolie, "John Milton Chivington, The Misunderstood Man," The Denver Westerners' *Monthly Roundup*, November, 1956.
Myers, Pvt. Frank, *Soldiering in the Dakotas among the Indians*, Huron, Dakota, 1888.
Neill, Edward D., *Fort Snelling, Minnesota*, N. Y., N. Y., 1888.
Payne, Doris Palmer, *Captain Jack, Modoc Renegade*, Portland, Ore., 1938.
Riddle, Jeff C. D., *The Indian History of the Modoc War and the Causes That Led to It*, San Francisco, Calif., 1914.
Smith, Cornelius C., "The Fight at Cibicu," *Arizona Highways*, May, 1956.
Stuart, Granville, *Forty Years on the Frontier* (2 vols.), Paul C. Phillips, ed., Cleveland, Ohio, 1925.
Tallent, Annie D., *The Black Hills*, or *The Last Hunting Ground of the Dakotahs*, St. Louis, Mo., 1899.
Taylor, Joseph Henry, "Bloody Knife and Gall," *North Dakota Historical Quarterly*, July, 1947.
Tilghman, Zoe A., *Quanah, The Eagle of the Comanches*, Oklahoma City, Okla., 1938.
Vestal, Stanley, *Siting Bull*, Boston, Mass., 1932.
Vestal, Stanley, *Warpath*, Boston, Mass., 1934.
Vestal, Stanley, *Warpath and Council Fire: The Plains Indians' Struggle for Survival in War and in Diplomacy, 1851–1891*, Random House, N. Y., N. Y., 1948.
Vestal, Stanley, compiler, *New Sources of Indian History, 1850–1891, The Ghost Dance, The Prairie Sioux: A Miscellany*, Norman, Okla., 1934.
Wellman, Paul I., Death on the Prairie, N. Y., N. Y., 1934.
Wharton, Clarence, *Santana: The Great Chief of the Kiowas and His People*, Dallas, Tex., 1934.
Wissler, Clark, *North American Indians of the Plains*, American Museum of Natural History, N. Y., N. Y., 1927.

Manuscripts in the Manuscript Room, New York Public Library

Brown, Edwin M., trumpeter, B Company, letters.
Cresson, Lt. Charles Clement, 1st Cavalry, description of a punitive expedition, June 4–August 10, 1878.
Forsyth, James B., defense of his actions at the Battle of Wounded Knee.
McClellan, James, diary of the expedition against Dull Knife, 1876–1877.
Miers, Col., letters from Fort Leavenworth, Kans., 1876, 1877.
Struckman, William, bugler, 3rd Regiment, U. S. Cavalry, 1858–1862, letters.

CUSTER AND THE LITTLE BIG HORN MASSACRE

Adams, Jacob, "A Survivor's Story of the Custer Massacre on the American Frontier," *Journal of American History*, Vol. III, pp. 227–32, 1909.
Barry, David F., *Indian Notes on the Custer Battle*, ed. by Usher L. Burdick, Baltimore, Md., 1937.
Brackett, William S., "Custer's Last Battle on the Little Big Horn in Montana, June 25, 1876," contributed to the Historical Society of Montana, Vol. IV, 1903.
Brininstool, E. A., *The Custer Fight: Captain F. W. Benteen's Story of the Battle of the Little Big Horn*, Hollywood, Calif., 1940.
Brininstool, E. A., *Troopers with Custer: Historic Incidents of the Battle of the Little Big Horn*, Harrisburg, Pa., 1952.
Brinkerhoff, Henry, "Account of the Custer Battle," *Custer Scrapbooks*, Billings Public Library, Billings, Mont.
Britt, Albert, "Custer's Last Fight," *Pacific Historical Review*, Vol. XIII, 1944.
Byrne, Patrick E., "The Custer Myth," *North Dakota Historical Quarterly*, Vol. VI, April, 1932.
Coughlan, Col. T. M., "The Battle of the Little Big Horn," *Cavalry Journal*, January–February, 1934.
Custer, Elizabeth B., *Boots and Saddles*, N. Y., N. Y., 1885.
Dustin, Fred, *Echoes from the Little Big Horn Fight*, Saginaw, Mich., 1953.
Dustin, Fred, *The Custer Fight*, Hollywood, Calif., 1936.
Dustin, Fred, *The Custer Tragedy*, Ann Arbor, Mich., 1939.
Flying Hawk, *Flying Hawk's Tale: A True Story of Custer's Last Fight*, N. Y., N. Y., 1936.
Fougera, Katherine Gibson, *With Custer's Cavalry*, Caldwell, Idaho, 1940.
Garland, Hamlin, "General Custer's Last Fight as Seen by Two Moon," *McClure's*, September, 1898.
Ghent, William J., "Windolph, Benteen and Custer," *Cavalry Journal*, November–December, 1934.
Graham, Col. William A., *The Story of the Little Big Horn*, N. Y., N. Y., 1926.
Graham, Col. William A., *The Custer Myth: A Source Book of Custeriana*, Harrisburg, Pa., 1953.
Graham, Col. William A., *The Reno Court of Inquiry*, Harrisburg, Pa., 1954.
Hogner, Francis R., letters and articles relating to Custer and the Little Big Horn, Manuscript Room, New York Public Library.
Hunt, Frazier, *Custer, The Last of the Cavaliers*, N. Y., N. Y., 1928.
Hunt, Frazier and Robert, *I Fought with Custer: The Story of Sergeant Windolph*, N. Y., N. Y., 1947.
Kellogg, Mark, "Notes, May 17 to June 9, 1876, of the Little Big Horn Expedition," contributed to the Historical Society of Montana, Vol. IX, 1923.
King, Capt. Charles, "Custer's Last Battle," *Harper's Magazine*, August, 1890.
Luce, Edward S., *Keogh, Comanche and Custer*, St. Louis, Mo., 1939.
Luce, Edward S. and Evelyn S., "Custer Battlefield," National Park Service *Handbook Series 1*, Washington, D. C., 1955.
Roe, Charles F., *Custer's Last Battle*, N. Y., N. Y., 1927.
Stewart, Dr. Edgar I., "The Literature of the Custer Fight," *The Pacific Northwesterner*, Vol. I., winter, 1956–57.

WESTERN PHOTOGRAPHERS

Brown, Mark, H., and Felton, W. R., *The Frontier Years: L. A. Huffman, Photographer of the Plains*, Henry Holt and Company, N. Y., N. Y., 1955.
Carvalho, S. N., *Incidents of Travel and Adventure*, reissued N. Y., N. Y., 1959.
Cunningham, Robert E., ed., *Indian Territory: A Frontier Photographic Record by W. S. Prettyman*, University of Oklahoma Press, Norman, Okla., 1957.
Dellenbaugh, Frederick, *A Canyon Passage*, New Haven, Conn., 1926.
Dix, Ross John, *Amusing and Thrilling Adventures of a California Artist While Daguerreotyping a Continent*, Boston, 1854.
Farquhar, F. P., *Place Names of the High Sierra.*
Hurt, Wesley R., and Lass, William E., *Frontier Photographer: Stanley J. Morrow's Dakota Years*, University of Nebraska Press and University of South Dakota, 1956.
Jackson, W. H., and Driggs, W. R., *The Pioneer Photographer*, N. Y., N. Y., 1929.
Newhall, Beaumont, *The History of Photography*, N. Y., N. Y., 1949.
Root, Marcus A., *The Camera and the Pencil*, N. Y., N. Y., 1864.
Taft, Robert, *Photography and the American Scene: A Social History*, 1839–1889, The Macmillan Company, N. Y., N. Y., 1938.
Taft, Robert, *Artists and Illustrators of the Old West, 1850–1900*, Charles Scribner's Sons, New York and London, 1953.
Wheeler, George, *Preliminary Report of Explorations and Surveys in Nevada and Oregon in 1871*, Washington, D. C., 1872.

PIONEER PHOTOGRAPHIC TRADE JOURNALS

Anthony's Bulletin
Daguerrean Journal, The
Philadelphia Art Journal, The
Philadelphia Photographer, The
Photographic Art Journal, The

PAMPHLETS AND ARTICLES

Haynes House Bulletin, March, 1922.
Jackson, William H., *Descriptive Catalogue of Photographs of North American Indians*, Miscellaneous Publications, No. 9, U. S. Geological Survey, 1877. (The U. S. Geological Survey, Miscellaneous Publications, No. 5., 1875, also includes a catalogue of Jackson's negatives.)
Jackson, William H., an article on early western photographers in the *Kansas Historical Quarterly*, Vol. III, February, 1926.
Taft, Robert, an article on Alexander Gardner's stereoscopic views of frontier Kansas in the *Kansas Historical Quarterly*, Vol. III, No. 1, and Vol. VI., 1937.

CATTLE AND COWBOYS

Abbott, E. C., and Smith, H., *We Pointed Them North*, N. Y., N. Y., 1939.
Aldridge, Reginald, *Life on a Ranch: Ranch Notes in Kansas, Colorado, the Indian Territory and Northern Texas*, London, 1884.
Ambulo, John, "The Cattle on a Thousand Hills," *Overland Monthly*, March, 1887.
Applegate, Jesse, *A Day with a Cow Column*, Chicago, Ill., 1934.
Armour, Philip D., *The Present Condition of the Live Cattle and Beef Markets in the United States*, Chicago, Ill., 1889.
Ashton, John, "The Texas Cattle Trade in 1870," *Cattleman*, July, 1951.
Barnes, Will C., "The Chisholm Trail—For Whom Was It Named?" *Producer*, January, February, 1929.
Bronson, Edgar Beecher, *Cowboy Life on the Western Plains*, N. Y., N. Y., 1910.
Cook, James H., "The Texas Trail," E. S. Ricker, ed., *Nebraska Historical Magazine*, October, December, 1935.
Cox, James, *Historical and Biographical Record of the Cattle Industry and the Cattlemen of Texas and Adjacent Territory*, St. Louis, Mo., 1895.
Crawford, Samuel J., *Kansas in the Sixties*, Chicago, Ill., 1911.
Cross, Cora Melton, "Up the Trail with Nine Million Longhorns," *Texas Monthly*, February, 1930.
Cross, Fred J., *The Free Lands of Dakota*, Yankton, D. T., 1876.
Cushman, George L., "Abilene, First of the Kansas Cow Towns," *Kansas Historical Quarterly*, August, 1940.
Dick, Everett, "The Long Drive," Kansas State Historical Society, August, 1940.
Dobie, J. Frank, "The Chisholm Trail," *Country Gentleman*, February 28, 1925.
Dobie, J. Frank, *The Longhorns*, N. Y., N. Y., 1941.
Farnham, T. J., "Travels in the Great Western Prairies, 1839," *Early Western Travels*, Vol. XXVIII, R. G. Thwaites, ed., Cleveland, 1906.
Fink, Maurice, *Cow Country Cavalcade*, Denver, Colo., 1954.
Haley, J. Evetts, *Charles Goodnight, Cowman and Plainsman*, Boston, Mass., 1936.
Harger, Charles Moreau, "Cattle Trails of the Prairies," *Scribner's Magazine*, June, 1892.
Hastings, Frank S., "A Ranchman's Recollections," *The Breeders' Gazette*, Chicago, Ill., 1921.
Hebard, Grace Raymond, and Brininstool, E. A., *The Bozeman Trail* (2 vols.), Cleveland, Ohio, 1922.
Herrington, George Squires, "An Early Cattle Drive from Texas to Illinois," *Southwestern Historical Quarterly*, October, 1951.
Hershfield, John, "When War Broke Out on Wyoming Range," Omaha *Daily Journal-Stockman*, Omaha, Neb., June 19, 1928.
Hough, Emerson, *The Story of the Cowboy*, N. Y., N. Y., 1897.
Hunter, J. Marvin, ed., *The Trail Drivers of Texas*, Vol. I, 1920, Vol. II, 1923, Cokesbury Press, Nashville, Tenn.
Kohrs, Conrad, "A Veteran's Experience in the Western Cattle Trade," *Breeders' Gazette*, Chicago, Ill., December 18, 1912.
Love, Clara M., "Cattle Industry of the Southwest," *Southwestern Historical Quarterly*, Austin, Tex., April, 1916.
McCoy, Joseph G., *Historical Sketches of the Cattle Trade of the West and Southwest*, Kansas City, Mo., 1874.
Moody, Dave, "Tales of a Cow Camp," *The Trail*, February, 1910.
Nimmo, Joseph, "The Range and Ranch Cattle Traffic of the United States," *Report on the Internal Commerce* of the United States, Part III, Bureau of Statistics, Washington, D. C., 1886.
Nimmo, Joseph, "The American Cowboy," *Harper's Monthly*, November, 1886.
Osgood, Ernest, *The Day of the Cattleman*, Minnesota, 1929; N. Y., N. Y., 1958.
Paxson, Frederic L., "The Cow Country," *American Historical Review*, October, 1916.
Ponting, Tom Candy, *Life of Tom Candy Ponting*, Decatur, Ill., 1904; Ill., 1952.
Potter, Jack, *Cattle Trails of the Old West*, N. M., 1935.
Prose and Poetry of the Livestock Industry, the U. S. National Livestock Association, Kansas City, Mo., 1904.
Rollins, Philip Ashton, *The Cowboy*, N. Y., N. Y., 1921.
Rossel, John, "The Chisholm Trail," *Kansas Historical Quarterly*, February, 1936.

Siringo, Charles A., *A Lone Star Cowboy*, Santa Fe, N. M., 1919.

Siringo, Charles A., *Riata and Spurs*, Boston, Mass. and N. Y., N. Y., 1927.

Streeter, Floyd Benjamin, *Prairie Trails and Cow Towns*, Boston, Mass., 1936.

Stuart, Granville, *Montana As It is*, N. Y., N. Y., 1865.

Taylor, T. U., *The Chisholm Trail and Other Routes*, San Antonio, Tex., 1936.

Tenth Census of the United States, 1880, Vol. III, Government Printing Office, Washington, D. C., 1883.

Thoburn, Joseph B., "Jesse Chisholm, A Stalwart Figure in History," *Frontier Times*, April, 1936.

Vestal, Stanley, *Queen of the Cowtowns: Dodge City*, N. Y., N. Y., 1952.

"Vivid Story of Trail-Driving Days," Missoula *Missoulan*, August 20, 1922.

Von Richthofen, *Cattle Raising on the Plains of North America*, N. Y., N. Y., 1885.

Webb, W. P., "The American Revolution and the West," *Scribner's Magazine*, February, 1927.

Wellman, Paul I., *The Trampling Herd*, N. Y., N. Y., 1939.

"Wild Cattle-Hunting in Texas," *Leisure Hour* No. 632, February 6, 1864.

Wilkeson, Frank, "Cattle Raising on the Plains," *Harper's Monthly*, April, 1886.

THEODORE ROOSEVELT

Hagedorn, Hermann, *Roosevelt in the Bad Lands*, Boston, Mass., 1921.

Lang, Lincoln, *Ranching with Roosevelt*, Philadelphia, Pa., 1926.

Roosevelt, Theodore, "Sheriff's Work," *Century Magazine*, 1882.

Volweiler, A. T., "Roosevelt's Ranch Life in North Dakota," *Quarterly Journal of the University of North Dakota*, October, 1918.

BET-A-MILLION GATES, BARBED WIRE

Warshow, Robert Irving, *Bet-A-Million Gates*, N. Y., N. Y., 1932.

Wendt, G., and Kogan, Herman, *Bet-a-Million Gates: The Story of John Warne Gates*, N. Y., N. Y., 1948.

Clippings, articles, etc. from the American Iron and Steel Institute Library, N. Y., N. Y., and the United States Steel Corporation, N. Y., N. Y.

WINDMILLS

Barbour, E., "Wells and Windmills in Nebraska," U. S. Geological Survey No. 29, *House Document N 299*, 55th Congress, Government Printing Office, Washington, D. C., 1899.

Bates, Walter G., "Water Storage in the West," *Scribner's Magazine*, January, 1890.

Hayden, F. V., *Preliminary Report of the U. S. Geological Survey of Wyoming and Portions of Contiguous Territory*, Government Printing Office, Washington, D. C., 1872.

Letters of a windmill-maker, Nebraska, 1870, owned by the author.

Morris, R. C., "The Notion of the Great American Desert East of the Rockies," *Mississippi Valley Historical Review*, September, 1926.

Newell, F. H., "Irrigation on the Great Plains," *U. S. Department of Agriculture Yearbook*, Government Printing Office, Washington, D. C., 1896–1897.

Powell, J. W., "Institution for the Arid Lands," *Century*, May, 1890.

Shaw, Lucien, "The Development of the Law of Waters in the West," California Supreme Court *Report No. 189*, San Francisco, Calif., 1922.

Smythe, William E., *The Conquest of Arid America*, N. Y., N. Y., 1911.

Washburn, Charles G., *Industrial Worcester*, Worcester, Mass., 1917.

Wiel, Samuel C., *Water Right in the Western States*, San Francisco, Calif., 1911.

HOMESTEADS AND PUBLIC LANDS

Adams, R., "Public Range Lands—A New Policy Needed," *American Journal of Sociology*, November, 1916.

Dick, Everett, *The Sod-House Frontier*, N. Y., N. Y., 1937.

Hibbard, Ben H., *A History of the Public Land Policies*, N. Y., N. Y., 1924.

Munson, Judge Lyman E., "Pioneer Life on the American Frontier," *Connecticut Magazine*, Vol. XI, Montana State Historical Society library.

U. S. Land Office Report, 1875, Government Printing Office, Washington, D. C., 1876.

SHEEP

Chapman, Arthur, "The Sheep Herders of the West," *The Outlook*, June 24, 1905.

Gilfillan, Archer B., *Sheep*, Boston, Mass., 1929.

Harger, Charles Moreau, "Sheep and Shepherds of the West," *The Outlook*, November 22, 1902.

Randal, Henry S., *The Practical Shepherd*, N. Y., N. Y., 1875.

Wilcox, E. Vernon, "Sheep and the Forests," *The Forum*, Vol. XXXI.

BUFFALO

Allen, Joseph Asaph, "The American Bison, Living and Extinct," Publication of the Museum of Comparative Zoology, Vol. IV, No. 10, Cambridge, Mass., 1876.

Davis, Theodore R., "The Buffalo Range," *Harper's Magazine*, Vol. XXXVIII.

Garretson, Martin S., *The American Bison*, N. Y., N. Y., 1938.

Holden, W. C., "The Buffalo of the Plains Area," *West Texas Historical Association Yearbook*, Vol. II, 1926.

Hornaday, William T., "The Extermination of the American Bison," *Smithsonian Institution Report*, Washington, D. C., 1887.

Jacobs, John Cloud, "The Last of the Buffalo," *The World's Work*, Vol. XVII.

LUMBERING

Bullen, C. A., "Lumbering in Chippewa Valley," The *Daily Telegram*, Eau Claire, Wis., April 12, 1916.

BAD MEN AND THE WILD WAYS

Adams, Ramon F., "Billy the Kid's Lost Years," *Texas Monthly*, Dallas, Tex., Vol. IV, September, 1929.

Aikman, Duncan, *Calamity Jane and the Lady Wildcats*, N. Y., N. Y., 1927.

Breckenridge, William M., *Helldorado*, Boston, Mass. and N. Y., N. Y., 1928.

Burns, Walter Noble, *The Saga of Billy the Kid*, Garden City, N. Y., 1926.

Burns, Walter Noble, *Tombstone, An Iliad of the Southwest*, Garden City, N. Y., 1929.

Clum, John P., "It All Happened in Tombstone," *Arizona Historical Review*, Phoenix, Ariz., October, 1929.

Coolidge, Dane, *Fighting Men of the West*, N. Y., N. Y., 1932.

Cunningham, Eugene, *Triggernometry*, N. Y., N. Y., 1934.

Dalton, Emmett, and Jungmeyer, Jack, *When The Daltons Rode*, Garden City, N. Y., 1931.

Dobie, James Frank, "Clay Allison of the Washita," San Antonio *Light*, reprinted in *Frontier Times*, February, 1943.

Forrest, Earle Robert, *Arizona's Dark and Bloody Ground*, Caldwell, Idaho, 1936.

Gard, Wayne, *Sam Bass*, Boston, Mass. and N. Y., N. Y., 1936.

Gard, Wayne, "Texas Robin Hood," *Southwest Review*, Dallas, Tex., autumn, 1935.

Garrett, Patrick Floyd, *The Authentic Life of Billy the Kid*, Santa Fe, N. M., 1882.

Haley, James Evetts, *Jeff Milton, A Good Man with a Gun*, University of Oklahoma Press, Norman, Okla., 1948.

Holbrook, Stewart H., "Robbing the Steam Cars," *American Mercury*, October, 1946.

Jennings, Alphonso J., *Beating Back*, N. Y., N. Y., 1914.

Lake, Stuart N., *Wyatt Earp: Frontier Marshal*, Boston, Mass. and N. Y., N. Y., 1931.

McNeal, Thomas Allen, *When Kansas Was Young*, N. Y., N. Y., 1922.

Mercer, Asa S., *The Banditti of the Plains*, Cheyenne, Wyo., 1894.

Myers, John, *The Last Chance*, N. Y., N. Y., 1950.

O'Connor, Richard, *Bat Masterson*, N. Y., N. Y., 1957.

O'Connor, Richard, *Wild Bill Hickok*, N. Y., N. Y., 1959.

"Picturesque Characters among Women of the Wild West," the Kansas City *Star*, January 20, 1932.

Raine, William MacLeod, *Famous Sheriffs and Western Outlaws*, Garden City, N. Y., 1929.

Raine, William MacLeod, "Taming the Frontier: The Apache Kid," *Outing*, N. Y., N. Y., August, 1905.

Rascoe, Burton, *Belle Starr, the Bandit Queen*, N. Y., N. Y., 1941.

Santee, Ross, "Tales the Cow Punchers Tell," *Travel*, N. Y., N. Y., August, 1932.

Sonnichsen, Charles Leland, *Roy Bean*, N. Y., N. Y., 1943.

"Story of Billy the Kid, A," extracts from the Laredo *Times*, July 13, 1881, August 10, 1881.

Sutton, Fred Ellsworth, *Hands Up!* Indianapolis, Ind., 1927.

Tilghman, Zoe Agnes, *Outlaw Days*, Oklahoma City, Okla., 1926.

Walrath, Ellen F., "Stagecoach Holdups in the San Luis Valley," *The Colorado Magazine*, Denver, Colo., January, 1937.

Walters, Lorenzo, D., *Tombstone's Yesterday*, Tucson, Ariz., 1928.

White, Owen Payne, "Come A-Smokin'," *Collier's*, August 28, 1926.

White, Owen Payne, *Lead and Likker*, N. Y., N. Y., 1932.

THE CARLISLE INDIAN SCHOOL

Scrapbooks, Hamilton Library, Carlisle, Pa.

Tousey, Lt. Col. Thomas, *Military History of Carlisle and Carlisle Barracks*, Richmond, Va., 1939.

OKLAHOMA—LAST FRONTIER

Nix, Evett Dumas, *Oklahombres*, St. Louis, Mo., 1929.

Rainey, George, *The Cherokee Strip*, Guthrie, Okla., 1933.

Tilghman, Zoe, *Oklahoma Stories*, Oklahoma City, Okla., 1956.

Picture Credits

Bureau of American Ethnology = BAE
American Museum of Natural History = AMNH
University of Arizona Library = UAL
Arizona Pioneers' Historical Society = APHS
F. Bourges Collection = FBC
Brown County, Minn., Historical Society = BC
California State Library = CSL
J. Duncan Campbell = JDC
State Historical Society of Colorado = SHSC
Culver Service = CS
Denver Public Library Western Collection = DPL
George Eastman House = GEH
Nick Eggenhofer = NE
Hamilton Library and Historical Association of Cumberland County, Pennsylvania = HL
Hispanic Society of America = HSA
Stewart Holbrook = SH
James D. Horan Civil War and Western Americana Collection = JDH
Idaho Historical Society = IHS
Jackson County Historical Society = JCHS
A. C. Jancovic = ACJ
J. Leonard Jennewein, Mitchell, S.D. = JLJ
Church of Jesus Christ of Latter Day Saints = LDS
Kansas State Historical Society = KHS
Library of Congress = LC
Alvin J. Lucke Collection = AL
Fred and Jo Mazzulla Collection = FJM
Missouri Historical Society = MHS
Historical Society of Montana = HSM
Robert N. Mullin = RM
National Archives = NA
National Park Service = NPS
Nevada Historical Society = NHS
University of New Mexico = UNM
New Mexico Department of Development, Santa Fe = NMDD
New-York Historical Society = NYHS
New York Public Library = NYPL
Oklahoma Historical Society = OHS
Pinkerton's, Inc. = P
County, State Records and Archives, Santa Fe, N.M. = CSA
Blanche Schroer = BS
Richard D. Shinchak Collection = RSC
Smithsonian Institution = SI
Museum of the University of South Dakota = MUSD
Library of the University of Texas = LUT
Collection of The Travelers Insurance Companies = TIC
Union Pacific Railroad = UPR
United States National Museum = USNM
United States Steel Corporation = USSC
Utah State Historical Society = USHS
State Historical Society of Wisconsin = SHSW
Wyoming University Library = WUL
Coe Collection, Yale University Library = YUL

9–10. NYPL.
11. *t*, Roswell Museum and Art Center, Roswell, N.M.; *b*, NYPL.
12. ACJ.
13. *l, c, Das Trachtenbuch des Christoph Weiditz Von Seinen Reisenbrach Spanien* (1529) *und Den Neiderlanden* (1531–32) edited by Theodore Hampe, Berlin, 1927. HSA. *r*, BAE, *14th Annual Report*, Plate LV.
14–15. JDH.
16–17. HSA.
18–19. JDH.
20–21. *Hoofs, Claws and Antlers of the Rocky Mountains, by the Camera*, Frank S. Thayer, Publisher, Denver, Colo., 1894.
22. HSA.
23. LC.
24. CS.
25. *tl, tc*, CS; USNM; *b*, JDH.
26. NA.
27. *t, John C. Luttig's Journal of a Fur Trading Expedition on the Upper Missouri*, 1812–13, edited by Stella Drumm. Courtesy Missouri Historical Society. *c, bl, br*, from *Across the Wide Missouri*, Bernard De Voto. Courtesy of the Houghton Mifflin Company, Boston, Mass., 1947.
28. *The Mounted Riflemen* by James Parker, Banta Publishers, Menasha, Wis., 1916.
29. *t, c, bl, br*, courtesy SHSW.
30. *l*, LUT; *r*, JDH.
31. *l*, YUL; *r*, LUT.
32. *t*, YUL; *b*, NA.
33. ACJ.
34. Photo by T. Grady Gallant, Chattanooga *Free Press*.
35. USHS.
36. *t*, JDH; *c*, ACJ; *b*, BAE.
37. *c*, MA; *b*, LC.
38–39. NA.
40–41. *t*, LDS.
41. *b*, USHS.
42. NA.
43. *t*, GEH; *b*, courtesy *Arizona Highways*.
44. *t*, GEH; *b*, NYHS.
45. JDH.
46–47. NYHS.
49–65. JDH.
66. APHS.
67. *l*, NYHS; *r*, MA.
68. *t*, CS; *b*, USHS.
69. *bl, bcr, br*, JDH; *bcl*, NA.
70. JDH.
71. BC.
73. *l*, DPL; *r*, OHS.
74. SHSC.
75. *t*, MUSD; *c, bl, br*, JDH.
76. *t*, NA; *cl*, HSM; *cr*, NE; *b*, LC.
77. *tl*, JDH; *tr*, NE; *b*, NYHS.
78. CSL.
79. *tl, tr, cl, cr*, JDH; *b*, UPR.
80. UPR.
81. *l*, JDH; *tr*, Bettmann Archives; *cr*, UPR; *br*, IHS.
82. *t*, UPR; *b*, IHS.
83. *tl, tr, cl, br*, JDH; *cr, bl*, NE.
84. *l*, NA; *r*, LC.
85. NA.
86. *l*, LC; *r*, APHS.
87. NA.
88. *t, c*, BAE; *b*, HSM.
89. *t, c*, NA; *cl, cr, br*, HSM; *bl*, JDH.

90. HSM.
91. NA.
92. *t, bl*, NA; *br*, JDH.
93. *t, bl*, NA; *br*, JDH.
94–96. NA.
97. MA.
98. *tr, bl, Indian Fights and Fighters*, Cyrus Townsend Brady, Doubleday, Page & Company, N.Y., 1909; *br*, MA.
99. *b, Indian Fights and Fighters*, Cyrus Townsend Brady, Doubleday, Page & Company, N.Y., 1909. *t*, NA.
100. NA.
101. MA.
102. *t*, JDH; *c, Pioneers of the Black Hills*, or *Gordon Stockade Party of 1874*, David Aken, Milwaukee, 1920. *b*, courtesy Way Museum, Custer, S.D.
103. NA.
104. *l*, JDH; *r*, courtesy Historical Division, U.S. Army.
105. *t*, NA; *b*, MUSD.
106. *l*, JDH; *r*, JDH.
107. JDH.
108–9. JDH.
110–11. JDH.
112. *t*, BAE; *b*, NA.
113–14. NA.
115–29. JDH.
130. GEH.
134–54. JDH.
155. *tl, tr*, JDH; *b*, HSM.
156. *t*, MUSD; *b*, JDH.
157. JDH.
158. *t*, NE; *b*, JDH.
159. NE.
160. JDH.
161. *l*, NE; *r*, LC.
162. LC.
163. JDH.
164. *tl*, JDH.
165. JDH.
166. JDH.
167. HSM.
168. *t*, NA; *b*, JDH.
169. JDH.
170. JDH.
170–75. JDH.
176. *The Iron Age*, June 24, 1926.
177–78. Courtesy USSC.
179. *t*, NE; *b*, courtesy M. T. Jensen, Vice President, Aermotor Company, Chicago, Ill.
180. Drawings by Evelyn Curro from *The Look of the Old West* by Foster-Harris, The Viking Press, N.Y., 1955.
181. LC.
182. JDH.
183. *t*, FJM; *b*, NA.
184. JDH.
185. NA.
186. SH.
187. *t*, LC; *b*, JDH.
188. Courtesy Pat McDonough.
189. *c*, NYHS; *b*, NE.
190. *t*, JDH; *c, b*, NE.
191. *The American Bison* by Martin S. Garretson, American Bison Society, N.Y., 1934.
192. *t*, MUSD; *b, The American Bison* by Martin S. Garretson, American Bison Society, N.Y., 1934.
193. NPS.

194. *The American Bison* by Martin S. Garretson, American Bison Society, N.Y., 1934.
195. *t*, NE; *b*, MA.
196. *l*, NYHS; *cr*, MA; *br*, MUSD.
197. *t*, NA; *cr*, NE; *br*, MUSD.
198. *t*, NA; *b*, MUSD.
199. *t*, NE; *c*, JDH; *b*, IHS.
200. JDH.
201. NE.
202. *t*, NE; *b*, SH.
203. JDH.
204–5. SH.
206–7. JDH.
208. SH.
209. JDH.
210. *tl*, P; *tr*, JCHS; *br*, JDH.
211. *bl*, JDH; *tr*, MHS.
212. JDH.
213. *l*, MHS; JDH.
214. *tl*, JDH; *tr*, LC.
215. JDH.
216. *t*, RSC; *b*, JDH.
217. *t*, KHS; *b*, CSL.
218. JDH.
219. *tl*, WUL; *tr*, JDH; *br*, P.
220–22. RM.
223. *b*, NA.
224. CSA.
225. NA.
226. *tl*, UAL; *br*, JDH.
227. CSA.
228. *tl*, UAL; *tr*, RM; *b*, UNM.
229. *tr*, MHS; *b*, AL.
230. AL.
231. AL.
232. *tl*, UP; *br*, P.
233. P.
234. P.
235. *bl*, WUL; *tr*, JDH.
236. JDH.
238. JDH.
240–44. BS.
245. JDH.
246. JDH.
247. *t, bl*, JDH; *br*, MA.
248. *l*, JDH; *br*, courtesy Emily Driscoll.
249. JDH.
250. JDH.
251. *tl, tr*, JDH; *tc*, MUSD; *bl, Photography and the American Scene* by Robert Taft, The Macmillan Co., N.Y., 1938; *br*, courtesy Miss H. M. Baumhofer.
252. *t*, SI; *b*, NA.
253. *tl, tr*, NA; *br*, JDH.
254. *t, b*, JDH; *br*, IHS.
255. JDH.
256. JDH.
257. JDH.
258–59. JLJ.
260. *r*, JLJ; *b*, JDH.
261–65. JDH.
266. NA.
267–71. JDH.
272. *t*, BAE, FJM.
273. HSM.
274. HL.
275–76. HL.
277. *t*, HL; *c*, W. Cann, Reno, Nev., *r*, NHS.
278. HL.
279–81. OHS.
282. JDH.
283. JDH.
284–88. OHS.
289–93. DC.

Index